# DEVON FIREFIGHTER

## A CENTURY OF COURAGE & SERVICE

*Firefighters damp down the smouldering remains of a fire at Victoria Mills, Rolle Quay, Barnstaple, in 1966. Left to right, the crew comprises Leading Firefighter Barry Dibble (who later became Devon's Assistant Chief Fire Officer) with firefighters Roy Barnes and George Kettle. This was the Devon County fire kit, little changed from the war years: tarpaulin 'wetlegs' leggings, cork-covered high-combed helmets and the long 'Lancer' tunic with belt and axe.*

# DEVON FIREFIGHTER

## A CENTURY OF COURAGE & SERVICE

EDITED BY IAIN RICE

CONTRIBUTORS

StnO Mark Willkins

StnO Nigel Toms

StnO Doug Smith

SubO Dave Crawford

David Rumble

Les Morris

HALSGROVE

First Published in Great Britain in 2000 by Halsgrove

**British Library Cataloguing in Publication Data**

Data for this publication is available from the British Library


ISBN 1 85522 760 6


**HALSGROVE**

Halsgrove House
Lower Moor Way
Tiverton
Devon EX16 6SS
Tel: 01884 243242
Fax 01884 243325
www.halsgrove.com


**All profits from the sale of this book go to the Fire Service National Benevolent Fund**


Printed and bound in Great Britain by Cromwell Press Ltd, Trowbridge

# CONTENTS

# ACKNOWLEDGEMENTS

Dennis Bellworthy
Ivy Boddy
John Chambers
Bill Cherry
Mr Chubb
John Colley GC., Torquay
June Collins
Ron Conway
Cliff & Geoffrey Coombes & Family, Bovey Tracey
Brian Dearnaley
Mike Drew
Neil Faithfull
John Ffoulkes
Teddy Francis
Ellen Grindley
Marc Hill
Mandy & Duncan Holden
Mrs Hull of Crediton
Mr A E Labbett
Gary Larkworthy
Mr D. Lashbrook
Kevin Lott
Les Mogridge
Finbar 'Baz' Nolan, Ex SubO, Plymouth
Cliff Palmer, ex-SubO Princetown
John Popham
Thomas F Rawlings & Family
Mr R. T. Rawlings
Ken Rowe
Barbara Rumble (for helping Dave!)
Mrs Smith of Exmouth

Alan Spear
Barry Stevens
Brian & John Stevens & Family
Heather Stotesbury
Fred Tozer
Brian Underhill
Colin Wallace
Mick Ward
Mrs Muriel Warren of South Molton
Bill Webber
Mrs S. E. West
Les Woodman

The late R Clemson-Young of Torquay
The late John Hughes of Cardiff
The late Peter Tully of Paignton
The late Roy W. Yeoman of Moretonhampstead

From Devon Fire and Rescue Service:
FF Ken Bickerton
StnO Tony Heywood
StnO Gerry Holmes
FCop Dave Honeywill
Joan Hopper, DFRS Personnel Dept.
SubO Ian Land
LFF Paul Lee
FF Brian Margrie
DO Mike Nevitt
FCop Peter Regan
StnO Dick Osborne
FF Rod Ousley

ADO Trevor Shaddick
David Trist, DFRS Media Resources
LFF Peter Trott
SubO Neil Whitemore
ADO Trevor Wright

All personnel (serving and retired) on stations throughout the Devon Fire and Rescue Service who ransacked their personal albums, station albums and logs, diaries and notebooks and sent in photographs, information and reminiscences.

Plymouth Area Members of the Fire Brigade Society

*Western Evening Herald*
*Western Morning News*
*Herald Express*
*Express & Echo*
*North Devon Journal*

Ashburton Museum
Barnstaple Museum
Devon Library Services
Devon County Council
Devon Books (Halsgrove) archive
Ilfracombe Museum
Newton Abbot Town Museum
South Molton Museum

*Editorial team: L-R: Back Row: StnO Mark Wilkins, StnO Nigel Toms, Judey Ford, StnO Doug Smith.*
*Front Row: SubO Iain Rice (Editor), Dave Rumble (Fire Brigade Society), SubO Dave Crawford, Ex-Firefighter Les Morris.*

# FOREWORD

I am delighted to have the opportunity to introduce this history of the fire service in Devon. It represents the first attempt to produce a comprehensive record of the service in this county and as such will itself form an important part of our history in the years to come. It would not have been possible, of course, without the determination and sheer hard work of the authors and I would like to place on record my congratulations to them for producing such an interesting and informative book. All of the profits from the publication will go to the Fire Services National Benevolent Fund and, as the President of that charity in Devon, I would like to express my sincere thanks.

The history of our fire service here in Devon throughout the last century is one of dedication, excitement and, sometimes, sacrifice. During that one hundred years, much has changed in firefighting. Fire engines have developed from horse drawn manual or steam-powered pumps to the powerful diesel-engined vehicles that we see today. The role of the firefighter has also changed radically. In 1900 Devon firefighters – other than those in the cities and larger towns – were often enthusiastic amateurs who had to rely on basic equipment and primitive protective clothing to supplement their own determination and courage. One hundred years later, the modern firefighter is a professional who needs intelligence, resourcefulness and a wide range of technical skills. The need for courage, however, remains unaltered.

In 1900 the fire service was highly fragmented across Devon, with dozens of separate fire brigades. Those brigades varied enormously. In Exeter, for example, the City Council maintained a professional brigade housed in a purpose-built fire station. But in many small towns and villages, the brigades consisted of volunteers who collected the horses from the field and hitched them up to the fire engine – which was probably stored in a friendly farmer's barn! By the outbreak of the Second World War, little had changed other than the introduction – in some cases – of petrol-engined vehicles. It was because of this lack of modern, compatible equipment and a unified approach that in 1941 the government created the National Fire Service – which brought about major change. The need to fight the huge fires caused through widespread bombing resulted in the provision of standardised equipment and procedures and the creation of professional organisational structures. In 1948, the government kept an earlier promise and returned the fire service to local government control – but not as it had been in 1939. Things had changed forever and fire protection was never to return to the fragmented and often amateur service of the past.

For the next 25 years the Plymouth and Exeter brigades and the Devon County Fire Service protected Devon. However, in 1973 change came again with local government re-organisation and the creation of the new Devon Fire Brigade, covering the whole of the county. With 58 fire stations, 1,400 staff and 200 vehicles, covering an area of 2,500 square miles, the Devon Fire Brigade became one of the largest county fire brigades in the country. In 1987 the brigade was renamed Devon Fire and Rescue Service in an attempt to better reflect the diversity of rescue work undertaken – a change of title which has since been copied by many other brigades.

With the creation of the county-wide brigade in 1973 it became an integral part of Devon County Council. However, this only lasted 25 years as local government re-organisation came once again in 1998. The creation of a unitary

Plymouth City Council and Torbay Council alongside the remainder of Devon meant that it was necessary to create an independent Devon Fire Authority, with elected representatives serving on it from all three principal councils. The new authority commenced work on 1 April 1998 and is the democratically elected public body to which I am responsible for the management of Devon Fire and Rescue Service.

This book is the story, not only of the organisation and equipment of the fire service, but of the people who delivered that service. It is about the brass-helmeted firemen who clung onto the horse drawn fire engine as it galloped through the streets of Exeter in 1900. It is about the eleven firefighters killed during five consecutive nights in April 1941 whilst they courageously fought the devastating fires that swept through Plymouth as a result of enemy bombing. It is about Leading Fireman John Colley who was awarded the George Medal in recognition of his brave rescue of people trapped in a serious hotel fire in Torquay on the night of 25 May 1974. The outward symbol of the fire service is the shiny red engines, the uniforms and the fire stations. However, behind that image we rely on the commitment, dedication and determination of the people that work within the service to make it the success that it is today.

The role of the firefighter changed dramatically during the twentieth century. In 1900, his job was almost entirely one of fighting fires. By the end of the century, that had changed entirely. The modern firefighter has to be ready to tackle a huge range of different incidents including fires, chemical incidents, road traffic accidents and numerous other types of rescues. However, the modern service is about much more than simply reacting to emergencies; firefighters teach fire safety in our schools and inspect buildings. They install domestic smoke alarms, demonstrate first aid firefighting for the home and workplace, and give fire safety advice to community groups of all kinds. Some go on to become specialists in fire investigation, firefighter training, fire safety, research and development and much more. The world has changed greatly during that 100 years – and so have the fire service and firefighters.

Finally, I cannot end this introduction without reference to those Chief Fire Officers that led Devon Fire Brigade, and more recently Devon Fire and Rescue Service, from its creation in 1973 to the end of the twentieth century. I know that Ralph Havery (1973–1977), John Killoran (1977–1987), Neil Wallington (1987–1991) and Robin Currie (1991–1997) felt as privileged as I do to have the opportunity to lead this Service.

*Paul Young*
*Chief Fire Officer*
*Devon Fire and Rescue Service*
*July 2000*

# FIREFIGHTING IN DEVON 1800-1939

This may seem rather a broad swathe to cut through the history of firefighting in Devon in a single chapter, but the story up until the outbreak of the Second World War was one of piecemeal evolution proceeding at very different rates across the county. As, indeed, it was throughout the country – the situation which so alarmed the Riverdale Committee that reported to the Home Office on the state of Britain's fire service in 1936. One factor, however, set Devon apart from other places: the prevalence of cob-and-thatch building construction in those areas of the county away from the granite moorlands and other ready supplies of building stone. But first – a little general history.

## PARISH BRIGADES AND MANUAL PUMPS

Organised firefighting on any scale is generally held to have originated with the Romans, who appointed the Corps of Vigiles to watch for and tackle outbreaks of fire in their cities. Judging by the number of Roman cities that burned down, the Vigiles weren't all that effective, but then the science of firefighting had not yet been born. Doubtless, the major Roman settlements in Britain had their own Corps, but with the departure of the Romans little else was done in the way of establishing any form of organised fire protection in Britain until a certain catastrophic event in 1666 brought home to the rulers of the country just how devastating – and disrespectful of rank, wealth or piety – an uncontrolled fire in a densely-packed city could be.

The legacy of the Great Fire of London was the introduction of an Act of Parliament in 1707 placing the responsibility for providing fire protection upon the churchwardens of each parish in the land, who were required to have available 'leathern buckets, squirts, preventers, ladders and other appliances for the quenching of fires' as well as organising bodies of men to assist in the event of an outbreak. The equipment was usually kept in the church, often in the porch where it was readily accessible in case of need, and the alarm was traditionally raised by 'clashing' the church bells ringing two or three bells haphazardly, a method that certainly makes a mighty din.

These measures had but limited effect. While a few primitive appliances might have been provided, there was still no developed science of

*Chief Officer Barry Jones of Crediton Fire Brigade*

firefighting and when the need arose the equipment was often found wanting. Rats were notoriously fond of the 'leathern buckets' while the 'preventers' – long-handled implements with a sharpened hook similar to a military pike, used to cut and tear down thatch – suffered from the depredations of woodworm and corrosion. The net result was that fires usually defeated the best efforts of the 'Parish Brigade' to control them, and the history of the period is rife with accounts of conflagrations destroying great swathes of buildings in towns; Devon suffered many such fires in the sixteenth and seventeenth centuries.

The first significant development in the science of firefighting was the invention of the manual fire pump, a device capable of applying water onto a fire from a distance. There were accounts of all manner of such 'fire engines' going right back into antiquity, including of course the ubiquitous 'squirt' – effectively, a large syringe – which dated from Roman times. But it seems fairly certain that the first effective manual machines were developed in Germany and the Low Countries around the beginning of the seventeenth century. These primitive appliances were usually in the form of a large wooden tub – sometimes wheeled but often not – in which was located a simple piston force pump, similar to the pumps used to draw water from wells. These pumps were worked by long handles, by means of which the brawn of a dozen or so men could be used to send a jet of water onto the fire from a fixed nozzle on top of the apparatus. The pump was kept supplied by buckets emptied into the tub, so sustained firefighting required a lot of people and plenty of buckets, not to mention a suitable source of water.

While they were a great advance on squirts, these primitive fire pumps were still alarmingly ineffective once a fire took hold. They could only project water over a short distance, and the jet was a series of pulses rather than a continuous stream. Also, the lusty efforts of the pumpers could easily outstrip the ability of the bucket-chains – often made up of women and children – to keep the pump supplied. The fire engines were also heavy and unwieldy, requiring a lot of effort both to get them to the site of an outbreak and to manoeuvre them into position to keep the water directed accurately at the fire. Their lack of manoeuvrability also placed them at risk if the fire should get out of hand, and many a manual engine went up in flames with the building it was supposedly protecting.

However, the manual fire engine was improved steadily in performance and efficiency over the next two centuries, and modern firefighters are often surprised at what a powerful jet a good manual engine crewed by a dozen brawny pumpers can produce. In England, the Newsham style of manual, patented in 1721, which used a chain and sprocket pump drive system attached to long handles on each side parallel to the centreline of the machine, allowed many more men to apply their muscle to the job of pumping. Larger Newsham machines also had foot-treadles on top of the pump so that yet more men – anything up to a total of thirty – could provide the power. A large Newsham No. 5 engine could pump more than 150 gallons a minute and throw a jet 165 feet in the air – an effective performance that made it possible to tackle even large fires.

The Newsham design proved a turning point in firefighting in Britain. Amendments to the act of 1707 now required the churchwardens to provide 'a large engine, a hand engine (squirt) and leather pipes and sockets' – by means of which the engine could be connected to the 'stop-blocks and fire cocks' that the churchwardens were also charged with installing

*Opposite page: This fire at Silverton is typical of the manual age of firefighting, although the date is very late for this type of appliance to be seen in action. It shows the scene at the Faraday family home at Milcott, Silverton, in 1934. Essentially, this represents the fire-fighting scene throughout the previous century, with the power for the manual pump being supplied by bystanders. A small wheeled escape has been brought into use and is pitched against the hapless cottage which, as was usually the case, has lost its roof entirely and most of the first floor to boot. The fire engine and escape belong to the local brigade and a brass-helmeted firefighter can just be seen at the rear of the escape. There is also a small hand hose-cart visible, and this may also have been Silverton's own firefighting provision. The young ladies of the village at front left seem to be treating the occurrence with a certain degree of levity!*

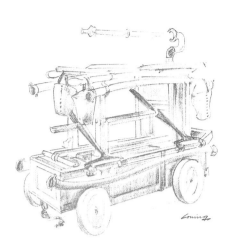

*One of the oldest fire engines recorded as being used in Devon was this Newsham Manual bought by the town of South Molton in 1736.*

in leats, pipes and other water supplies. With the combination of a Newsham engine and hose to supply it with water, the parish brigades at long last began to have some effect – although it must be said that many churchwardens were lax in their duties and failed to keep the equipage in good order, risking a fine of £10 if found negligent. The £10 stick was replaced with a smaller but attractive carrot – a payment of thirty shillings 'to the first person who brings in a Parish engine or other large engine with a hose and socket when any fire happens', with the second and third engines to attend receiving twenty and ten shillings respectively. This was the type of equipment with which the best of the earlier Devon brigades faced the risk posed by the local vernacular architecture – cob and thatch.

## COB AND THATCH, FIRE AND CANDLE

Cob is a building material compounded of clay, straw and manure. Well mixed – traditionally, by the trampling of cattle – and rammed down between shuttering on a stone foundation, cob made an economical and effective building material for a relatively poor rural county. The thick, uneven walls associated with cob construction gave rise to what is widely regarded as the archetypal Devon cottage or farmhouse, with small windows and low doorways beneath timber lintels and having a wide-eaved straw-thatched roof. Internally, partitions in such cob buildings were of timber panelling or lath-and-plaster. The only masonry apart from the vital footings (for cob must 'keep its feet dry') was the fireplace and chimney, built in stone rubble up to roof level but often brick above that.

In many Devon towns and villages, whole streets of cob-and-thatch buildings were built as terraces or as tight-packed groups separated only by 'drangs' – narrow alleyways scarcely a yard wide. Cob-and-thatch construction has many virtues, including simplicity, low cost and good thermal insulation properties, making the buildings warm in winter but cool in hot weather. However, it also possesses a fatal flaw; thatched cob buildings are painfully vulnerable to fire, and – in the rural household of the seventeenth, eighteenth or nineteenth century, there were many ill-guarded sources of ignition. It is not surprising to find, therefore, that numerous towns suffered devastating conflagrations that destroyed whole streets or even entire quarters in a single blaze. Chulmleigh lost 95 houses in 1803, North Tawton suffered two major fires in the 1830s which destroyed a total of 150 out of the town's 270 dwellings – not to mention several inns and a part of the church – while Ottery St Mary lost 111 buildings as late as 1866, about a third of the total.

But where were the parish fire brigades amid all this mayhem? They were there, certainly, and by all accounts they did their valiant best. But so fire-prone is a cob-and-thatch building that even today it is frequently difficult to save such a structure once it becomes involved in fire. The first problem lay in the roofs; straw thatch – unlike the older heather thatch still used on Dartmoor up until the nineteenth century – catches fire readily and, once ignited, burns rapidly and often vigorously, especially where the thatch is new or when the weather has been dry for a period. The only way to prevent a thatched roof fire spreading is to create a firebreak in the thatch ahead of the fire-front, a laborious and time-consuming business. It also requires a bit of science and a fair bit of luck to make the break in the right place, for the fire within the attic of the house on the lower side of the thatch may well be some way in advance of the visible fire on the outside.

Where a row of thatched houses formed a terrace with a common attic void running the entire length of the street – as was common in most Devon villages and country towns – it was almost impossible to confine the fire, and almost invariably the whole terrace was lost. Once the straw roofs had spread the fire along the street, often at bewildering speed if there was any sort of wind, the burning thatch dropped into the inter-ior of the houses, firing the wooden partitions and floors, burning the timber lintels of doors and windows and baking the cob so that it cracked and spalled. When the burned lintels gave way the walls were destabilised, and the whole building usually collapsed. In the fiercer fires, the very binding straw and dung within the cob mix burned, reducing the walls to little more than dry clay powder. All that was usually left after one of these cob-and-thatch conflagrations was a series of stone chimneys, stand-ing like sentinels amid the ashes and dust. The evidence of these past fires is often found today in ancient chimney stacks that are not quite aligned with the buildings that now surround them, where new construction has taken place around the fire-ravaged remnants of older dwellings.

## DEVON PARISH-PUMP FIREFIGHTING

The tactics, such as they were, of the parish fire brigades confronted by cob-and-thatch fires depended very much on the speed with which the brigade was able to reach the fire; which, by modern standards, was very slowly indeed. For a start, before the advent of the electric telegraph (developed in the 1840s but not widely available in rural areas until much later in the nineteenth century), the fastest speed of communication was that achievable by a good horseman on a fast horse – about twenty miles an hour, once the horse was caught and saddled and the rider mounted. If the fire was some little way from the parish church – the usual alarm point – then it might easily be twenty minutes or more before the alarm could be raised, bearing in mind that even two hundred years ago many parishes were quite large and might contain several hamlets as well as the church village or town. (By comparison, twenty minutes is the *maximum* time allowed for the fire brigade to reach any but the remotest fire in Devon today.)

Once the alarm was raised, the engine had to be got out and crewed. The care of the engine frequently fell to the lot of the local blacksmith, as being the craftsman most fitted to effect repairs when needed, and it might well be kept adjacent to the smithy. He and the other tradesmen and shopkeepers of the town were most likely to form the initial response to the fire call, as they were usually in their workshops or otherwise working close to the town centre; the rest of the manpower needed was dispersed around the fields and farms of the parish, often some miles distant. It was then necessary to get the engine to the scene of the fire, often relying on manpower, although horses might be used if there was any great distance to travel and they could be speedily procured. As well as the engine, there was need to transport the other firefighting apparatus that the churchwardens had – hopefully – provid-ed; the vital buckets, thatch-hooks and ladders, not to mention the equipment needed to set the engine into whatever water supply was available. A raggle-taggle procession of townsfolk or villagers hurried toward the billowing column of smoke by now threatening the build-ings around the original outbreak, carrying stop-planks for leats, boring irons and bungs for pipes, leather suction hose, squirts, and such other implements as they thought might be useful.

Frequently, all was in vain so far as the buildings immediately involved were concerned, and all that could be attempted was to save surrounding properties by dousing the thatch and dealing with the embers and flaming brands that rained down from the blazing cottages. Aid might be summoned from adjoining communities, but again the slow speed of communication and the time needed to manhandle pumps or other equipment over any distance meant that it was usually impossible to concentrate enough firefighting resources in any one place to be effective. Churchwardens were anyway often reluctant to let engines leave one parish to aid another, for fear of an outbreak at home during their absence. Matters were further compounded by a lack of any sort of organisation, training or chain of command on the fireground, where the local gentry usually saw fit to take charge and issue orders – almost invariably totally impracticable – rather than leaving the conduct of operations in the more capable hands of the smiths and masons, who at least had some idea of what was possible.

It is scarcely surprising, therefore, that more drastic measures were often needed to contain these fires, and resort was had to the technique that ultimately checked the fire of London, that of pulling down or blowing up buildings in the path of the fire to create firebreaks. Even then, a change of wind could spell disaster, and fires often burned for days until they either burned themselves out or were brought under control by yet more firebreaks. The resulting devastation amid what were already impoverished communities was far-reaching and long lived, and it might take a town several years to recover from a serious fire and to rebuild the affected streets, for many of the losses were uninsured. Loss of life in these fires was, however, mercifully small, as people were usually able to escape the flames; it was the aftermath that caused the greatest suffering.

Very many Devon parishes suffered severe fires due to this prevalent building construction and lack of elementary fire precautions, such as

*All hands take a rest and pose for the camera at this fire at Clyst Honiton, near Exeter, on 7th July 1909. This was a farm fire involving a range of barns, and was tackled by the Exeter brigade who are here 'shouldering axes' – one suspects they had been engaged in chopping-out charred woodwork. Note the length of the branchpipe and the separate screw-in nozzle. Branches in those days were non-adjustable and the only way to go from a half-inch to a one-inch jet was to change the half-inch nozzle for an inch one! The farmhands in the foreground have doubtless been supplying brawn for the pump, unless the steamer 'Devonia' was used.*

firestop walls to divide roof spaces or streets wide enough to form fire-breaks. Frank Gentry, in his account of eleven disastrous nineteenth-century Devon town fires, *Take Care of Your Fire and Candle* (Devon Books, 1985), has an appendix listing no less than 146 major fires affecting 66 Devon towns and villages in the century, not including the most serious fires studied in the text! Top of the list was Crediton, with nineteen major conflagrations between 1832 and 1893, followed by Tiverton with sixteen in much the same period. Obviously, something had to be done.

## THE INSURANCE FACTOR

Two factors started to ameliorate the situation in the latter years of the century. The first was the growth of the concept of insurance, which spread out from the cities to the larger towns and eventually to the more prosperous elements of the countryside – notably, the fashionable country houses then being built by the *nouveau riche* of the manufacturing classes. The second was the involvement of the landed classes, who stood to lose much by fire.

The insurance companies that already maintained fire brigades in the larger towns like Exeter found themselves in the mid-nineteenth century carrying substantial risks in rural areas, where fire protection was so limited as to be, from all practical points of view, useless. This lead, in due course, to insurance brigades being set up in areas that previously had enjoyed little or no fire protection. A good example of this is the case of Chagford, a small stannary town on the north-eastern slopes of Dartmoor that became, during the 1850s and early 1860s, very fashionable as a 'country retreat' after the Moor had been popularised in books like Crossing's *Amid Devonia's Alps*. By 1864, the Royal Insurance Office of Exeter had some tens of thousands of pounds of risk in the Chagford district, with country houses and large fashionable hotels as well as substantial woollen mills. So the Royal stationed a Shand, Mason manual fire pump in the town, recruited a dozen firefighters and a 'Captain', and trained them in standard insurance-brigade firefighting techniques.

*Here is an early insurance-pattern Nuttall 'vertical manual' of the late eighteenth or early nineteenth century being used for fund-raising and PR purposes by Plymouth firefighters 'Baz' Nolan at left and Dave Brooks (now a BA technician) at right. This type of manual had the handles across the ends – they were fitted with extension pieces to accommodate about a dozen pumpers. There is a fixed nozzle on top of the pump, but suction and delivery hose could be attached.*

*A later insurance manual was this 1864-vintage Shand, Mason stationed at Chagford when the brigade was formed by the Royal Fire Office of Exeter. It passed to the parish in 1894 and was still in use in 1940, at which point it was widely reckoned to be the oldest fire appliance in use by a public brigade in England. It is now preserved in the museum of the Chartered Insurance Institute in London, and was photographed at Chagford Agricultural Show in about 1950.*

Another way in which the growth of insurance helped to improve fire protection in the countryside was through the increasing prosperity of the larger towns, particularly where manufacturing industry, milling and other commercial activities supported a larger population and also brought about a greater insurance risk. The insurance companies carrying this risk sought to minimise their exposure by improving their fire brigade provision, re-equipping their brigades with the latest generation of lightweight, high performance horse-drawn manual engines and increasing their establishments to include full-time or retained stations – Exeter had four such brigades by the middle of the century, able to respond swiftly over quite a large area.

This had two effects; firstly, a number of second-hand but serviceable fire engines came on to the market, and communities that previously had little or no provision were able to acquire such machines at affordable prices. The insurance companies were also increasingly selling insurance in the countryside to farmers, landlords and merchants, and they saw it as very much in their interest to improve firefighting facilities even in places that did not warrant the establishment of a full-blown insurance brigade. So they started to assist the parish brigades with equipment and training, to make them more effective. And it soon became the rule that the insurance brigades from the larger or more prosperous towns would respond to outbreaks of fire in smaller, outlying places, swiftly bringing their discipline and expertise to the situation and thus helping to reduce the incidence of widespread conflagrations.

## The Gentry Lend A Hand

The majority of the cottages destroyed in the major conflagrations that swept through towns like North Tawton or Cullompton belonged, not to their occupants, but to the local landed proprietors. It was they who ultimately lost out, not just because they had to bear the cost of rebuilding the affected properties, but also because the disruption to the local economy resulting from a major fire affected their own incomes and prosperity. In studying the history of many Devon fires, it is evident that the county's landowners took their responsibility in these areas quite seriously. There are many instances of destroyed cob-and-thatch cottages being replaced by new 'fireproof' buildings in brick or stone with slate roofs, and in the later part of the century there are accounts of fires that burned unchecked until they reached such properties, which caught fire much less readily and were far easier to protect, thus effectively forming firebreaks.

There was also considerable sympathy among the wealthier sections of the community for those burned-out in a fire, and subscriptions were sometimes swiftly raised for the relief of the suffering of fire victims. After the major fire in Moretonhampstead on 12th September 1845, a subscription was opened in the *Exeter Flying Post* newspaper, and by 16th October the same paper carried a notice to the effect that 'enough has already been received to indemnify the sufferers'. Some more far-sighted individuals advanced the idea that it might be better to organise such a subscription *before* any outbreak of fire, thus furnishing the means to purchase more effective fire appliances and other equipment. In fact, this was not a new idea even in the mid nineteenth century; some towns had raised money for fire engines in this way a full century earlier – South Molton purchasing a 'large four-wheeled engine' (A Newsham manual) as long ago as 1736. It still exists today.

However, with the long succession of severe fires from about 1830 onwards, when a succession of dry summers brought about the fatal combination of tinder-dry straw thatch and low water supplies, the matter of fire protection was never far from the public mind, aided by a local press which took a lively interest in reporting (in lurid detail) on outbreaks of fire and the plight of the victims. It soon became quite fashionable to be associated with fire engine funds, and by this means many towns at last acquired equipment that enabled an effective response to be made. The situation was further helped by the major fire-engine makers like Merryweathers producing smaller, easily-handled and economically priced – but still highly efficient – manual fire engines, machines which were ideally suited to the needs of the small country brigades. The report of the 1845 Moretonhampstead fire mentions the fact that the town possessed 'two good engines' (one of which was provided by the West of England Insurance Office) and that these were successful in preventing the fire spreading into many parts of the town.

The combination of some on-the-spot firefighting capability together with the speedier response of the insurance brigades, especially from Exeter, helped reduce the effect of major fires, such as that which afflicted Cullompton in July 1839. Although there were, at one time, no less than six large fires burning in different parts of the town, the town's two fire engines started an enthusiastic attack and three Exeter insurance brigades – the Little West, West Middlesex and Sun – were on the scene within two hours. Although damage was extensive – a hundred houses burned and fifty damaged – the potential of the outbreak was for far greater destruction than this. With the rebuilding of the affected parts of the town, many property owners decided to insure their new homes and businesses – which meant that by 1852 the West of England Insurance Company (the proprietors of the 'Little West' engine) had decided that Cullompton warranted its own insurance brigade. The *Exeter and Plymouth Gazette* of 22nd May 1852 recorded that a fire had broken out in a Cullompton bakery, but that 'the West of England Fire Brigade with their engine were swiftly on the spot and ... the adjacent property was saved...'. One wonders whether the speedy attendance of the 'Little West' to the 1839 fire – it was the first insurance engine to arrive, as it invariably seems to have been – won for the West of England office the bulk of the Cullompton insurance business.

The other contribution made by the gentry to rural firefighting came about as the result of a little healthy self-interest. While not as fire-prone as cob-and-straw thatched cottages, the grander mansions of the land-owning classes were by no means immune from fire, and the records of the eighteenth and nineteenth centuries are not short of accounts of disastrous country-house fires. With their large staffs of grooms, gardeners, farmworkers and domestic servants, such places were not short of the manpower needed for firefighting, and the fire-engine makers, ever alive to new markets, were soon producing country-house fire engines intended for private use. These were often quite substantial and effective appliances, and by the early years of the nineteenth century many a country house and its adjoining estate had a level of fire protection far greater than any of the surrounding towns and villages. The more magnanimous of such landed proprietors would despatch their private brigade to assist at outbreaks on farms or villages in the area; Sir Thomas Acland sent the Killerton House engine to the fire at Stoke Cannon on 21st April 1841, when some 30 houses were destroyed but many more were saved.

*Axminster was another town with a well-established brigade, of which five members pose here; Axmister went in for beards and mutton-chop whiskers, it would seem! The men here are: standing left to right – W.E. Pitfield Chapple (Captain) – Solicitor; W. Enticott , Plumber; Walter Connett, Cabinet Maker. Sitting , left to right – Levi Welch, Landlord of the Red Lion Inn; W. Frost, Haulier. Axminster had a modern (c.1870) manual pump, and were hot on the marketing front with a neatly-printed scale of charges.*

### AXMINSTER FIRE BRIGADE.

#### SCALE OF CHARGES
FOR ATTENDING FIRES

|  | £ | s. | d. |
|---|---|---|---|
| For Calling ... ... ... | 0 | 5 | 0 |
| „ Horses—according to distance |  |  |  |
| „ Use of Engine ... ... | 2 | 2 | 0 |
| „ Firemen each—2/6 for the first hour, 1/6 the second hour, and 1/- every hour after ... ... |  |  |  |
| „ Pumpers—6d. per hour ... |  |  |  |
| „ Additional help—2/6 per man for 4 hours or less, and 6d. per hour after ... ... ... |  |  |  |
| „ Refreshments—according to time men are at work ... ... |  |  |  |
| „ Watchers—according to time employed ... ... ... |  |  |  |
| „ Cleaning Engine, Hose, Stand-pipes, &c., afterwards ... | 0 | 10 | 6 |

All damage to Engine, Hose, or other appliances to be paid for by the Company who have the property insured where the fire happens.

#### W. E. PITFIELD CHAPPLE,
February, 1898.                                    CAPTAIN.

*Above: South Molton Fire Brigade in the 1890s – an exceptionally well-set-up brigade for a small market town, with a relatively modern and large Merryweather manual dating – it would seem – from 1886. They also had a very smart one-horse hose cart and an escape ladder. The sixteen firefighters have smart uniform and a wondrous selection of moustaches.*

*Top right: Country house fire provision was often 'of the best', in keeping with the status of the owners! Many a public brigade would have given their collective eye teeth for something as splendid as this 'Little Gem' Merryweather steam pump of the 1880s, which was bought new for Trehiddy House in Cornwall. It is here seen at one of the post-war Plymouth City Fire Brigade Gala Days at the Raglan Barracks.*

*This view of the serious fire at Southwood's stationers and printers, Exeter, in 1906 is full of interesting detail. Two escape ladders are in use, of which the nearer is the Shand, Mason sixty-foot escape bought for the Exeter City Fire Brigade fitted with props to allow it to be used standing free of the building as a water tower (this before the days of turntable ladders, at least this side of the Atlantic). The Shand, Mason ladder has the 'underneath' extension typical of its maker; the other escape has convention top-sliding ladders and a fly-ladder at its head.*

The steamer 'Devonia' on parade at Exeter's Nothernhay Place drill ground about 1900, showing the sort of horses used to pull a typical steamer – which weighed about 30 c.w.t. – small and handy but strong. Somewhat stronger horses are seen on the Escape Van at the rear of the picture – these usually tipped the scales at a couple of tons; wheeled escapes are heavy pieces of equipment.

## THE FIRE PROFESSIONALS – EXETER'S FIRE BRIGADES

While the situation in the countryside ranged from the shambles of the untrained parish pump-men to the part-time professionalism of the insurance brigades, the latter had long been the standard in the larger towns and the cities of Exeter and Plymouth. From all accounts, Exeter was particularly well-covered, with at least five fire offices – the West of England, the Sun, West Middlesex, Royal and Norwich Union – maintaining brigades in the city. It was just as well that the insurers made this provision to protect Exeter, as the city's own contribution amounted to a solitary manual engine dating from as long ago as 1626! Like all insurance establishments, these Exeter brigades were primarily set up to protect and preserve property, and had little equipment and no mandate to save life, although the West of England brigade – the biggest and from all accounts most proficient – did posses an escape. But otherwise the insurance brigades were equipped with manual pumps, mostly horse-drawn, carrying suction and delivery hose, a few hand tools and maybe a short ladder, but little else. The firemen did, however, have very smart uniforms!

All this changed after the disastrous Theatre Royal fire of September 1887, which claimed a total of 166 lives. Subsequent upon this dreadful event, the insurers and the city council met in December 1887 and resolved to provide Exeter with a fully-constituted public fire brigade equipped and trained to save life as well as property. This followed the purchase by public subscription of a new steam fire engine to replace the city's antique pre-Newsham manual pump, which finally gave out in 1837. This steamer, a Merryweather 'Little Gem' with a 350-g.p.m pump, was named 'Devonia' and was presented to the citizens as part of the Jubilee celebrations in October 1887; it soon came to form the nucleus of Exeter's new public brigade.

The Municipal Fire Brigade was founded on 1 March 1888 and as well as the fine new steam fire engine also took over the equipment of two of the insurance companies – the West of England and the Sun – amounting to three manual engines and the West of England's escape. The new brigade also assumed responsibility for the two street escapes stationed in the city, and based itself at the former West of England brigade station in New North Road. There were eighteen firemen, six whole-time with

*Right: The St Thomas Brigade station in Cowick Street also survives today, latterly used as a community centre. It was last used to house AFS machines and crews after the war.*

*Far Right: This is the original Exeter fire station in New North Road as it is today; originally, it was somewhat larger, but part of it was demolished in 1832 after the new Dane's Castle station opened. Originally built for the 'Little West' insurance brigade, it became the first headquarters of the Exeter Municipal Brigade and was used until 1931.*

quarters on the station and the remainder retained on the insurance company scheme, plus an engineer and two messengers, all serving under their newly-appointed 'Superintendent', William Pett. As well as the four fire engines, the brigade owned a hose cart and an equipment cart, plus a considerable quantity of hose, nozzles, standpipes, axes, buckets and so on. The new fire brigade also installed street telegraph alarms, twenty of them situated at key points about the city.

The new Exeter municipal brigade proved very successful, and in 1889 a second independent brigade was set up west of the Exe in the parish of St Thomas, with a fire station in Cowick Street, the main doorway of which is still visible today. The St Thomas' engine was a horse-drawn manual, and there were ten retained firemen and a chief, trained by Exeter's

*Two Exeter firemen enrolled to fight in the Boer War. They are here pictured with 'Superintendant' Pett – in full regalia – in front of one of the ex-insurance manual machines.*

The Exeter steamer 'Devonia'. This is described in some sources as being a Merryweather 'Greenwich Gem' but this picture looks very much like a Shand, Mason 'Double Vertical' with twin upright cylinders and pumps behind the boiler and the characteristic elongated air vessel. It also lacks the characteristic Merryweather footboard and other salient details. Unfortunately the maker's plate on the side of the boiler is not visible – but the name and Exeter City arms are.

Superintendent Pett. The Exeter brigade was modernised over the years, replacing the original hinged street escapes with two 60-foot sliding-carriage escapes and adding a Shand, Mason telescopic escape with props that could also be used as a free-standing 'water tower' to project water onto a fire from above. The 'Devonia' remained the main appliance until the brigade received its first motor pump-escape, the solid-tyred 'Exonia', from Merryweathers in 1914. A further motor appliance, a Fiat ex-WD truck, was purchased in 1921 and fitted out as a chemical first-strike engine; it was also used to tow the 'Devonia' in place of horses. The gallant old steamer was finally retired in March, 1924, when a second Merryweather pump-escape was purchased. 'Exonia' then became purely a pump, being modernised and fitted with pneumatic tyres.

The original Exeter Merryweather motor pump 'Exonia', as later modified with pneumatic tyres and running as a pump rather than a PE as originally supplied. Note the electric gong – an unusual fitment. When new, this appliance was identical to the Devonport and Plymouth Merryweathers illustrated later in this chapter.

21

*Exeter City Fire Brigade in 1927: Back row, left to right – F. Maunder, F. Webber, R. Gard, F. Fry, C. Rookes, S. Shepherd, W. Bowden, F. Penberthy, S. Burford, R. Paskell, W. Gibbs, S. Clapp.*

*Middle row, left to right – F. Parker, L. Holmes, W. Mogridge, S. Davey, E. Avery, J. Tancock, F. Woodland, T. Combes, P. Down, S. Clapp, L. Woodland.*

*Front row , left to right – H. J. Hartnoll (Sub Engineer), J. Hartnoll, W. Melluish (Foreman), R. Shepherd (Engineer), William Pett (Chief Officer), W. Hill (Second Officer), J. Kelley, F. Sculpher (ex-cabinetmaker, responsible for out-fitting the Bedford appliance).*

William Pett oversaw all these developments, and by the time he finally retired in May 1927 after 39 years service, the City of Exeter Fire Brigade, as it became after absorbing the St Thomas Brigade around 1900, was one of the most progressive and best-equipped in the country. But by the late 1920s, the old headquarters fire station at New North Road had become quite inadequate for the enlarged and re-equipped brigade, and the city council were actively considering the construction of a new central fire station. The site chosen was Dane's Castle, near the prison, and the new station opened in 1931; at the time, it was one of the largest and most modern fire stations in the country outside the major cities, with room for four appliances, a drill yard and tower, and living quarters – in the form of substantial houses – for the six full-time firefighters, plus accommodation in the main station for the new Chief Officer, Mr F. Richards and his deputy, Second Officer Wain.

*Dane's Castle from the air – a modern picture taken from the top of the 'Bronto' aerial ladder platform, but showing the station essentially as built in 1931. The three semi-detached houses at the rear were built to house firefighters, while the CFO's accommodation was at the left-hand side. The building with the pale-coloured ridged roof at the rear is the brigade workshop – still in use – with the well-tended gardens to the fore.*

Under CFO Richards, the brigade expanded and modernised still further. A third new motor engine, built by the brigade themselves on a Bedford chassis, was placed in service in 1933. This 'No.3 engine' had an early example of the 'New World' style of coachwork, with the crew safely seated along the centre of the equipment lockers rather perched on top or hanging onto the sides of the traditional 'Braidwood' body that originated with the horse-drawn manual. The new engine carried a side-mounted 35-foot Bayley wooden extending ladder as well as hook and roof ladders, and towed a Merryweather 'Hatfield' 250-g.p.m. trailer pump. It could carry a crew of twelve men and, being fitted with pneumatic tyres, was both speedy and comfortable.

*The opening of Dane's Castle on 25th November 1931, with a full complement (46) of firefighters. The appliances are, from the left, the new Merryweather pump-escape FJ 2939 bought in 1924 – which had an enclosed cab, unusual at that time – with 'Exonia' in the centre and the ex-WD Fiat first-aid tender FJ 1530 on the right.*

*This is Exeter's home-built 'No. 3' appliance, constructed over a Bedford 2-ton 'long' commercial chassis of a type usually used for buses. This came from Ried and Lee of Exeter and cost £183 10s 0d in April 1933. The progressive 'New World' coachwork (first seen in Birmingham in 1930) was built in the brigade workshops at Dane's Castle under the direction of Chief Officer Richards, who had succeeded William Pett when the latter finally retired in 1927. The excellent finish of the coachwork was down to ex-cabinet-maker Fireman Sculpher. The machine had a 'long Bayley' ladder on the offside and hook ladders on the nearside, with plenty of locker space and seating for a crew of twelve – so perhaps it was nearly a bus! It towed a Merryweather 'Hatfield' trailer pump of the type shown above – a powerful reciprocating pump, but very heavy to manhandle if needs be.*

*In 1934, Exeter obtained its first TL, a new Merryweather all-metal mechanically-operated ladder on an Albion chassis. This must have been one of the first all-steel TLs made by Merryweather, who up till this point were using steel-trussed wooden ladders. The reach was 85-feet and Fireman Shepherd is on the monitor in this 1935 view taken from the top of the drill tower.*

*A studio portait of Exeter fireman G. Rookes, taken in October 1933.*

Early in 1935, the Exeter brigade received two further new appliances from their preferred supplier, Merryweathers – an 85-foot mechanically-actuated turntable ladder and a new pump-escape to replace 'Exonia'. The TL was fitted with a powerful Dorman, Long petrol engine and a turbine pump and had, apparently, a surprising turn of speed. The new PE was on Merryweather's favoured 'Albion' chassis, with a self-priming reciprocating pump (Merryweathers preferred piston pumps when Dennis and most rivals had gone for turbines by 1914 or so) and servo brakes. This machine was sold to a private industrial brigade and is believed to be still in existence today. Under the immediate pre-war provisions, when money was made available to many municipal brigades to purchase additional equipment, Exeter acquired a further motor PE in the form of a Leyland 'Cub', then a very popular appliance with a fine reputation. This had pneumatic tyres and a 30hp 6-cylinder engine with dual ignition, making it speedy, good on hills and a very reliable starter.

## PLYMOUTH CITY FIREFIGHTING

Plymouth in the nineteenth century was a lot smaller than the 'greater Plymouth' of today, and places like Stonehouse, Devonport, Plympton and Plymstock were very much separate towns with their own administrations and hence their own firefighting provision. The history of firefighting in Plymouth city proper up to the time of the formation of the first municipal 'police brigade' in 1891 is unfortunately a lot less well-documented than the equivalent period of development in Exeter, but it is known that at least four insurance brigades were operating in Plymouth in the first part of the nineteenth century. These were the Commercial Union, Sun, Phoenix Fire Office and the Eagle Insurance company. There was also a fire engine called the 'Firefly' which may well have belonged to the West of England office, which preferred to name its fire engine companies.

However, it seems apparent that by mid-century Plymouth had some form of 'Local Board' or municipal fire brigade, which may well have incorporated some of the older insurance brigades. In the later part of the nineteenth century, the city did rather well so far as modern equipment was concerned, the first steam fire engine to arrive being none other than Merryweather's famous 'Sutherland' which had gained the first prize in the 1863 Crystal Palace fire engine trials, after which it was acquired by the Admiralty for Devonport Dockyard. Three years later, Plymouth city proper was presented with a steamer by The 'London & Liverpool' and 'Globe' insurance companies. This was described as a 'Merryweather Light Steam Fire Engine', possibly one of the original single-cylinder 'Deluge' type. In 1888, the Western Insurance Company provided a second Merryweather steamer, although the type is not recorded.

As well as the two Plymouth steamers, the adjoining brigades in Stonehouse and Devonport were also equipped with up-to-date firefighting apparatus. Stonehouse Fire Brigade were presented with a Shand, Mason 'double vertical' steam pump by a 'prominent local resident' in 1894, while at roughly the same date Devonport also had a steamer – described as a Merryweather, although from the photograph reproduced here it would also seem to be a Shand, Mason. (Merryweather steamers generally had their twin-cylinder horizontal pumps in front of the boiler, whereas Shand, Mason placed their vertical pump aft of the boiler, as here.) The Devonport picture also shows a late-model manual and a underneath-extending escape with props. Both these appliances also look to be of Shand, Mason & Co.'s manufacture.

*Stonehouse Fire Brigade in 1900 with their Shand, Mason vertical steam pump, presented by a 'prominent local resident'.*

*Devonport Fire Brigade with their steamer in 1904, described as a Merryweather but of the vertical design, so possibly a also Shand, Mason vertical type.*

The Naval Dockyard was always self-sufficient in firefighting facilities – a move that was only prudent given the high degree of risk in an establishment that stored large quantities of timber, tar and pitch, canvas and cordage – not to mention gunpowder and other munitions! Nineteenth-century plans of the dockyard show a number of 'fire engine houses': an 1879 plan of the site has 'fire engine house No.2' marked adjacent to the officer's quarters as part of the Strong Room building – the No.1 house being in the South Yard – while an 1883 plan of the Keyham seaman's barracks has a further 'fire engine room' shown beneath the 'glasshouse' and guard room. An 1888 plan marks 'stables for Team and Fire Engine horses', while by 1912 there is a new, separate 'fire engine house' adjoining the police station on the New Saltash Road entrance, with 'Fire Engine House No.1' shown in the South Yard next to a further new and substantial fire station marked 'fire engine house and sleeping quarters for fire party'.

*Devonport's Chief Officer Burns – typical of a brigade commander of his day. At this time, firefighting was still very much a local affair, and each brigade – no matter how small – had its hierarchy.*

A classic studio portrait of Fireman Boaden of Devonport, taken in 1902.

A very interesting photograph of Plymouth's Merryweather Fire King self-propelled steamer at work at a fire in a storeroom at the Devonport Military Hospital in 1912. The nursing staff have obviously been evacuated while the fire crews get to work. The Devonport brigade would presumably also have attended this incident.

Plymouth Fire Brigade's Merryweather Fire King self-propelled steamer of 1906. Many attempts had been made to produce a self-propelled steam fire engine, but the Merryweather Fire King of 1899 was the only commercially successful design. A Fire King would do 20 m.p.h. on the level and could climb a steep grade at a steady 10 m.p.h. – ideal for a hilly city like Plymouth. Steam could be raised fully in six minutes from cold, far less if the boiler water was kept hot by a gas burner on the station, when only 1–2 minutes was needed to get enough steam to start off. The early Fire Kings had 300 g.p.m. pumps, but later versions (the machine remained in production until 1922) could move 1,000 g.p.m.

Several fire engines are listed for the naval dockyard in returns for the later nineteenth century, including: 'Three large double-cylinder manuals, 2 Merryweather 'Greenwich Gem' steam pumps, 1 'vertical Greenwich' stationary pump and two small 'Valiants' – believed to be hand-pulled manuals. There is no mention of the 1863 'Sutherland', but it is hard to believe it would not also still be in use at this time. All of which indicates a substantial establishment, at least part of which was full-time. Indeed, it may well have been the case that the naval firefighting establishment in the dockyard was larger than the civilian provision in the city.

The development of the Plymouth Police Fire Brigade after its formation from the old insurance and local brigades in 1891 paralleled that in Exeter in several respects. But there was one important difference; being a 'police brigade', Plymouth operated as a branch of the police force rather than as a separate, dedicated organisation in its own right. This was a common arrangement at the time, but one which inevitably suffered from clashes of interest, particularly where the same men and financial resources were needed to undertake two quite disparate jobs. As was usually the case, the fire service was very much the subordinate partner, and its organisation and operations were directed essentially by police officers rather than professional firefighters. This was to have serious consequences in the later history of the Plymouth brigade, especially during the war.

The establishment of the Plymouth brigade in 1891 was quite modest in respect of the risk to be covered, although the levels of provision were undoubtedly influenced by the presence of the substantial naval fire brigade based in the Devonport dockyard and the well-equipped adjoining brigades of Devonport and Stonehouse. There were also a number of private brigades, such as that of the *Western Morning News* newspaper office, which were recorded as assisting the 'Police Brigade' on occasions. In Plymouth proper, there was a principal station called Penlee, situated in Molesworth Road, Stoke, with a further station at Torr in the Mannamead area. Stonehouse and Devonport remained as separate brigades and did not become part of Plymouth City until later – Stonehouse amalgamated in 1916, but Devonport was independent until 1941.

*Plymouth Fire Brigade ranged outside the Guildhall some time after the arrival of the Fire King, which has now been joined by a Merryweather motor pump/escape of about 1912 vintage. This was the first real production type of Merryweather motor appliance, although Merryweathers had built their first motor fire engine in 1904 and had supplied a number of different designs in the interim. In this view, the escape has been slipped and a number of men have mounted the ladders.*

At around the turn of the century, Plymouth took delivery of a Merryweather Fire King self-propelled steam fire engine, the last word in fire-fighting apparatus at that time. Although little faster than a horsed steamer, a Fire King was ready for instant action and had superior hill-climbing capability – important in Plymouth. Two escape ladders are also listed at this time, and one of these appears to have been mounted on the first Plymouth motor fire engine, a solid-tyred Merrweather. This is shown – together with the Fire King – in the picture taken outside the Guildhall, from which evidence it appears that the machine may also have a pump, making it a very early 'pump-escape'. Devonport acquired a similar Merryweather pump-escape in 1914, shown in the official Merryweather 'works portrait' reproduced here. In 1920, Plymouth is recorded as having acquired a Belsize pump-escape with a Morris wooden escape ladder, and this may well have replaced the Fire King. Devonport also had a Merryweather motor pump of the same type as the Plymouth and Devonport machines, and this passed to Plymouth in 1916. In 1930, a new Dennis 30-h.p. motor pump was bought by the Plymouth brigade, a machine with a pumping capability of 700 g.p.m. In 1933, the city

*Devonport's 1914 Merryweather, the same type as the machines supplied to Plymouth and Exeter. These sturdy appliances usually had a 4-cylinder Aster petrol engine of 30-h.p. which drove the road wheels via a 3-speed gearbox and a chain final drive. The gearbox was connected to the engine by a shaft which also carried a simple sliding-pinion power-take-off to drive the 250-g.p.m. 'Hatfield' pump mounted at the rear – essentially, the prototype of almost every motor fire pump built since. These machines could carry either a fifty-foot wheeled escape, as here, or a simple extension ladder. They also had a small first-aid water tank of 40-gallons capacity which fed a hosereel via the pump.*

*Here is Plymouth's first TL, which arrived in 1933 – a year before Exeter's machine. So this was one of the last Merryweather TLs built with wooden ladders trussed by steel rodding – from the following year, the lightweight all-steel design was introduced, a development which made longer ladders of 100-foot reach possible. This was almost certainly a 70 or 75-foot ladder. Most 1920s Merryweather appliances were built on chassis by the Scottish lorry-builder Albion. This TL was later sold, being replaced by a 100-foot Leyland/Merryweather early in the war.*

*Right: Merryweather's main rivals in the motor fire appliance field were Dennis Bros. of Guildford, Surrey, still building fire appliances today. Their famous model 'N' with a Gwyne turbine pump was introduced in 1914, and was technically more advanced than the Merryweather with its reciprocating 'Hatfield' pump. Plymouth turned to Dennis for a new appliance in 1930, when they took delivery of this pump fitted with a 30-h.p. Dennis petrol engine driving a powerful Tamini-designed centrifugal pump with a 500 g.p.m output. This appliance had pneumatic tyres and electric lighting, and remained 'on the run' at Station 'B' Penlee into the 1950s.*

*Plymouth Police Fire Brigade at the fire which severely damaged the Plymouth workhouse in 1936. This picture sums up somewhat ironically the problem with a joint police force/fire brigade; people aren't quite sure which role they belong in...*

*Opening of Greenbank fire station, 1935. Plenty of civic dignitaries, plenty of policemen; but ne'er a fireman in sight!*

received its first turntable ladder, a Merryweather. From the photo reproduced here, it is seen to be an older design of TL with trussed wooden ladders in three sections, probably of about 75-foot reach. The chassis is believed to be an Albion. The last pre-war appliance to be delivered new was a 1938 Leyland PE with 'cross-bench' bodywork, received under the provisions of the Fire Services Act of that year. At the same time, Plymouth acquired its first Emergency Tender, an adaptation of a very handsome coachbuilt horsebox on a Bedford chassis.

In the 1930s Plymouth, like Exeter, opted to erect a brand new purpose-built headquarters fire station at Greenbank, Mutley. Although not quite as grand as Dane's Castle in the first instance, Greenbank was conceived as a two-stage project, with the basic fire station being completed in 1935. Provision was made to add a further floor to provide headquarters accommodation, but this work was not in fact completed until after the war. The photo of the opening ceremony reproduced here says everything there is to say about the status of firefighters in a police brigade; civic dignitaries and policeman by the mile, but barely a fireman to be seen. The parade is led by the Chief Constable A. K. Wilson who was also, ex-officio, the Chief Fire Officer.

## THE FIRE BRIGADE IN FASHIONABLE TORBAY

Throughout the nineteenth and early twentieth century the popularity of Torbay as a 'watering place' grew steadily, especially once the Great Western Railway – with their ground-breaking publicity department – took a hand. This led to rapid development in the area, with bespoke villas for the well-off jostling with fashionable hotels, theatres and amusements of all kinds and a wide range of commercial property. Most of this construction was new and substantial, and masonry buildings with slate or tile roofs predominated. Much reconstruction of older settlements took place, however, so that while the new promenade areas adjacent to the seafront were elegant and spacious, with many gardens, squares and open spaces along the wide boulevards of the emerging 'English Riviera', behind this relaxed elegance lay a jumble of narrow, winding streets packed with new buildings upon the street-plan of the old fishing port. The fire risk, both in terms of property value and life, was substantial, and the 'local board' and the West of England Insurance Company soon had brigades in the area.

The first of these was an early example of the town authorities assuming the responsibilities of the churchwardens. The Local Government Board took over from the parish in 1832, and their 22-man brigade was equipped with a horse-drawn manual fire engine – although the horses had to be hired when needed. In 1841 a fire station 'to house two engines' was built next to the site of the Town Hall. This seems to have been a temporary affair because subsequent to the 1851 building of the 'Old Town Hall' the fire station was recorded as being 'under the town hall in Lower Union Street'. In 1880, the Local Board built a new fire station in Market Street with accommodation for ten firefighters and stabling for dedicated fire brigade horses, and these premises were in use until 1955. They were recorded as being 'connected to the telephone exchange' in 1892. In 1889, the Torquay brigade opened their first sub-station at Torre, which seems to have been primarily an escape station although there was also a stock of hose. In 1890, a separate volunteer brigade was formed at Cockington. This was no ramshackle affair, but a very smart and professional brigade equipped with a brand-new Merryweather steam fire engine that must have been the envy of Torquay! The Cockington brigade had

*Torquay Fire Brigade's horsed 'escape van', a classic example of this relatively short-lived type of appliance, taken in 1900; this fine vehicle also had chemical first-aid apparatus. However, the far speedier motor appliance was the obvious candidate to carry life-saving apparatus like the escape as soon as it became sufficiently reliable. Most horse-escapes had gone by 1915 or so.*

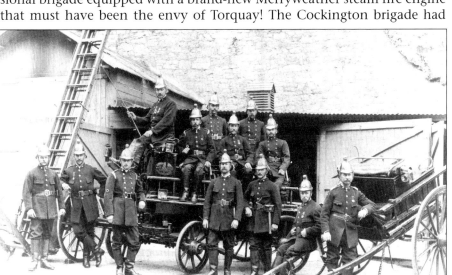

*The yard of the Market Street fire station some time between 1900–1910, with a fascinating array of equipment in view. The shed at the far left housed the ex-Cockington brigade Merryweather steam fire pump, while the less-than-prepossessing range of sheds leaning against the rear wall of the yard were home to the large manual machine in the centre, a further ex-insurance manual and the racy-looking hose cart at right. At the left is a three-section fixed-carriage escape ladder with wire trussing and underneath extensions – a lightweight design intended for manual handling. The heavier sliding-carriage escape was carried by the escape van. The thirteen men seen here were almost certainly those recorded as living on the premises at this time.*

the patronage of Squire Mallock, but was absorbed into the expanding Torquay brigade in the early years of the twentieth century. Further sub-stations were also opened at St Marychurch, Chelston (the old Cockington brigade station) and Wellswood. These were primarily escape stations – St Marychurch having two escapes and a hose cart, Chelston one escape and a hose cart and Wellswood one escape plus a stock of hose.

By 1910 the Torquay Corporation Fire Brigade, as it became in 1894, was quite substantial. Its headquarters was still the 1880 Market Street station, which was very awkwardly situated in a confined yard behind 'Corporation Buildings' – the block of flats housing the firemen – with the exit through an arch into Market Street. The flats had call-bells on the landings to rouse the crews, and are still in existence as 'Albert Court'. Market Street station housed a steam pump (presumably the 1890 Cockington machine), a horse-drawn escape van with chemical apparatus, a horsed manual pump (probably the ex-West of England insurance machine, passed to the Board when the insurance brigade disbanded in the early 1890s), an additional escape and a single-horse hose cart. The establishment was 'Superintendent' T. S. Weeks, two officers and 25 men, of whom 13 lived at Market Street. St Marychurch had an officer and six men, Chelston an officer and five men, and Wellswood and Torre seem to

*Steam fire pumps needed regular overhaul, as with any machinery. This view of the Torquay Merryweather undergoing major work shows the characteristic boiler design, with a water jacket around the firebox and water-tubes through the heart of the fire to ensure the maximum heating surface and hence the rapid evaporation needed to get a quick head of steam. The notice reads: 'Good luck to all you boys' with, beneath, a list of names – Drum, Webber, Hearn, Melhuish and Vosper. This suggests the picture might date from 1914 and enlistment. One wonders what today's Health and Safety culture would make of the way in which the appliance has been raised to allow the firebox to be dropped out!*

*Torquay's second motor appliance was this handsome Leyland which arrived in 1930.*

have been manned either on a retained basis or by volunteers. The total of seven escapes in the town was a remarkable provision for the time and reflected the high life risk represented by the many hotels and boarding-houses; at this date, Exeter had three escapes and Plymouth only two. Chelston was upgraded to a full fire station in 1913, although the appliance allocated there is not recorded; it may well have been the old West of England manual.

Torquay's first motor appliance, a chain-driven solid-tyred Merryweather pump-escape, arrived in May 1920, being christened the 'Firefly' by the mayoress. This machine was modified with pneumatic tyres in the later 1930s and remained in service into the war years. It was later joined by a Leyland pump/ladder DV 5732 in the later 1920s, and in 1939 the famous Torquay TL /pump arrived. This was on a Leyland chassis and had a 100-foot Metz ladder in five sections rather than the usual three, to keep the appliance short enough to negotiate the turn into the Market Street station; even so, there were problems, and on receipt of a 'shout' for the TL a firefighter used to rush to the street exit of the arch and yell 'Up blinds!' at the top of his voice – whereupon the butcher opposite would hurry out, pole in hand, to furl his shop-blind before the speeding TL carried it away.

As well as the public brigade, the West of England insurance brigade operated in Torquay from a small station in the Market Hall. This brigade commenced operations around 1850, and was equipped with a seven-inch (cylinder bore) horse-drawn manual pump and had a strength of six men under 'foreman' John Chilcott, pumpers presumably being hired as needed along with the horses. By 1890 the insurance brigade had eight men under foreman Stephen Warren, but by 1892 it had been disbanded and its equipment given to the Torquay Corporation. The Market Hall station was used for some time as an annex to the cramped Market Street station. It is not recorded whether the insurance firefighters became part of the public brigade, although this is quite likely as the strength of the Torquay Corporation establishment went from 'three superintendents and fourteen men' in 1892 to four officers and 34 men in 1910. The expanded Torquay brigade participated keenly in the various fire brigade competitions popular in the

*Paignton Fire Brigade about 1905 with their Shand, Mason steam pump, complete with hand-cranked blower in the chimney to help with quick steam-raising. The splendid shield was won in one of the popular drill competitions organised by the West of England Fire Brigade Society – it probably put their neighbour's nose out of joint, as Torquay were accustomed to triumph in these events! Note the bare-foot lad looking on, and the old fire station in Palace Avenue.*

early twentieth century, and in 1910 became the National Lifesaving Champions, to great acclaim in there town.

The Torquay brigade were by no means isolated, and in times of need could reckon on plenty of support. There was a separate municipal brigade at nearby Paignton, a smart and well-equipped outfit with a Shand, Mason 'Vertical' steam pumper and an escape ladder. They were based at a station in Palace Avenue street. Before the Second World War, Paignton acquired a very fine Leyland PE which remained in service into the 1950s. Elsewhere in Torbay, Brixham also had a substantial fire brigade, and the town brigades at Newton Abbot and Totnes were close at hand; these latter two brigades, along with the 'local board' engine, were recorded as attending a fire at Marchetts (now Queens) Hotel as long ago as 1833.

**Torquay Corporation Fire Brigade**

GENERAL OUTLINE OF DUTIES, &c.

The following General Instructions are to be observed with reference to Station Duties and the Brigade's attendance at Fires, Drills, etc.

1. The Senior Fireman on Station Duty is responsible for receiving all calls, either by telephone or messenger.

2. On receipt of a call, the Officer or Fireman in charge for the time being will give instructions to switch on the call bells at Headquarters, and for the opening of the doors of the Fire Station, and will detail a Fireman to remain in the Station on telephone duty, and make a Brigade call, if necessary.

3. An entry of the time at which the call is received, also the exact situation of the fire, must at once be recorded in the Log Book, and full information as to the nature of the outbreak obtained.

4. In all cases of DOUBTFUL calls for the services of the Brigade, the information must be immediately conveyed to the Chief Officer, by telephone or otherwise.

5. Police Headquarters must be notified of all calls as soon as possible.

6. The saving of life is the first duty of the Fire Brigade, and the sending out of *adequate life-saving appliances* is the *first duty* of the Officer or Fireman in charge.

7. Every Fireman is expected to obey without a moment's hesitation all orders he may receive from his superiors in the Brigade, *and he is strictly forbidden to obey an order from any other person* ; but if a suggestion appears to be of sufficient importance, he can submit it to the Officer in command. Nothing tends in a greater degree to the efficiency of a Fire Brigade than *silence, strict discipline, and perfect steadiness on duty.*

8. A Senior Fireman is expected to set an example to the Firemen of alacrity and skill in the discharge of his duty, and of regularity and punctuality at all drills. In the absence of his superior officers he will take command. He must be careful to place the engines in such a manner that the men who work the appliances

*Rules of Torbay Corporation Fire Brigade*

*Severe flooding in the basement of Williams & Cox on The Strand Torquay on 4th of August 1938, just over a year before the major fire which swept through the store and adjoining property. Torquay's Leyland Pump/Ladder DV5732 is doing the pumping out. Such flooding was fairly common in this area of the Strand, with properties in Union Street and Fleet Street encountering a similar fate, invariably this also coincided with a high tide, the floodwater being unable to drain away quickly enough, merely back filled the drainage system forcing water out back into the streets.*

## BARNSTAPLE, BIDEFORD AND ILFRACOMBE BRIGADES

The other main centre of population in Devon has always been in the north, particularly the ancient borough of Barnstaple and the equally ancient port of Bideford. Also of increasing importance in the nineteenth century was North Devon's own fashionable watering-place, Ilfracombe. All three of these towns represented extensive risks at the turn of the nineteenth century and quite early in the period of growth that took place in the Victorian era their firefighting establishments were put on a firm public footing.

Barnstaple was, in the earlier part of the nineteenth century, protected by one or more insurance company brigades; the offices providing engines are not recorded, but it seems likely that at least one was from the West of England fire office. From about mid-century, the Local Board assumed the Parish responsibilities and set up a 'Borough' brigade, responsible for attending fires within Barnstaple Borough boundary, working in concert with a 'Barnstaple Rural' brigade covering the outlying areas. The 'Borough' brigade apparently took over the insurance company provisions and was housed beneath the Guildhall, using the adjacent Pannier Market for training. The 'Rural' brigade was actually a private works brigade, that of Shapland and Petter's cabinet works on the south bank of the River Taw. This brigade made themselves available 'to attend fires throughout North Devon and to assist the Borough Brigade on request.' Both brigades were initially equipped with the usual manual appliances, but by the end of the century the Borough brigade had a Shand, Mason steamer named 'Artavia One'.

With the growth of the town and following a series of serious fires in the North Devon area, the Barnstaple Borough brigade was modernised by the

*This Major Fire started in Williams & Cox store on The Strand, Torquay on the evening of Thursday, September 21st 1939 and was one of Torquay's largest ever, quickly spreading to three other shopping premises including the well-known Bobby's next door, together with shops occupied by Messrs, Maynard, confectioners, and Messrs T. Swift and Son, Tobacconist, and two or three flats at the back of these premises. Members of all A.R.P. services, as well as Territorials and the Brigades of five towns (Paignton, Newton Abbot, Brixham, Dartmouth, and Totnes) assisted the Torquay brigade who were quickly on the scene, but the fire was already well established and burning fiercely on their arrival.*

Barnstaple Fire Brigade in 1926 – medals and moustaches to the fore!

acquisition of a Dennis motor pump, 'Artavia Two', to serve alongside the steamer. New premises were required to house the extra machine, and these were found when the fire station moved to Castle Street, next to Queen Anne's Walk. This station also housed a former street escape, thus concentrating the town's firefighting resources at a single location. By this time, the 'Rural' brigade had disappeared from accounts, as by the late 1920s Barnstaple, Bideford and Ilfracombe all had motor appliances capable of responding swiftly over greater distances. In 1934 the steam pump 'Artavia One' was sold to a timber yard in Braunton, who sold it on to a factory in Chard, Somerset. It was replaced, in 1937, by a Leyland 'Cheetah' pump 'Artavia Three', probably under the Home Office arrangements resulting from the Riverdale Report of the previous year; it is notable how many Devon brigades received new appliances – almost all Leylands – in 1937/8.

As elsewhere, Barnstaple's firefighting provision was substantially bolstered during the war with an AFS detachment and strengthening of the regular brigade. New premises for the expanded brigade were provided by adapting the former Allendale & Walker's garage in Boutport Street, opened in 1941 just before Barnstaple became an NFS station. From here, regular and AFS crews attended blitz fires in Plymouth and Exeter as well as travelling further afield, to Bristol and even being mobilised to Coventry, although on this occasion the Barnstaple men were re-directed to Avonmouth Docks. After the war, Barnstaple fire station continued at Boutport Street as station B1 and North Division headquarters of the Devon County Service until the new North Road station opened in 1964.

## BIDEFORD FIRE BRIGADE

Bideford was early in the field with a public fire provision, the town – helped by the Bridge Trustees – buying a manual fire engine in 1770; this, from contemporary illustrations, appears to have been a Nutall vertical type with pumping handles at either end, equipped with leather fire hose. It was kept, as was so often the case, 'beneath the town hall' and was taken out and 'played off' every two months or so. In the early years of the nineteenth century, the town engine was joined by the West of England Fire Insurance Office, who also stationed a manual fire engine in Bideford. In 1847, this machine was replaced with a new manual built by Kingdons of Exeter, the main firm of iron-workers in Devon at the time. They also manufactured fire hydrants, and a few Kingdon hydrants are still in use to this day. Bideford's new machine was named 'Hero' in the customary manner. Thereafter, there was considerable rivalry between the West of England and the town brigades, resulting in some regrettable examples of non co-operation. By 1860, the Bideford Town Brigade also had a new manual, the three engines then available giving a substantial level of protection to the town. By 1870, Bideford had been provided with hydrants, or 'fire plugs', so called because they were, quite literally, wooden plugs driven into holes bored in the mains water pipes at the bottom of a pit. In use, the plug was removed, the pit flooded and the engine pumped from there. For reasons no longer clear, the Town Brigade was disbanded around 1880, although the engines were kept on hand.

This reliance on insurance cover only did not last long; a series of serious fires in the mid-1880s demonstrated the need for greater provision, and when the local brewery at Littleham burned down in March, 1885 it was resolved that the Town Brigade be reinstated under the Local Board as a volunteer brigade with a paid (£2 per annum!) 'Captain'. The new brigade formed early in 1887 with ten men under Captain Henry Chowins, the Borough Surveyor. A couple of handcarts with standpipes and hose and an escape ladder were added to the equipment, together with 'twenty four new buckets', purchased in 1903. There were two fire stations at this time, the main one on the Quay and a handcart shed in the Market Place. A new appliance finally arrived in 1917 when second-hand Shand, Mason steamer was bought from the Barnet Fire Brigade in Hertfordshire. This was a small steam pump but was still a great advance on the manual. It was housed in the Pannier Market building and the horses were stabled at the New Inn.

*'Grenville' again, on a melancholy occasion, the funeral of Bideford fireman Sherbourne, who died in 1832 at the early age of 47. The escape has been unshipped and the coffin mounted on the ladder gantry. The weather seems as doleful as the event.*

Bideford's 'Great Fire' was that which completely destroyed the important Edgehill College – a girl's boarding school – in June, 1920. Lack of a water supply to sustain the steam pump hampered operations, and the large range of buildings were a total loss. This caused a considerable upset, and

led eventually to the purchase in 1927 of the 'Grenville', Bideford's first motor fire engine. This was a solid-tyred Merryweather pump-escape with a Hatfield 250 g.p.m main pump and a second Hatfield 150 g.p.m. trailer pump. A new fire station was opened in what was left of Bideford Old Town Boys School, which had largely burned down in 1926! This station was rebuilt and refitted in 1928, by which time the brigade was known as the 'Bideford, Northam and District Fire Brigade' This brigade acquired a second motor appliance in the immediate pre-war period in 1938, presumably under the Riverdale Arrangements which subsidised such purchases. This was 'Kippling' a Merryweather machine on a six-cylinder Morris-Commercial chassis of 80 b.h.p., with a 400 g.p.m Hatfield pump. It took over the role of pump-escape, as 'Grenville' was a little slow on the hills when fully laden.

As with the other 'town' brigades in Devon, Bideford was reinforced by regulars and AFS men in the war, with seven trailer pumps and crews housed in a temporary fire station in Torrington Street, Bideford-East-the-Water. In 1941, Bideford became part of B division of NFS Fire Force 18. Bideford also improvised a fire barge, the 'Good Hope', from the old Ilfracombe lifeboat. This had two NFS ex-trailer pump units and was propelled by reaction from a fire jet. The worst wartime incident in Bideford was the crash of a Wellington bomber on the east bank of the river in 1945.

Ilfracombe's sixteen-man voluntary 'Local Board' brigade was formed at a public meeting called in 1874 and led by a retired artillery officer, a Captain Huxtable. The brigade was maintained by public subscription, and was provided with a fire station under the old town hall and a pre-existing parish manual engine. However, this machine was obviously somewhat wanting; a report of the first 'Exercise of the Fire Engine' in the *Ilfracombe Gazette* of 17th October 1874 concludes, after a jocular account of antics which resulted in elements of the citizenry getting very wet, that 'there is much room for amendment; the hose needs looking to (it was of two different sizes and types), and, in case of fire, it would not do to have the various parts of the apparatus in such a disorderly state...'. How disorderly the apparatus was can perhaps be judged by a further report in the *Gazette* of 12th August 1876, recording the first test of the 'New Fire Engine', a 24-man manual that would throw a 170-ft jet. However, when Ilfracombe's 'Great Fire' of July 1896 raged through Fore Street, The Arcade, Downs Court and part of Portland Street, the best efforts of the brigade and many volunteer pumpers using both old and new manual engines and a wheeled escape ladder could not contain the fire, which burned with great ferocity for four hours and destroyed 30 shops and houses.

As a result of the 'Great Fire', funds were speedily raised to re-equip Ilfracombe with a Merryweather 'Greenwich Gem' steam fire pump, named – as was the custom in those days – 'Victoria'; the brigade now became an Urban District retained establishment. The fire station was moved to more spacious premises in Wilder Road, and the reformed 14-man brigade had soon attained a good standard of efficiency, demonstrated by success in the drill competitions organised by the West of England Fire Brigades Union, which were very popular at that time. The steam pump was retired in 1927, the last fire at which it saw action being the Grand Hotel in March of 1926; it was replaced by 'Capstonia', one of the well-known Dennis Model N 350-g.p.m. turbine pumps, in January 1927. This had solid tyres and a 40/50h.p. petrol engine, boasted electric lighting and carried a 35-foot Bayley ladder. It also had a 40-gallon first-aid tank and hosereel. 'Capstonia' was tested in anger at the severe fire in outbuildings of the Imperial Hotel which occurred in March 1928, in bitter winter weather. In spite of difficulties with frozen hose, the Ilfracombe Brigade were successful in bringing the fire under control within an hour, and prevented it spreading to the main hotel. The Dennis remained in service until the end of the Ilfracombe Brigade's independent existence when the NFS formed in 1941.

## PUBLIC BRIGADES IN THE RURAL AREAS

The 1894 Local Government Act finally took firefighting in Britain out of the ad-hoc era of independent, unregulated parish, voluntary, retained and insurance brigades and placed the responsibility for fire protection squarely on the shoulders of the newly formed parish, rural district and urban district (town) councils. However, these new authorities had very considerable discretion as to what constituted the 'adequate' measures demanded by the Act. Inevitably, the consequences of the legislation varied widely across the country and, nowhere more so than within counties like Devon, which encompassed extremes of population density ranging from overcrowded Devonport to moorland hamlets with only a dozen or so dwellings. While the cities and the larger towns like Ilfracombe, Newton Abbot or Totnes already had substantial and efficient municipal brigades, the provision elsewhere varied widely.

*Above and right: Typical of a well-set-up country town brigade around the turn of the century – Cullompton had an insurance brigade by the mid-nineteenth century, a good foundation to build on. This would have been taken over by the Parish Council or Local Government Board under the 1894 Local Government Act as a municipal brigade, and here are the Cullompton Parish Council Brigade in 1910. The second picture was posed following a fire at the Rectory, Plymtree, in August 1911. They are equipped with a large Merryweather manual pump of about 1880 vintage.*

Some country towns – Cullompton being a good example – already had competent and well-equipped insurance or parish brigades that the new authorities could simply take over wholesale. Probably most notable of these pre-existing brigades was that at South Molton, which had a public brigade with a Newsham manual pump funded by public subscription as long ago as 1736, a very early date for such an institution. South Molton remained progressive, and by 1886 had a state-of-the art Merryweather horse-drawn manual, a Wivell type fly-escape with canvas chute, a 'jumping sheet' and a horse-drawn hose cart; the establishment was four officers and ten men. The town also had a system of fire-stops and hydrants, as set out in a 'directory' which gave exact positions of these water supplies. The fire station was in the Pannier Market – a common location shared by other Devon towns. South Molton became a RDC retained brigade and was motorised in 1926 with a solid-tyred Merryweather with a 250 g.p.m pump.

### List of Hydrants & Wells.

#### HYDRANTS.

**Broad Street**
Outside Lock's Shop, No. 11. Near North West Pillar of Town Hall. 5 ft. East of Skinner's side door, No. 2. 2 ft. from Telephone pole, New Walk Steps.

**East Street**
Near Allen's Steps, No. 3. 2 ft. out by side of Stediford's side door, No. 127. 1ft. from kerb, 3ft from gully opposite Miss Couch's No. 9. 3ft from kerb opposite United Methodist Ministers House, No. 21. 2ft out and 1ft East of Mr. G. Smiths Double-doors, No. 111. Centre of Mr. F. F. J. Sander's Bay Window, 4ft out and 10ft from end of flagging. Poplar Place, 9ft west of entrance. Children's Home, in slope west of steps, No. 41. Adam's Garden, No. 82, 1ft. east of door. Tan Yard, 16ft. east of steps. Lieut. Peuler's, No. 71, 1ft. bottom of steps. Collar Factory, at entrance oy Lamp-post.

**Station Road**
55ft. down from Lamp-post opposite Mr. F. F. J. Sander's, "Loughrigg." 4ft. South of gate, South of Tinto Hotel.

**North Street**
Drill Hall, 14ft. east of railings on opposite side. Snow's shop, No. 6, 2ft. from west end. 6ft. east of lamp near Mr. J. Avery's No. 20. Congregational Church—east end of railings.

**Parsonage Lane**
3ft. from Mr. Holdup's Garage, No. 9. Mr. Bodley's, No. 9 4ft. out and 2ft. below rear entrance.

*South Molton Fire Brigade Water Directory*

Crediton Fire Brigade in 1920 outside their fire station in Searle Street (which is now the Conservative Club) ready for carnival celebrations. Noah Balson is holding a hose in the front row. To the right of the picture can be seen a large ball of cotton waste suspended on a chain from the rear of the fire engine, which is decorated 'en fête'. For the carnival procession, this would be soaked in paraffin and set alight resulting in a dramatic ball of fire as the engine led the parade. For a town as fire-prone as Crediton, this old Merryweather manual was hardly a generous provision in 1920!

Elsewhere, however, arrangements were a lot more ad hoc, and smaller parishes often chose to band together to make common provision, either by supporting, or subscribing to, existing brigades in the locality, by concluding fire-cover agreements with the nearest sizeable town brigade, or by strengthening their existing provisions by means of mutual aid agreements. The more progressive small towns, like Moretonhampstead – painfully aware of the potential of unchecked fire – already had quite substantial firefighting resources that they could build on – which they did. Moreton had an ex-London Fire Brigade 1916 Dennis Model 'N' turbine pump in service by 1934 which replaced a manual engine mounted on a speedy Talbot touring-car chassis, while neighbouring Chagford was still soldiering on with their 1864 manual inherited from the 'Royal' insurance brigade, even if they did now take it to fires on the back of a builder's lorry! Elsewhere, provision was at an even more basic level. The village of Drewsteignton, for instance, relied on a 'village fire party'; the equipment, kept in a small lean-to shed by the vicarage gateway, consisted of a standpipe, three or four lengths of canvas fire hose and a brass nozzle, a stirrup pump, buckets and, of course, a 'preventer'. The hose relied on the pressure in the newly-installed water mains which, as Drewsteignton sits on top of a hill, was not great.

Moretonhampstead was another town with a history of bad fires but which was still relying on a manual pump in the 1930s – although they had at least persuaded the Parish Council to purchase a second-hand Talbot car chassis on which to mount it by 1931.

*The manual age finally came to an end in Moretonhampstead in December 1933, when an ex-London Fire Brigade Dennis Model N – latterly used by the Salvage Corps – was offered by Merryweathers, who had taken it in part-exchange. They refused a similar deal on Moreton's old Talbot-mounted manual! The solid-tyred Dennis was named 'Miss Moreton' with due ceremony and, it is said, champagne – not a common commodity in rural Devon in 1933! In 1937 the old Dennis was fitted with pneumatic tyres, after being taken over by the Newton Abbot RDC brigade under the Riverdale Arrangements.*

*A fire at Topsham on August 19th, 1909 – yet another thatched roof fire, attended by brigades from Topsham and Exeter. The thatch has been 'ripped' and the adjoining roof saved. In the foreground is an escape ladder, probably a Shand, Mason 'underneath extending' type, while a stout 'preventer' or thatch-hook lies against the front of the ruined cottages, which seem to have suffered some structural collapse.*

However, the medium-sized towns, particularly those that had a more industrial aspect, soon realised they needed to equip themselves far more adequately. Bovey Tracey, home to the famous Bovey Potteries and several other manufactures, had, by the turn of the century, a very professional and well turned out brigade of some twenty men equipped with a relatively modern manual fire engine, and by the 1920s they had a solid-tyred model 'T' Ford pumping appliance with a Braidwood body and wooden Bayley extension ladder. By the time the second world war broke out, Bovey had progressed to a brand new Dennis 'Ace' turbine pump with a 'New World' body, first-aid apparatus, a magnificent spotlight and a thirty-five foot Ajax ladder. Neighbouring Newton Abbot also had a substantial

*Top & left: Bovey Tracey, with its clay-pits and potteries, was an industrial town of some note by the early years of the 20th. century. Here is the fire brigade in a funeral procession about 1920, with the old manual engine being paraded ahead of the new motor appliance that had replaced it. This was a slightly unusual appliance, built on a Ford model T commercial chassis with equipment by Stanley – a midships-mounted pump with deliveries both sides and a simple Braidwood body. A 25-foot Bayley-pattern ladder was carried, but very little additional equipment. The brigade was quite large and had smart traditional uniform.*

*In 1935, Bovey bought a brand-new state-of-the-art appliance from Dennis Bros. for the not inconsiderable sum of £900, raised by public subscription. This was one of the well-known Dennis 'Ace' pumps with 'New World' bodywork of compact dimensions, a type somewhat unflatteringly known as 'pigs' to a generation of firefighters. With a short wheelbase and good steering lock, this was a highly suitable type of appliance for a country town like Bovey. Here, the appliance is presented to the townspeople at a ceremony outside the Town Hall, which was also the fire station. The machine was loyally christened 'Queen Mary'.*

and well-equipped brigade, progressing from a steamer at the turn of the century to a fine new Bedford appliance that appears to be a close copy of the 1933 Exeter appliance.

It is perhaps not surprising to note that it was those Devon towns that had suffered the most from fire in the nineteenth century which often had the most professional and best-equipped brigades in the earlier years of the twentieth. The example of Moretonhampstead has already been noted, and other examples included Axminster, Ottery and Tiverton. However, even in 1920 the Crediton brigade were still relying on a large manual pump, although by 1930 they had progressed to a solid-tyred Dennis motor pump. Tiverton Borough Brigade at this time had a similar pump-escape, and this type of equipage may be regarded as typical of the country town brigades in the county from the later 1920s onward. Much older machinery lasted into the war years, and in view of the antiquity of so much of it it is perhaps not surprising that the government was panicked by the 1936 Riverdale Committee report on Fire Services in Britain, which noted that 'the equipment of some of the smaller brigades is obsolete and quite useless', into providing newer appliances for rural brigades.

Following Riverdale a series of brigade amalgamations took place, designed to bring together neighbouring small brigades into larger 'district' brigades with a unified command, which might hopefully be better equipped to face the large-scale incidents that hostilities might bring. Thus, in 1937 the Moreton and Bovey brigades, together with those from Chudleigh and Ashburton, were merged with Newton Abbot's borough brigade to form the Newton Abbot & District Fire Brigade, a relatively large and well-equipped establishment having six motor fire engines and around 60 retained and volunteer firefighters. At the same time, Chagford's venerable 1864 manual passed to the Okehampton Rural District Fire Brigade, who were probably less than overjoyed to come into possession of what was widely held to be the oldest – and last surviving manual – fire engine in service in a public brigade anywhere in the country. The new owners wasted no time in consigning this relic to a museum, replacing it with one of the new government-issue trailer pumps.

*Crediton came into the motor age in 1930 with a Dennis motor pump of late-1920s vintage, but still solid-tyred. It is odd that so many rural brigades specified solid-tyred fire appliances well into the age when most other motor vehicles were running on pneumatics; it may have been cost, or worries about punctures on unmade country roads. This machine is generally similar to Okehampton's example, though a year or so younger. Note the naval-rating style caps – many fire service traditions have maritime origins, as many early firefighters were ex-seamen.*

*Fire at Moretonhampstead, the 1926 blaze that claimed several properties between New Street and The Square. The fire broke out shortly after 3 a.m. on the morning of 23rd March, and Moreton's manual pump arrived at 3.30 to find the fire spreading rapidly. Help was summoned by telephone from Exeter and Newton Abbot. Exeter responded with Merryweather pump 'Exonia', and Newton with their similar Merryweather, and a total of six jets were got to work using water pumped from the Mill Leat. Oddly, Bovey Tracey brigade do not seem to have attended. Four properties – including the National Provincial Bank – were destroyed.*

And so, at the threshold of war in 1939, we find Devon meagrely provided with firefighting resources, with the situation in the cities giving most cause for concern due to their greater vulnerability to air attack. This was particularly true of Plymouth which, as a naval base, was a prime target. As the threat of hostilities grew nearer, the Auxiliary Fire Service, hurriedly set up in 1938, started to recruit men to swell the ranks of the regular firefighters, whole-time or retained. An 'auxiliary' generally received but 60 hours training, much of which was theoretical rather than practical. It would seem more valuable for a potential firefighter to know how to slip and deploy an Ajax 35ft-ladder rather than to know it had strings of Douglas Fir and rounds of seasoned Ash, and weighed 200lbs! However, manpower was manpower, and the auxiliaries would soon find out the hard way just what the job involved. One suspects that they were viewed with some scepticism by the regular men, but the extra hose, pumps and other equipment that came with them was doubtless welcome.

*Tiverton, like neighbouring Crediton, went for a solid-tyred Dennis, equipped with electric lighting, a 50-foot wheeled escape and a fine dog. The wire-braced underneath-extending escape is probably by Morris.*

*Bovey Tracey's Dennis Ace 'Queen Mary', photographed about 1951 in Devon County Fire Service days with Mr Geoffrey Coombes at the wheel. Ask anyone at Bovey Tracey a question about the history of the town's Fire Service and one name will immediately come to the fore – that of Coombes. Not surprising, as the Coombes family have given nearly 150 years service to the local brigade. Geoff Coombes' grandfather, a lamplighter, was in the Bovey Brigade, his father Albert was second in command and spent 24 years with the Bovey crew, and his brothers, Roy and Leonard, both served for 25 years. Geoff Coombes joined the service as an NFS retained fireman in 1946 and as a child remembers waking other firemen for a fire call by running around to their homes during the night. 'Each fireman's house was identified by a white pole attached to a gatepost or wall,' he recalls.*

*The end of an era occurred recently with the retirement of Sub-officer Clifford Coombes as Officer-in-Charge of Bovey Station after over 30 years service to his community. The Coombes family have seen the service through from the manually operated horse-drawn pump before the first world war to the latest modern appliances, have fought thousands of fires and attended many road traffic accidents at all times of the night and day. It is a record of service which will be difficult if not impossible to beat.*

# THE SECOND WORLD WAR
# & THE NATIONAL FIRE
# SERVICE 1939-1948

Following the alarming report of the Riverdale Committee in 1936, the years immediately preceding the outbreak of the Second World War saw much hasty activity to reorganise, unify and reinforce Britain's inadequate and understaffed fire service which, compared with fire services in France, Germany and the USA, was woefully inadequate. And, for the first time serious consideration was given to tackling large-scale outbreaks of fire in cities which might well have suffered major damage.

## AN ALTERNATIVE FIREFIGHTING STRATEGY

The greatest weakness of the existing fire provision in British cities was the almost total reliance on the street water mains and their associated fire hydrants for the primary firefighting water supply. Although the pumping appliances themselves were equipped with suction hose which enabled them to draw water from 'static' or 'open-water' sources such as ponds, reservoirs or rivers, there were insufficient pumps and nowhere near enough hose to move this water over any distance. Thus, if the water mains were disrupted, there would be no practicable way of getting water onto a fire unless it happened to be close to some convenient water source. In Exeter and Plymouth – both cities built on hilly sites with all the main water sources at the foot of the hills – this was a crucial weakness. The problem was further compounded by the fact that, with the exception of a few having small 'first-aid' tanks of 40–80 gallons capacity, the fire appliances of the day did not carry any water with them.

The other great problem lay with the fire hose and hydrant fittings on hand. These had been produced by a variety of manufacturers to their own specifications, and came in a huge range of different sizes, types and qualities. As each manufacturer was intent upon getting its customers to standardise on their own pattern of hose and fittings, there was no commonality of any sort and a myriad of different types of hose composition,

*The core of AFS provision was the Utility trailer pump and its ten-man crew. In this case, the pump is a Dennis 'medium' unit with a 25-h.p. petrol engine driving a 500 g.p.m. pump. Note the single 25-foot length of suction with basket strainer - more reliable than shorter lengths with joints. The crew are carrying their gas-masks and wearing the wartime 'tin pimple' helmet. This crew was photographed in Plymouth in 1940.*

*A Ford 7V Heavy Pump Unit with a five-man crew. The vehicle has simple bodywork with a crew shelter faired in behind the cab and lockers for hose and fittings beneath the load-bed. The pump itself consists of a power unit – a commercial truck engine of about 40 h.p. – coupled to a powerful turbine pump of around 900 g.p.m. capacity in a casing on the load bed. A gantry above the pump carries a couple of basic 25-foot extension ladders, and there is a bell on the roof of the crew shelter. A further trailer pump could be towed if needed. This vehicle was stationed at Newton Abbot.*

pressure rating and, most crucially, coupling, were in use. This meant, of course, that brigade A could not couple its pumps and equipment to that of brigade B – a critical weakness that prevented adjoining brigades operating together. The brigade amalgamations of 1937 were in part intended to address this weakness, but the intervening period had not really been sufficient for these amalgamated brigades to bring all their equipment into line with one standard.

To meet this need, the Fire Brigades Act of 1938 called – amongst the other emergency measures that included the formation of the Auxiliary Service – for the procurement of a large quantity of equipment. This was to include several hundred 'Utility' fire pumps and a huge quantity – over 900 miles – of large-diameter high-pressure canvas fire hose. And, most importantly, all this new equipment would be fitted with the 'instantaneous' type of hose coupling as standard, while adapters were produced to allow existing fire appliances to use this hose. These new 'Home Office' fire pumps were very spartan appliances, built onto trailers or on ordinary commercial vehicle chassis of the day, and were designed for a limited role – principally, that of moving quantities water over a distance.

There were three principal pieces of equipment produced under this 1938 act – the light, medium and heavy Utility pump units. The light units consisted of a small petrol-powered first-aid pumps of 50–150 g.p.m. capacity fitted with a hosereel and mounted on a light trailer which could be manhandled or towed by a light car. These pumps were meant for ARP (Air Raid Precautions) work and were not usually allocated to fire brigades, but rather to the ARP Emergency Committees. The medium pump, how-ever, had a centrifugal or turbine fire pump of 350–500 g.p.m. capacity powered by its own petrol engine, mounted on a heavy two-wheel trailer which could be towed by a larger car or light commercial vehicle. These medium pumps were equipped with suction hose, a few lengths of deliv-ery hose, a nozzle, and a standpipe, key and bar to set into hydrants. The last type was the heavy or major pump which was much larger, having a 900/1,000 g.p.m capacity and being powered by large commercial-vehicle petrol engine. They were mounted either on a lorry chassis as a 'Self-Propelled Pump' (SP unit), or on a heavy four-wheeled trailer that could be moved by a lorry or tractor. The SP units usually had Austin K series or Ford 7V 'V8' chassis, and in addition to the pump and the associated suc-tion hose, standpipes and so on had a crew shelter, lockers for a large quantity of hose and a short extension ladder on a gantry. They could also tow a trailer pump and had a nominal crew ten men.

The bulk of the medium trailer pumps were initially towed behind requi-sitioned civilian vehicles, light lorries, vans or taxicabs, but the Auxiliary Towing Vehicle (ATV) was eventually developed for this role. The ATV was really little more than a van filled with hose, although they did have specially-reinforced roofs to protect the crew in the event of a structural collapse. Most ATVs were on Austin K4 chassis, carrying a crew of eight (two in the cab, six inside) and some 40 75' lengths of rolled $2^{3/4}$-inch can-vas hose in racks. A 25-foot and a short extension ladder were carried on the roof. All these new appliances were painted in flat Admiralty grey rather than the traditional red. They had hand-operated bells, but other-wise lacked most of the usual appurtenances of a fire engine.

*Another Utility appliance was the 60-foot manually-operated TL produced by Merryweather on the Austin K3 chassis. The ladders were elevated by cables and winches built into the turret, and the crew rode in a shelter behind the cab. This is GXM 206, stationed at Barnstaple and Ilfracombe during the war. Modernised and fitted with a pump in front of the radiator, it remained at Ilfracombe until the mid-1960s.*

*Torquay's unique 5-section 100-foot 1939 Leyland TL in wartime condition, with Home Office area instructor Leading Fireman Philpotts. The 'short' ladders were to ease access to the Market Street station.*

*An Exeter AFS unit in Plymouth during the early stages of the 1941 blitz. This is representative of a typical AFS unit in the earlier part of the war – a ten-man pump crew riding a requisitioned civilian lorry towing – in this case – a Dennis medium trailer pump of 500-g.p.m. capacity. The following unit has requistioned a large car – it appears to be an American Packard saloon.*

These Utility pumps were allocated to the various brigades throughout Devon to replace or reinforce the regular equipment. Exeter City brigade received 10 Home Office pumps in 1938, although it is not recorded whether these were of the medium or heavy type. A photograph of an AFS drill on Exeter Quay taken immediately before the war shows one Ford 7V SP heavy unit and three medium trailer units, so there was probably something of a mixture. The additional appliances were initially garaged in Goldsmith Street but it was soon realised that putting all the firefighting eggs in one basket was not a good idea, and the equipment was then dispersed about the city at 'sub stations' protected by sandbagging and linked by field telephone. There were temporary fire stations at Heavitree and Butts Road as well as deployments to the main Danes Castle headquarters station, the old headquarters station at New North Road, the St. Thomas' station in Cowick Street, and to Topsham.

Under the provisions of the 1938 Act, at times of need firefighting resources could be required to move wholesale from one place to another. Thus, in the run-up to the Plymouth blitz in March and April 1941, much

*Be prepared! Newton Abbot firefighters ready for gas attack – all in gas masks, and six men in full gas-precautions rubber suits. This was in preparation for a gas-attack training exercise directed by military personnel.*

*Practice – in this case, for decontamination after a gas attack, under the direction of a soldier. Rubber capes and gas-masks provide protection, and a water spray removes the gas by dissolution and displacement. (Well, that was the theory! Fortunately, it was never put to the test.)*

of Exeter's firefighting strength was sent to Plymouth, where it was based at Stonehouse.

By recruiting additional strength – mostly retained men – plus the provision of raw AFS recruits and their Utility equipment, the hurried upgrading of the rural and urban district brigades gave a 'second wave' of reinforcement that could be used to assist hard-pressed city brigades. During the blitz periods in both Plymouth and Exeter, men and machines from the surrounding countryside and neighbouring towns were brought in to help, either to bolster the immediate firefighting effort or to provide relief to exhausted fire crews at protracted fires.

Later in the war, after the formation of the NFS, the 'Flying Column' tactic extended this concept to move large numbers of men and appliances over substantial distances quickly, so that it proved possible for reinforcements from all over southern England to be rapidly deployed to Exeter when that city was attacked in 1942. Before the fire service was nationalised in August 1941, such arrangements were very 'ad hoc' rather than being carefully pre-planned, and when Plymouth requested firefighting aid from other cities during the 1941 spring blitz the response seems to have been patchy and often largely ineffective due to failures of command and incompatible equipment

The London blitz of Autumn 1940 exposed many weaknesses of the proposed fire-fighting arrangements in the face of intensive aerial bombardment, which in reality proved to be even more of a nightmare than had been foreseen by the Home Office planners. The wisdom of not relying on the water mains was quickly established, but the alternative provisions proved quite inadequate to the task of establishing adequate water supplies for large-scale firefighting. Laying the required quantities of hose for long-distance water supply by traditional manual running-out methods proved impracticable. Hose-running is heavy and tiring work, even today it is used as a stamina test for would-be firefighters, and required huge manpower resources that just were not available, especially after both the regular and auxiliary strength had been depleted by the release of fire personnel for military service during the period of the 'false war' in late 1939 and early 1940. The result was that the fire crews were often exhausted by hose-laying before they ever got to start fighting the actual fires.

*Leading Fireman R. Clemson Young from Torquay drew this Sketch of a 500 g.p.m. trailer pump in action during the blitz. He invented many pieces of Fire Brigade equipment, including the device mounted onto this trailer pump, shown being operated by the steel-helmeted fireman. Lfm Clemson Young had it patented and he called it, appropriately enough, 'The Clemson Water Gun'.*

*Monitor branch holder, another R. Clemson Young invention. On the rear of the picture is the following information: 'On test at the Fish Quay Torquay, this Monitor held steady (unattended) with over 150psi delivered from a Dennis pump through a 1-in nozzle; has good range of elevation, folds straight & is easy to carry, with a weight of 14lbs.'*

There were three answers to the problem. The first was to create many more 'static' supplies in vulnerable areas, so that there would be at least some water on hand to commence immediate firefighting without the need to run out miles of hose. These static supplies came in two forms: large purpose-made canvas or steel 'dams' erected at strategic road junctions or on other suitable sites, usually holding from 5–20,000 gallons of water; and extemporised supplies created by the deliberate flooding of basements, tunnels and even bomb-craters to form ponds or underground reservoirs. These static water reserves enabled the pumps to set-in and get to work quickly, and gave time for long-distance supplies to be established to keep the dams or ponds full.

The second part of the solution was to make the implementation of long-distance pumped water supplies effective and relatively quick, to which end the formal 'water relay' was established. This used the Home Office pumps in a fixed configuration to set up and maintain the supply at an adequate volume and pressure, and led to the introduction of an extra type of appliance, the Utility high-speed hoselayer. This was based on the design of the hose-laying lorry developed pre-war by the London Fire Brigade, and consisted of a medium commercial chassis, usually a 7V Ford, carrying a box body containing a mile of large-diameter fire hose stowed 'flaked' – folded to and fro along the length of the body and pre-coupled. There were two compartments on the lorry, one on each side holding half a mile of flaked hose which could be laid as 'twin lines' over the special tailboard of the vehicle at speeds of 15m.p.h. or so. To maintain pressure, medium trailer pumps were set into the hose line at intervals, while a heavy pump unit formed the 'base pump' at the main water source. The whole relay was co-ordinated with semaphore pump signals, field telephones and runners. Twin lines were used not just to increase the volume of water that could be delivered, but to maintain at least some supply should a hose burst or a pump fail.

The third answer to blitz firefighting was the development of the water-carrier or 'mobile dam unit'. Initially, these were again improvised from requisitioned civilian vehicles, either flatbed lorries or small buses. The portable dam was of canvas in a steel frame, with inward-sloping sides to maintain stability and a wooden 'milkmaids cross' floating on top to prevent slop; it could be folded and stowed when not in use. The virtue of the mobile dam was that it could take a reasonable water supply – typically 4–500 gallons – to a fire while it was still in its early stages, no matter where it might be, and thus facilitate effective first-aid action that could contain the outbreak before it got out of hand. Most of the major blitz fires resulted from a lot of smaller fires, that could not be tackled quickly enough, developing until they joined to give a major conflagration, which would then propagate itself by radiating huge amounts of heat and showering burning debris onto adjacent structures.

## PLYMOUTH PREPARES...

In Plymouth, where the scale of risk was far greater than elsewhere in Devon, a larger contingent of emergency equipment was placed in service alongside the Plymouth City brigade's establishment. The city received about 30 Home Office pumps and one new regular fire appliance plus an Emergency Rescue Tender in 1938–9, and efforts were made to recruit and train many extra firefighters. It was reckoned that 500 men were needed, but this figure was never reached. The situation in Plymouth

*A regular brigade on a war footing. Members of the Plymouth Police Fire Brigade pose in front of two of their machines about 1940. On the left is the 1932 Dennis 'Big 6' 45-h.p. PE that arrived in 1932, and on the right the smaller Dennis 30-h.p. pump from 1930. These machines are believed to have been stationed at Penlee. Note the white visibility paint around the wheel arches of the pump.*

was, however, aided by the presence of several well-drilled teams of military and industrial firefighters – the Navy had its own extensive firefighting establishment at the Naval Dockyard, and there were several works brigades including a railway brigade at Laira. The naval dockyards, the railway yards and the commercial port of Millbay were an obvious target, and all were uncomfortably close to the city centre.

Early on it was realised that the traditional concentration of city firefighting resources at large central fire stations – such as Plymouth's new Greenbank headquarters – made these resources very vulnerable in the event of a 'blitz' type air raid, although in fact the Greenbank station survived the war relatively unscathed. The new policy was to ring the city with the smaller type of sub-station having just one or two appliances, so that equipment would be moving *into* the city centre in several directions from the outskirts after an attack rather than trying to fight its way outwards through rubble-choked streets from a central location. And, of course, there was always the chance that a central station would itself be hit and disabled in a raid, which might well knock-out a substantial proportion of the brigade's strength – something that was far less likely when it was dispersed in small units over a wide area.

There were 15 such sub-stations in the Plymouth area by 1940. Establishments were listed at Cattedown, Stonehouse, Devonport, Keyham, Camel's Head, Higher St Budeaux, Milehouse, Lower Compton, Crownhill and Millbay. Some of these were existing fire stations of the Plymouth, Stonehouse and Devonport brigades, but most of the others were temporary affairs set up in garages, schools and other requisitioned premises. In addition to these stations within the city, there were others in neighbouring areas. The Plympton St Mary's Rural District Council Brigade had been reinforced under the 1938 scheme, receiving a new 6-cylinder Leyland pump in 1940 to bolster its existing 1935 Leyland and 'Motor tender with Merryweather trailer pump'; doubtless, AFS units were also stationed at Plympton and probably at Plymstock, where the local brigade had a motor pump of unspecified type.

The strength of the Plymouth brigade itself is given in the same report, dated January 1941. The city had only twelve whole-time and fourteen retained firefighters, the rest of the strength being drawn as needed from police ranks under dual-service arrangements. There were now six regular fire appliances – a motor pump and pump escape of unspecified makes (probably the Merryweather and Belsize machines dating from 1914/1920), the 1930 Dennis pump and 1933 Albion/Merryweather turntable ladder plus the 1938 Leyland pump-escape allocated under the 1938 Act, now joined by a second TL, a 1941 Dennis/Merryweather hundred-foot version. All the wartime TLs were by Merryweather, as for obvious reasons the German Metz and Magirus ladders common before the war were no longer available!

As well as the land-based fire appliances, a large number of small fireboats had been improvised out of old naval whalers and similar stout craft, fitted with a Home Office 250 g.p.m. light portable pump amidships and carrying hose, branches and other equipment. There were eventually a total of 54 of these vessels, operated by small crews of 2–4 men, and they could be used either to supply shore-based appliances – particularly at low tide – or to fight waterside fires and fires involving shipping. Many of these were stationed around the naval dockyard, but in the various accounts of the blitz they do not seem to figure greatly.

## THE PYMOUTH BLITZ – MARCH 1941

The first heavy, concentrated raid on Plymouth commenced on 20th March 1941. Attacks up to that time had been confined to single-aircraft or small-group 'lightning raids', the most serious being a 25-bomber raid in December 1940. With the conclusion of the Battle of Britain and the London blitz, the Luftwaffe changed its tactics to concentrate on large-scale night raids on British manufacturing and seaport cities. Plymothians soon became convinced that their turn for 'blitzkrieg' could not be far off, and civil defence and air raid precautions were – somewhat belatedly – increased in early 1941. The recruitment of additional firefighters for the AFS establishment in the city became a matter of urgency; the total complement of the Plymouth AFS was only 267 men out of the 500 plus authorised. At the same time, the problem of firefighting water supplies was addressed by the hurried erection of a number of street dams and the creation of emergency reservoirs, although these were to prove far too few. Many of the citizens also left the city for the surrounding countryside at this time, leading to problems with locked, empty premises and some areas being almost deserted. A raid in January 'tested' these preparations, but a poor assessment was made of their effectiveness – leading to the Plymouth Emergency Committee declaring them 'adequate'. As events were to show, they were anything but.

Although the raids up until the beginning of March 1941 had caused substantial damage across the city, they in no way approached the scale of what was to come, while the Emergency Committee were by now hopelessly behind with effective preparations to meet the threat. That threat materialised with dreadful suddenness on the evening of 20th March, only hours after the King and Queen had left the city after inspecting naval and civil defence establishments. The sirens sounded a few minutes after 8.30, swiftly followed by AA fire from the batteries on the outskirts of the city. And then all hell, quite literally, broke loose. Among the ordnance that rained down on Plymouth that night in the space of a few tortured hours were 34 delayed action bombs, 17 1-ton 'blockbusters', and 12,500 incendiary and high-explosive bombs.

*Plymouth's baptism of fire was exactly that, with the first major raid on the city resulting in conflagrations of virtually unprecedented size and intensity. Here, crews battle with a sea of flame as the bombers drone overhead. At least this crew has a water supply to feed their jet; many crews were left struggling and helpless when supplies failed.*

*The smoking ruins of Plymouth on the day following a major raid. Notice that every flammable element of these buildings has been consumed, leaving just the hot stonework of the few remaining walls to steam in the spring sunshine. Effective firefighting was just not possible against blazes of this intensity, and the scene resembles the aftermath of an uncontrolled eighteenth or nineteenth century town fire.*

Plymouth's emergency control room in the Guildhall basement, to which all the ARP and civil defence posts reported and from where the fire, police, ambulance and rescue services were co-ordinated, received its first report of a major conflagration, at Dingles store on Royal Parade, not long after nine p.m. In a short time, this fire had extended along the whole of Royal Parade toward St Andrew's church, with numerous other serious fires breaking out across the city. The fire service was, quite simply, over-whelmed. The mobilisation arrangements broke down so that of the total strength of 537 part-time, retained and AFS men that should have been available, only 236 reported for duty, while the water supplies failed total-ly. Attempts to set in pump relays were hampered by the fact that, at the time, Plymouth had only received two of the new hose-laying vehicles and thus the men had to try and run out literally miles of hose manually. And much of that hose had ill-matched couplings, leading to delay and wasted effort. The fires were soon burning on a scale hitherto unseen in the city, and an urgent assistance call went out to eighteen surrounding brigades for reinforcements, while the military brigades at Devonport and elsewhere in the area sent 21 pumps into the fray, setting up a major water relay from Sutton Pool to a large 20,000 gallon reservoir in the city centre close to the Guildhall. Navy despatch riders maintained emergency communications after the telephone system, permanent and field, was almost totally knocked out in the first hour of the raid.

With many of the fires now totally out of control, the fire aid plans were put into action, and AFS and civilian brigade fire units were requested to proceed to Plymouth from Birmingham, Bristol, Gloucester, Swindon and Salisbury. By now, the entire city centre was on fire, with scarcely a building remaining intact, and firestorm conditions developed. This is the phenomenon whereby the huge mass of superheated air rising at high velocity above the conflagration creates near gale-force winds at ground level as fresh air is sucked in to replace that displaced, effectively feeding the flames in the same manner as a blast-furnace is fanned to greater heat. The glow from the fires could be seen for miles in all directions – AA gunners on Nattadon Hill, Chagford, some 35 miles to the north, could see them clearly – and the column of smoke was rising thousands of feet into the sky. Such was the confusion in Plymouth that the Home Security Intelligence Unit, the body charged with the job of assessing damage and informing central government, quite failed to indicate that the damage report that they sent to London next day was grossly incomplete, leading to initial reports describing the raid as 'slight'.

*This is a famous photograph, somewhat posed, of rescue workers taking a break during the Plymouth blitz. Centre is an AFS firefighter with a mug of tea, standing next to a schoolboy amid what looks like a debris-clearing working party. Where the tea has come from is anybody's guess, as one of the criticisms levelled against Plymouth's Emergency Committee was the lack of planning for the sustenance of relief workers and fire crews.*

The blitz continued the next night in spite of cloudier conditions, preceded by a pathfinder force dropping coloured flares to identify targets. The planes came in by a wide circuit over lightly-defended Dartmoor to attack from the north-east before tearing out to sea at full throttle once their bomb loads were despatched. The pathfinder unit was largely unneeded, for many of the fires started the night before were still burning. Due to the cloud, the bombing raids were conducted from lower level, about 9000 feet, and the still-burning fires were soon surrounded by hundreds of new outbreaks. Once again, the fire service response was quite unequal to the task; the Plymouth establishment found itself short of 174 men who had failed to report for duty, and the water supplies and telephone system soon broke down again. Matters were made worse by a combination of low tide, taking water out of the range of the fire brigade's suction hoses, and a brisk south-westerly wind that fanned the flames. The ARP wardens and street fire parties were also hampered by the many locked, deserted buildings; with no occupants to report outbreaks quickly or to douse incendiaries before they could start fires, the ARP men were additionally faced with the problem of trying to force entries to the locked houses and boarded-up shops to take first-aid firefighting action. In this way, many fires that could have been controlled if tackled swiftly soon got out of hand.

Communications once again failed completely; 52 part-time messengers were available but had no transport, not even bicycles, while the Emergency Committee had not yet got around to recruiting any of the 45 full-time messengers it was authorised to employ. Once again, it fell to the navy to bale out the inadequate civilian provision with manpower and equipment, particularly in ambulance work. And then the Guildhall was hit and set on fire, causing the emergency control centre to be abandoned and the city's operational HQ moved to the basement of Devonport Market, the back-up site, which was fortunately intact. This took time and led to a break-down in command at a critical stage of the raid. The fires were once again burning on a massive scale: Union Street was alight virtually from end to end, two large timber yards were blazing and the tar distillery at Castledown was an inferno. Firestorm conditions soon developed to raise the fires to new heights of intensity, and the authorities had

*Plymouthians pick their way through the rubble of their city, towards the scene of clearance operations. Note the large-diameter fire hose with instantaneous couplings lying in the gutter – the remains of a water relay. Some of this damage is obviously the result of high explosive bombs, but the more distant buildings have been burnt out.*

*A very large part of Plymouth's historic heart and much of the heritage of the city were wiped out by the blitz fires. The mediaeval buildings in the old city had very little fire resistance and were usually utterly destroyed.*

*Devastation in Plymouth*

to fall back on the oldest resort of all, that of demolishing and dynamiting buildings to create firebreaks. By a little after ten p.m., virtually every water main in the city – some 80 in all – had been knocked out, and the only mains water that could be used was that pouring into bomb craters, which was often mixed with sewage. The fire service was once again struggling to set up huge water relays which were frequently disrupted by the collapse of structures and bomb damage, as well as being hampered by the ill-matched equipment.

## AFTER THE FIRE-RAIDS

Of Plymouth's proud civic heritage, little survived by the next morning, 22nd March. St Andrews church was a mere shell, as were the Guildhall and Stonehouse Town Hall. Most of the city centre shops had gone, along with much of the infrastructure of the docks. Oil tanks at Stonehouse and Turnchapel were still ablaze, along with warehouses and factories of all kinds. The city had virtually no usable drinking water, the sewage system was disrupted, and there was a critical shortage of food, medicine, blood and general supplies of all sorts. Many fires still burned unchecked while the exhausted firefighters stood by their pumps, many of which had run out of fuel. There were at least 85 unexploded bombs located in the city centre area, and many of the streets were impassable. Much firefighting equipment had been destroyed or damaged, and many of the static tanks or other fixed installations were out of action, buried beneath countless tons of rubble. Relief from the surrounding area and further afield was slow to arrive, while the Home Security Intelligence Unit once again failed to make an adequate report, meaning that Plymouth's extreme plight was largely unknown in London, let alone the rest of the country.

Emergency measures taken in the wake of the two massive fire-raids included shutting the city off from incoming traffic, with road blocks manned by both civilian and military police. With no communications and a dislocated headquarters, the Emergency Committee were unable to gain a true picture of the situation until a survey could be made on foot, a process that took most of the day. Away from the total devastation of the

*The combination of high explosive and incendiary bombs created the necessary conditions for firestorm conditions to develop. Some of the largest HE bombs used in the whole Blitz campaign were dropped on Plymouth, with the potential to utterly destroy large buildings in a single blast.*

city centre, which had to all intents and purposes been wiped out, there was also widespread destruction in the residential areas; some 6,500 houses had been damaged or demolished, many roads were impassable and most services were non-existent. The fire crews, now relieved by men from rural brigades all over Devon and Cornwall, were still fighting several large fires and damping-down innumerable smouldering buildings. Spasmodic salvage work began as the fire service tried to regroup, retrieving hose and equipment, replenishing fuel stocks and trying to repair defective pumps and appliances.

There was something of a respite after the raids of 20–21st March, which were reckoned to have been the most severe yet seen in the war, more intense than the blitzes on London, Coventry, Birmingham and Liverpool. In the period following the March raids, the Plymouth fire service came under increasing criticism for its lack of preparedness and the inadequacy of its response to the consequences of the raids. This criticism culminated in a letter to the Town Clerk from the Home Secretary, Herbert

Morrison, regarding the fire protection arrangements for the city. This letter contained a whole raft of 'recommendations' (in effect, direct orders, given the authority of the source!) from the regional Inspector of Fire Brigades and the Chief Inspector of the South West fire division.

First and foremost of these reforms were the immediate separation of the fire service from police control, and the appointment of a professional chief officer with a proven fire service background. The control facilities, relying on the civilian Emergency Control Room, were also reckoned unsatisfactory, as were the associated communications. The establishment of a separate fire control was deemed essential, and the fire service should employ its own dedicated despatch riders and messengers who could not be deflected to other duties. The lack of provision of firefighting water supplies was also heavily criticised, and many more static sources were to be created. The system of pump relays had also proved inadequate, as there were still inconsistencies in the equipment, especially in the matter of hose couplings, while the city's fire hydrants did not use the universal connection system but an obsolete screw type that meant that fire appliances from outside Plymouth could not use them. The Devonport brigade used bayonet hydrant fittings, so not even they could work with the Plymouth equipment. Screw-fit hydrants with 3-inch female round threads – the new Home Office standard – were to be fitted without delay throughout the whole area and new standpipes provided, together with a good supply of hose adapters to ensure fire hose of different types could be coupled. Mr Drury, a Headquarters fire brigade inspector, was despatched from London to oversee these changes.

## THE APRIL BLITZ

It is not clear how much had been achieved by the time the Luftwaffe once again turned its attention to Plymouth a month after the first fire raid. On the night of 21st April, 120 bombers were used to mount a further devastating raid on the city. This started at 8.39 in the evening, when a 'pathfinder' force of Heinkels arrived to drop marker flares and to unleash no less than 10,000 incendiary bombs. These started numerous fires, several of which rapidly reached 'conflagration' status. The last of the path-finding Heinkels was still over the city when the next wave of bombers arrived, guided by the sea of fire now raging below; targets were easily found and whole areas of the western part of Plymouth were soon burning. The raid lasted six hours in all, and during that time no less than 35,000 incendiaries were dropped, plus 700 HE bombs including 31 of the dreaded 'blockbusters'.

This was a terrible night for the city and its people. A shelter in the city centre took a direct hit, leaving only two survivors from the 74 people inside, while 78 sailors died in a hell of fire and explosion when the Boscawen block at the dockyard was hit repeatedly. There are no detailed accounts of how the fire service fared on this occasion, but there seems little reason to suppose that things were any better than they had been a month previously. However, the spotlight of critical attention now swung to the city's civil rescue facilities, as in this raid much of the property set on fire or demolished by HE was domestic housing, leading to many civilian casualties. Sir High Elles, the Home Office Regional Commissioner, the official responsible for overseeing protection of the civil population, drove through the night to reach Plymouth to see for himself what arrangements were in place. He found them woefully inadequate, with no procedures to systematically search bombed buildings for survivors. When he sat in on that morning's meeting of the Emergency Committee, he could not believe the degree of detachment and lack of urgency in the deliberations. There were, he discovered, no arrangements in place to feed either the rescue parties nor those they rescued. Much of the discussion amounted to little more than petty wrangling over past failings. Some of the current failings proved bad enough; the back-up ARP control centre had no telephones...

The following evening, however, it was the fire service that was once more the centre of attention; within the first hour of that evening's raid, no less than 46 major fires were burning, and the city's firefighters were already stretched beyond their limits. High winds fanned the flames, and the masses of timber and other flammable debris that had not been cleared after the previous night's raids helped to spread the fires. Soon, whole streets were ablaze in Devonport, the main target that night. The military and naval headquarters, together with marine and naval barrack blocks were destroyed, along with whole tracts of the close-packed terraced and back-to-back housing of the town. The destroyer HMS *Lewes* was hit in the dockyard, and the railway yards were pounded by high explosive. Buildings in the South Dockyard were soon on fire, and the navy firefighters were fully committed and quite unable to aid the city. Plymouth's exhausted firecrews simply could not muster the strength to respond vigorously to yet another desperate fire situation, although sufficient equipment appears to have been available. Once again, aid was summoned from afar, and 100 London firefighters were despatched to the city by train. In the middle of the raid, the Devonport market – beneath which the city's ARP emergency control was now sited – took a direct hit, which meant the control room had to evacuated. It made little difference to the control situation, however, as the Devonport telephone exchange had also been hit and all communications were dead. The fire control, now located behind Greenbank fire station, was unaffected, although many fires were now burning out of control due to a lack of fire crews.

The same sorry story was repeated the following evening, 23rd April. Again, the target was Devonport and the dockyard, with over 10,000 incendiaries raining down. Huge petrol and oil fires broke out at the dockyard, with nearly 12,000 *tons* of fuel ablaze – fires which took four full days to extinguish. The fire situation in the city and dockyard rapidly became so serious that Sir Aylmer Firebrace, the nation's Chief Superintendent of Fire Services, was ordered to Plymouth to take charge. An RAF plane flew him to Roborough airfield, and he went straight to the Greenbank headquarters. Firebrace's first action was to order that Mr Drury, the Home Office inspector sent to implement the changes in Plymouth's fire defences demanded by the Home Secretary, be put in charge of operations on the ground. The senior Plymouth officers were apparently simply overwhelmed in the face of such a massive fire threat, whereas Drury had been through the London blitz and thus gained valuable experience. The London Fire Brigade had despatched another 100 firefighters during the day, and these men now started to relieve the exhausted Plymouth crews on the pumps. But relief brigades arriving from elsewhere in the hastily-organised mobile columns that were now rushing from one blitzed city to another were in little better shape than the Plymouth men, while once again the old bugbears of lack of water and ill-matched equipment reared their ugly heads. Huge areas of Devonport were lost to fire and many people deprived of their homes that night, due to inadequate water supplies.

*A strange normality. In this extraordinary image, two young Plymouth schoolboys trudge stoically through the rubble as a huge column of smoke from blazing oil tanks dominates the skyline. One must not be late for school!*

Next morning it was reported that major fires were still burning in many parts of the city and in Saltash, across the Hamoaze. Oil tanks at the Thankes oil depot were on fire, and a serious fire was burning in a basement below the South Dockyard's rope store, where a further 40,000 barrels of oil were involved. In the city centre, Union Street and The Octagon were ablaze, the firefighting effort once again hampered by the inadequacy of the static and pumped water supplies. The Plymouth crews had done their utmost and beyond, but many of the men were now at the limit of their endurance. The principal failings of Plymouth's blitz firefighting were organisational, and there was certainly no lack of valour or commitment on the part of the actual fire crews. Fire officers from other brigades commented that the Police Brigade heritage was only too evident in the lack of qualified personnel and, especially, experienced and well-qualified officers, while the Emergency Committee's lackadaisical approach to air raid precautions – in particular, the lack of sufficient static water supplies – had tied the firemen's hands from the start.

*In 1943, after the blitz was over and some normality had returned to the city of Plymouth, a civic service was held in the burned-out shell of St Andrew's church for the members of the NFS No. 19 Area who had served in the Plymouth blitz. The church today remains much as it is seen here – a monument to and reminder of Plymouth's ordeal by fire.*

After four days respite – just long enough to extinguish the oil fires and to make a start on the massive task of clearance and demolition of unsafe structures, the Luftwaffe returned once more in strength on the night of 28th. April. The main attack by 124 bombers was again to the west, and this time took in Saltash and Torpoint on the Cornish side of the river. Oil tanks at Torpoint were soon burning, and the St Budeaux and Camel's Head areas were torn apart by high explosive and fired by incendiaries. This attack included the dropping of two of the Luftwaffe's most powerful weapon, the 'Satan' bomb, weighing well over a ton. The naval dockyard was once again hit, the North Yard and Keyham taking the brunt, while the ammunition depot at Bulls Point was involved in a serious fire. The improvised fire floats and six regular fireboats were fully engaged on this occasion, mostly tackling the Bulls Point fire from the river. Virtually all the city's fire equipment and crews were committed in Devonport and St Budeaux, while twelve fire appliances were despatched to cross the Hamoaze by the ferry and aid blazing Saltash. So bad were conditions, however, that these machines were unable to reach the ferry slip on the Devon bank.

The final night of the Plymouth blitz (although by no means the final air attack on the city) was that of 29th. April. On this occasion the Luftwaffe stumbled a little due to poor visibility, and many bombs were fortunately dropped over open country and in the Mount Edgecombe woodlands, where forest fires were started. Once the bombers got their bearings, however, Devonport was once again in the front line, along with Milehouse and Keyham; Milehouse gasworks was soon ablaze, the huge gasometer catching fire in spectacular fashion, but the main destruction was among the crowded Devonport streets and in the dockyard, where several ships were hit. Some bombs fell on the remains of the city centre, the main loss on this occasion being the Central Library and its 100,000-book collection. The Swindon fire brigade, reinforcing Plymouth's fire defences, responded to the library fire but could not connect their pumps to Plymouth's non-standard fire hydrants and, once again, the battle was lost due to inadequate firefighting water supplies. Fortunately, the adjoining Art Gallery and Museum, with its fine collection of paintings, was saved, but it is symptomatic of the lack of foresight that such valuable national treasures had not been removed to the countryside for safe keeping

*The fire service throughout Devon was strengthened under the National Fire Service, and here is the NFS establishment at Holsworthy about 1942, consisting of the members of the regular brigade together with the town's former AFS detachment – which included a number of firewomen, as they were then called, who were tasked with administrative, control, communications and support functions.*

## THE NFS IN PLYMOUTH AND DEVON

With the cessation of the mass air raids, Plymouth and the rest of Devon had time to regroup and reorganise their fire defences. There was further criticism of the fire service organisation from both within and without Plymouth, but in point of fact the fire protection situation in Plymouth was little different to that elsewhere in the country. The simple truth was that the fire brigades nationally simply were not up to the job of firefighting on the sort of scale demanded by blitz attacks. The services were too disjointed, and lacked commonality of equipment, training, command and procedures. The horse had well-nigh bolted, but determined efforts were now made to shut the stable door.

The result was the abolition of all local fire brigades throughout the country, and the creation of a National Fire Service that took in every fireman and piece of firefighting equipment in the land, whether they be professionals from smart city brigades or volunteers from one-pump country stations. The NFS also absorbed the AFS and all railway, factory or similar private firefighting teams. From August of 1941, Britain had a single,

Emblems at Torr – Plymouth City, N.F.S. and Comodian Forces Fire Service.

Under the NFS, national standards for the various disciplines of firefighting were put in place, supported by a unified training and assessment scheme. Personnel were required to qualify in a number of areas, and on successful conclusion of the relevant training received certificates such as these – for driving and BA wearing.

Right & top centre: Fun drills for the spectators in this NFS display on Paignton Green: NFS crews lying in their beds 'at home' are woken from their slumbers by the siren, leap up out of bed and into their fire-kit, hurrying off to the 'station' to man the fire appliances. Trailer pump competition drills were part of the spectacle, and in the second picture a crew are connecting up the suction hose ready to pump water onto a pre-arranged target – all good practice for real firefighting.

unified fire authority organised on near-military lines. Equipment was re-allocated as to need, and rapid action was taken to procure much more hose, of larger diameter, together with many more pumps and hose-laying lorries, so that it would be possible to establish much more effective water relays. New appliances – notably the water carrier – were designed and ordered, a unified training scheme adopted and vigorously carried into effect. A temporary street water main system using surface run quick-fit steel piping was devised, and stocks of the requisite equipment built up.

Plymouth now became part of Area Fire Force 19, Plymouth & Cornwall under NFS Region 7. The rest of Devon formed Area Fire Force 18. Fire Force 19 was commanded locally by Fire Force Commander Drury, and ultimately from the regional HQ at Bristol. The 15 existing sub-stations were retained, and a workshops to maintain the equipment set up at Mumford's Garage in Salisbury Road, St Judes. Prince Rock School became the Fire Reception Centre, to which oncoming appliances from outside Plymouth would report if ordered to the city; this replaced the

previous rendezvous point at Devonport High School for Girls, severely damaged in the April raids. The NFS fire control was moved to the Torr fire station in Mannamead, further from the city centre, and a large training establishment was set up at Lee Moor, near Ivybridge. The fire stations at Yelverton, Ivybridge and Tavistock, together with Plympton and Plymstock, were brought into the Plymouth fire area under the direct control of Plymouth control. The firefighting strength of the city was bolstered by the arrival of a group of Canadian firefighters and their pumps and other equipment, stationed at the Torr headquarters. Much of the extra hose and additional trailer pumps needed for the relay system came from the USA, and American Chevrolet hose-laying lorries carrying large-diameter 3½-inch hose became available. By the spring of 1942, the state of Britain's fire defences presented a very different picture to the situation a year earlier – a state of affairs that Exeter was soon to have cause to be grateful for.

## THE EXETER BLITZ

Exeter had been spared the concentrated attentions of the Luftwaffe throughout the earlier stages of the war, doubtless due to its lesser military importance and smaller size. There had, of course, been lesser attacks, mostly single-aircraft raids or sporadic attacks by small groups of planes, starting in August 1940 and continuing throughout 1941 into the early spring of 1942, some 18 separate raids in all. These had caused some limited damage and a few casualties, but the resulting fires had not over-taxed the city's fire crews unduly, as only a few buildings were involved. Its fire-

*One of the best-known and most striking images of the Exeter Blitz, showing NFS units in front of the cathedral after tackling the fires that destroyed much of South Street in 1942. At the right, a self-propelled heavy pump on an Austin K3 chassis is set into a portable dam – just visible – which would have been supplied by pump relay, probably from the pumps that were kept on the Quay for the purpose. At the left are two Austin K3 Auxiliary Towing Vehicles, which would have positioned their trailer pumps where needed then been used for hose-laying purposes – each ATV carried around 3,000 feet of hose. Under magnification, a further ATV can be seen behind the large car, which is almost certainly an NFS staff officer's transport. Most of the hose seen here is the large-diameter two and three-quarter inch canvas delivery hose used to move water to the appliances, although a couple of lines of inch-and-three-quarters firefighting hose lead off from the deliveries of the SP pump. From the relaxed attitudes of the passers-by and the only firefighter plainly visible, the fires are obviously now all out and it is simply a matter of draining, drying and making-up all that hose... a backbreaking task in itself.*

fighters had, however, certainly not been idle, and besides dealing with these incidents on their own 'patch' many Exeter crews had fought the fires in Plymouth throughout that unhappy city's ordeal.

The NFS reorganisation in August 1941 substantially strengthened Exeter's fire defences, which now formed part of the NFS Fire District 18 – covering most of Devon – under the command of Fire Force Commander Coles. Exeter's preparations, especially in the matter of the static water supplies organised by the force water officer, Company Officer Shephard, were far more advanced than had been those of Plymouth, while the smaller size of the city presented less of a problem should water relays be needed. Nevertheless, Exeter would soon find that even these improved and battle-tested fire arrangements could not prevent massive fire damage to the historic fabric of the city when Hitler ordered his air force to make the series of attacks known as the 'Baedekar Raids'. These were named after the pre-war German tourist guidebooks from which the targets were allegedly selected. The Baedekar attacks were widely believed to have been intended as reprisals for British bombing of German cultural centres, in particular the devastating attack on the beautiful and ancient German port of Lübeck in March 1942, a city which many considered had relatively little strategic importance.

It is argued that it was precisely because of Exeter's rich artistic and architectural heritage that it was chosen as the target for the Lübeck reprisal raid; certainly, in strategic terms, the town was even less important than Lübeck had been, although there were inevitably some elements of military presence and war manufacture in both places. Whatever the reason for the action, the most severe raid commenced with a force of 30 Junkers JU88 bombers flying up the Exe at around midnight on 4th May 1942 to drop flares and high-explosive bombs ahead of the main attack that shortly followed. The next few hours changed forever both the face of Exeter and the status of its fire crews. Almost within minutes of the raid starting,

*Exeter firefighters at Dane's Castle during the war with a Royal Engineers UXB (Unexploded Bomb) unit and a few trophies. The appliance is a Ford 7V Heavy SP pump unit.*

the firefighters found themselves well and truly in the front line, with whole streets ablaze and the centre of the city a mass of fire and ruin.

Exeter had had longer to prepare than London or Plymouth, and been able to learn the lessons of previous blitzes. Her firefighting forces were thus dispersed widely around the city, with each crew having a pre-determined role in the event of a serious attack. The Exeter NFS fire companies were more numerous, better trained and better equipped than had been their AFS opposite numbers in Plymouth a year earlier; their control system was more effective and, most importantly, their water supplies were more numerous and more accessible than Plymouth's had been. The River Exe was not tidal within the city limits, and with the small size of the town it was never far away.

Nevertheless, the fires that broke out in the early morning of 4th May were a horrific baptism for any fire service, however well prepared. The High Street, Fore Street, Paris Street, Sidwell Street, South Street and the Newtown area of the city were soon all burning, and there were numerous smaller outbreaks elsewhere in the city. It could so easily have been Coventry or Plymouth all over again, but the hard lessons of 1941 had spawned a new order. Missing was the chaos that had characterised the initial reaction of firefighters in Plymouth; the response was now ordered, with each crew having clear objectives. Fires were swiftly assessed and prioritised by experienced fire officers, and the resources available were deployed to the best effect. There were enough pumps and hose-layers to set up the necessary water relays without delay, and the men charged with this task were well-drilled and efficient. Reinforcements from the surrounding rural and urban brigades were mobilised promptly, and routed effectively to their required scene of operations.

However, the crews making the initial attack on the large city-centre fires soon found themselves facing the familiar water supply difficulties, with fractured mains rendering hydrants useless and the access to many of the static supplies being blocked by debris or burning buildings. But here there were over a million gallons of water available in street dams, flooded cellars and from the flooded brickworks quarry at Clifton Hill, so the situation never became as desperate as it had in Plymouth. These static supplies were fed by a network of 8-inch steel pipes laid in the gutters and supplied by a large pump on the Quay, and as the firefighting effort built up more and more water supplies could be brought into use. The 6-inch deep main below the High Street, with its siphon pump, also kept a limited mains supply available.

On the communications front, matters were not so good. The NFS fire control at Exeter lost its telephones quite early on in the raid, and was unable to keep the 19 Fire District headquarters at Plymouth abreast of developments. Efforts were concentrated on protecting the main telephone exchange next to the fiercely-burning Central Library, but it was a brave group of post office telegraph operators who stuck to their posts long after the General Post Office building was well alight – and thereby managed to keep communications going via colleagues at Bristol Post Office – who were able to alert the outside world to Exeter's plight. Very soon, NFS Fire Columns were being mobilised to the city's aid from as far away as Reading. With the telephones knocked out, local fire communications were maintained by cycle-mounted messengers who guided oncoming fire crews to their objectives and carried situation reports back to HQ throughout the raid.

As the fire situation worsened, the value of effective control and informed pre-planning in extreme situations became evident; swift decisions were taken as to what was possible, and no efforts were wasted or men and machines jeopardised in trying to hold hopeless situations. This meant that operations were concentrated on preventing fire spread from the worst-affected parts, where fires were left to burn while the crews worked on protecting buildings not yet involved, or in extinguishing the many smaller fires that could easily have worsened the situation if allowed to develop unchecked. This strategy was effective, but still left an inferno at the heart of the city; while that burned, the danger of massive spread was always present. However, with substantial reinforcements on the way, the commanders on the spot undoubtedly had their priorities correct; the forces on hand were insufficient to mount a successful attack on the city-centre fires, so containment was the only realistic option.

Finally, as the scale of the main fires reached major conflagration status and firestorm conditions ensued, the NFS instituted their 'Fire Zone' procedure, effectively the 'last resort' in their overall strategy. This procedure recognised that the fire situation was now too widespread to be handled by any central control system however competent, and thus divided the problem up into more manageable areas, or Fire Zones. Each zone would be under the absolute command of a Zone Commander, who would have a major firefighting force at his disposal and absolute discretion to manage his tactics and deployments without reference to the situation elsewhere in the city. The procedure was implemented by the Chief Regional Fire Officer in charge of Region 7, who was now in Exeter. He ordered the main fire area divided into five zones, with Fire Force Commanders Drury from Plymouth and Coles from Exeter taking command of the two worst-affected areas, and Column Officer Bowden of the 18th area HQ, and two un-named Divisional Officers from Fire Force 17 assuming responsibility for the others. The Chief Regional Fire Officer established a 'Field HQ' at St Anne's Fountain. With the resources of three Area Fire Forces now committed to the attack some 300 assorted fire appliances and over 1,500 firefighters were deployed, and over the next 24 hours the fires were gradually brought under control and finally extinguished.

Although the degree of devastation suffered by the High Street and Bedford Circus area of the city centre was as bad as anything suffered in Plymouth, the area involved was nowhere near as large as the fires had been contained far more effectively. A number of important historic buildings, notably the Cathedral and Guildhall, miraculously escaped the flames, but much of the ancient fabric of the 'Jewel of the West' was irretrievably destroyed. However, the civilian casualty list, although severe at 161 dead and many more injured, was nowhere near as bad as might have been expected, and it is evident that Exeter's Civil Defence provision had also profited from the disaster of Plymouth. The organisation of the fire service, although tested to the limit, had held. Men had been relieved before they reached exhaustion point, and in spite of the difficulties of rubble-choked streets and the lack of telephones, the pumps had been kept supplied with fuel, hose and other necessities throughout. Problems had still been experienced with incompatible hydrant and hose fittings, but on nowhere near the scale that had occurred a year before.

With the Baedekar raid on Exeter, the major blitz period in Devon came to an end. Air attacks largely returned to the sporadic affairs of the 1939–40 'false war' period. Most of these raids did not cause the fire brigade too many problems, with one notable exception in 1942, when a

Another well-known image of the Exeter blitz, the High Street opposite the Guildhall on the morning after the great fire-raid of 4th May 1942. The roadway is littered with rubble and lined with fire-hose, while in the centre of the picture a jet is being used by a firefighter and two soldiers to knock down a hot-spot in the ruins of Colsons Department Store – the fore-runner of Dingles. An ARP warden stands in the foreground, with two more soldiers behind him. Two firefighters with another jet are damping down rubble on the left, and a thick haze of smoke hangs over the whole scene. Miraculously, the Tudor oriole windows of the building next to the Guildhall – now Liberty's store – stand relatively unscathed at the left.

Clearance work in Exeter after the May 1942 blitz. On the right are the remains of the National Provincial Bank.

lone aircraft attacked Teignmouth at 10a.m. in the morning. The town's fire station was then part of the town hall complex in Brunswick Road, and it was this prominent target the raider chose to attack. He unfortunately scored a direct hit on the fire station, severely damaging the Dennis pump-escape stationed there and killing fireman Maurice Mortimer who was on station watchroom duty. The wrecked Dennis was returned to its maker for rebuilding, and the Teignmouth unit of the NFS 18 area had to fall back on the old Teignmouth Town Council appliance, a solid-tyred Merryweather PE of around 1920 vintage. This machine was fitted with new wheels and pneumatic tyres, and stationed at a temporary fire station at the County Garage, Teignmouth.

Although there were further similar raids throughout Devon and several more major fires in Plymouth and elsewhere, the county's NFS strength became increasingly re deployed to other affected areas. Now it was Devon fire columns heading north to aid other cities when they came under attack. But gradually, as the war initiative swung in Britain's favour, the risk of air raids lessened over much of the country, and the fire and civil defence services were either reduced or re-directed to other work. Of course, there were still increased fire risks over peacetime norms, with huge numbers of troops and large quantities of supplies and munitions gathering in the south of the country ahead of the 1944 invasion, so the level of incidents remained relatively high. But none of these incidents were on anything like the scale associated with the Plymouth and Exeter blitzes, and the NFS now found itself responding with excessive resources rather than struggling to meet the need. Nevertheless, the NFS structure remained in place throughout the county until the reorganisation of March 1948 returned the responsibility for fire provision to local authority control, although on a very different basis to that pertaining before the war.

*The end of it all. Exeter's 1938 'war precautions' Leyland Cub pump EFJ 359 taking part in the Victory Parade in May, 1945. Virtually all of Devon's 'regular' fire appliances survived the war, although some of the older machines were completely worn out.*

# THREE BRIGADES
# 1948–1973

T he 1947 Fire Services Act was the biggest single peacetime reorganisation that the British fire service had ever seen. The 1941 national-
isation that created the National Fire Service was only ever regarded
as a temporary expedient in time of crisis, and the government had
assured the various authorities whose men and equipment had been
requisitioned that the fire service would be returned to local authority
control once the war emergency was over. (Although, as the home secretary was at pains to point out in the House, 'not necessarily in the form in
which it was taken over'). It was widely expected that the NFS would be
dissolved in 1946, but the government of the day wisely decided to take
their time in determining the future basis of firefighting in Britain. The
framework that they came up with has since been widely copied as an
organisational model throughout the world.

## THE RETURN TO LOCAL CONTROL

The breathing space created by the continuation of NFS control through
1946 and 1947 was time put to good use by the Home Office Fire
Inspectorate, who determined to take a thorough look at the whole organisation of the service from top to bottom, and to incorporate fully the
many lessons that had been hard-learned since the Riverdale Report of
1936. It was also not forgotten that, while the country might now be at
peace with Germany and the other Axis powers, new threats were emerging in the Soviet east and the possibility of further war could not be
discounted. And with the Pandora's box of the atom bomb now well and
truly opened, the potential existed for fire situations that would make the
Plymouth blitz look like a cosy bonfire.

The first and most obvious lesson, the need for standardisation of basic
equipment and working practices, had already been addressed and proven
during the NFS administration of the later war years. But there were other
factors to consider – factors that were perhaps more relevant to the peacetime situation than the more extreme conditions of wartime. As James
Kenyon remarked in his book *The Fourth Arm* – a review of firefighting
science and practice published in 1948 just after local control had
resumed – 'blitz' firefighting and peacetime firefighting were two totally

different disciplines, with different objectives and calling for a totally different approach. The former demanded broad measures and what was, in firefighting terms, a very crude tactic – simply stop the fire spreading, then to drown it out by main force. Peacetime firefighting, on the other hand, required far more precision and skill, as fires had not only to be extinguished quickly and safely, but with minimum consequential damage. And water damage can be as destructive as – and often more destructive than – the actual effects of fire. There was an apocryphal story circulating in fire service circles at the time about a supposed meeting in a pub between an 'old hand' from a rural district fire brigade and a young NFS fireman new-versed in blitz firefighting. 'You old boys,' says the young man, 'You don't know what a real fire is, with your little cottages and barns and hayricks.' 'Ah, that may be so', says the Old Hand. 'But from what I've heard, you boys always make it a hundred pounds of fire damage and a thousand pounds water damage.'

The new order established the underlying principle that the weight and speed of the fire service response should be in proportion to the risk. Even while the war still raged in Europe, far-sighted officers of the NFS were devising the new peacetime firefighting strategies, and were training selected officers in the risk-based approach. This meant that, at the war's end, there were sufficient fire officers skilled in the new science of risk assessment to undertake the task of categorising the degree of risk right across the country. The NFS, with a national organisation reaching down through a broad pyramidical structure to thousands of local fire stations, was ideally placed to implement such a nationwide scheme of risk categorisation. By the time the NFS was disbanded in March 1948, the Home Office national risk register was in place, as were the criteria for assessment of new construction following the war.

The initial 6-category scheme of risk assessment and categorisation devised in 1944 under the Central Fire Brigades Advisory Council proved a little too complex, and in 1958 it was simplified into four basic categories plus a 'catch-all' for areas that had so little risk to assess that they fitted none of them: the risk categories were A to D, plus the 'remote rural'. 'A' risk was the highest category, and included densely populated urban areas and special risks like hotels, hospitals or dangerous manufacturing processes. 'B' risk covered medium-density mixed urban and industrial areas, while 'C' risk was for the suburbs, country towns and other relatively low-density populations. 'D' risk covered the rest of the country – essentially, the populated rural areas, leaving the wilderness areas as 'Remote Rural'.

The risk category that an area was placed in determined the number and type of fire appliances that would be sent in response to a fire call, together with the minimum crews and the time within which they had to reach the incident. Generally, the level and speed of response proposed was set at a far greater level than had been the norm before the war over most of the country, with the objective of nipping any fire in the bud before it had a chance to grow beyond the resources of local control. One suspects that the architects of this scheme also had in mind that, in order to meet these new standards, fire brigades would have to provide far greater establishments than had been the case in the pre-war years. There was a determination that never again would Britain's fire defences be allowed to reach the low ebb that had so alarmed the 1936 Riverdale Committee. The standard of attendance times that were set for the various risk categories was: 'A' risk, two pumping appliances within five minutes of the time of call and a third within eight ; 'B' risk, one pumping appliance within five minutes and a second within eight; 'C' risk, one pump in ten minutes and two within twenty; and 'D' risk, one pump within twenty minutes. Remote rural risks would be attended 'as soon as practicably possible'.

As described in the first chapter, the Home Office – through its Joint Council for Design and Development – had also set down the specifications for the new types of appliance to be used to meet these requirements. Key to the new strategy was that an initial attendance appliance should carry with it enough water to mount an effective attack on the fire while a main firefighting supply was being established from a hydrant or open water source. The figure determined was 400 gallons, which would keep a firefighting branch with a half-inch nozzle supplied for around four minutes, or a hosereel branch fed by $^3/_4$-inch tubing for about twenty minutes.

The 1947 act set far more stringent limits on the types of local administration that would be permitted to maintain public fire brigades. The basic unit chosen was the county, with provisions for cities and other large towns to manage their own city or 'county borough' brigades. Under these criteria, the maximum number of brigades permitted for Great Britain as a whole would be 151, rather than the 1660 public brigades existing prior to 1937. In fact, when the dust settled in March 1948 there were 147 brigades in total, a few places that could have maintained independent brigades chose to form 'joint authorities'. Torbay, which might have expected 'County Borough' status, became part of the Devon County Fire Service. Devon County Council formed a 'Fire Brigade Committee' to oversee this new brigade, leaving Exeter and Plymouth to manage their own affairs as City brigades.

*A Home Office inspection at Exeter in the 1950s finds the Dane's Castle establishment on parade on the station apron, with the Dennis F8 pump that replaced the pre-war Leyland in the background. Note the topiary in the station grounds.*

*Seen in Devon Fire Brigade days, the Exeter City Fire Brigade emergency tender was built by Mumford on a Bedford TK chassis and was equipped as a Home Office class 'A' machine.*

*Opposite page bottom left: Re-naming of the Plymouth fireboat as Cissie Brock by Mrs Cissie Brock herself – the diminutive lady at the foot of the stairway. There are five pump deliveries a side on the boat, the foremost of which is fitted with a Home Office pattern monitor. There was also a swivelling monitor on the foredeck, behind the crew.*

*Opposite page bottom right: The old order prevails. Here is Plymouth's 1930 Dennis 30-h.p. pump DR 7555 photographed turning out from Station 'B' Penlee about 1950. This machine was on the run as a pump only at this time, carrying only a basic Home Office Utility-pattern ladder. The appliance has been modernised in detail, with new headlights and a rear searchlight. At this period, the escape at Penlee was being carried by a Utility Austin K4 escape-carrier modified as a pump-escape.*

# THE NEW ERA IN DEVON – THE CITY BRIGADES

On 1st April 1948 Exeter became one of the smallest new city brigades in the country, with just two operational stations, Dane's Castle (No. 1 station) and Topsham (No. 2). There was also initially a No. 3 station, but this was the AFS establishment which was never part of the Exeter City Brigade's front-line resources and was anyway disbanded in 1968. The manning at No. 1 station was part whole-time, part retained, while the No. 2 station was retained. There was a control room at No. 1 station, along with administrative offices and housing for firefighters. The new Exeter brigade was equipped with four pumping appliances, originally a mixture of the original pre-war pumps and Utility pump-water tenders, later replaced by modern Dennis pump-water-tenders to the JCDD specifications. There was also a pump-escape at No. 1 station together with a wartime 100-foot TL, an emergency tender and later, with the advent of multi-storey car parks, a Land Rover light pump to attend incidents in these and similar premises inaccessible to regular fire engines. The brigade also had a 'water carrier' at Dane's Castle, which was maintained to meet forest-fire risks within the Exeter area.

Both the Exeter stations were relatively modern and the brigade was quite well-placed to meet its requirements being, so far as was possible, self-suf-ficient. As well as the firefighting establishment of 46 whole time and 20 retained men plus 4 senior officers, there were 8 female control operators and a brigade engineering establishment with workshops at the rear of the Dane's Castle station, where all the appliances and equipment were maintained as well as contract work being undertaken for outside customers to use up spare capacity. Ambulances and City Council vehicles were among those worked on, while members of the brigade possessing their own cars could arrange to have them serviced at the brigade workshops. The Danes Castle station also had a large drill ground with a tall drill tower, and formed the Exeter Brigade's main internal training centre. However, as with many small brigades, Exeter was not self-sufficient in this respect, and sent recruits away to Birmingham for initial training by the City of Birmingham Fire Brigade. Later, when Birmingham ceased 'outside' training, Exeter men went to the Surrey Fire Service school at Reigate.

Obviously, with a total strength of only four pumping appliances and two 'specials', a large fire in the city would outstrip the resources of the Exeter City brigade, and there were extensive arrangements under 'Section 12' of the 1947 Act for mutual aid between the Exeter City and Devon County brigades. Many of the villages surrounding Exeter attracted a 'dual attendance' to fires, with one appliance attending from Exeter and any additional machines coming from Devon County stations, while Devon appliances would go into Exeter on standby duties or to back up the city brigade at larger incidents. Exeter's 'specials' saw use in the Devon County area from time to time, as the Devon County service only had such vehicles as TLs and emergency tenders at Torquay and in the far north of the county at Barnstaple.

## PLYMOUTH CITY FIRE BRIGADE

The Plymouth City Brigade was considerably larger than Exeter, with three large operational stations and a firefighting strength of some 250 whole-time men. The headquarters station was at Greenbank, Station 'A', where the control was also situated. Station 'A' had a good number of appliances:

It was the custom for the Pymouth City Fire Brigade to stage an annual display at the old Raglan Barracks, part of the Devonport Dockyard blessed with a large parade ground. This is believed to be the 1952 event and shows the brand new Dennis F12 pump-escape GCO 138 that had just gone on the run.

Also at the Raglan Barracks Display were the 1932 Dennis 44 hp pump-escape JY 956, while in the background is the 1938 Leyland 'cross bench' pump and two wartime appliances: a 1943 ATV converted to a hosereel tender with the reel on the roof (stationed at station 'C' Torr) and a Ford 7V heavy pump unit. Also seen are the splendid coachbuilt Bedford horsebox that became an Emergency Tender in 1938 and a loudspeaker truck converted from a US Army Dodge 'light 6' ambulance.

*Cissie Brock in the Sound off Millbay, with Drake's Island in the background. Built in 1942 as the Iris, the Cissie Brock remained in service until 1993, when it was replaced by a converted naval dory. At that time, it was the oldest piece of fire apparatus in use in a British public brigade. Latterly, it was based at Plymstock.*

*Below: The standard replacement for pre-war machinery used by all three Devon brigades from the mid-1950s was the Dennis F8, a compact appliance ideally suited to the county. Plymouth had several of these machines, this 1958 example lasting until 1971. One of these machines, LCO 318, is preserved at Greenbank fire station.*

*Below Right: This beautiful TL is actually a wartime Utility appliance on a modified Leyland 'Tiger' TD7 30-h.p. bus chassis, there being a shortage of specialist running gear at the time (most TLs used heavier 45-h.p. chassis). FDR 706 was built for the Navy in 1942 with Merryweather 100-foot ladders, and after the war was loaned to the Plymouth City Brigade who stationed it at Camel's Head. It lasted there until 1967, when it was replaced by the 70-foot 'Snorkel'.*

a dual-purpose (pump-escape or, later, water-tender-ladder) appliance and two pumps, plus one 100-foot TL, an emergency tender and four general-purpose vans. One of the pumps was also later replaced with a multi-purpose machine. Station 'B', Penlee (later replaced by Camel's Head), had one pump-escape and two pump-water-tenders, a 100-foot TL, a fireboat, a personnel carrier and a van. Station 'C' was at originally at Torr, replaced by Crownhill when the latter opened in 1954, where the new establishment was one pump-escape, one pump-water-tender, one foam tender, one 'special equipment tender' and a van, plus a wartime ATV (Auxiliary Towing Vehicle). Initially, there was also a Station 'D' – the fireboat mooring in the docks, which also had an allocation of Utility appliances including a heavy pump unit and two ATV/trailer pump units. It is believed Station D reverted to a fireboat mooring only after Crownhill opened, the extra appliances being stored there. In April 1967, the Plymouth brigade area was enlarged to take in Plympton and Plymstock, and these two retained stations passed from Devon County to Plymouth City. Plymstock had a pump-escape and Plympton a Commer type A water-tender, each station also being allocated a van.

Plymouth also had a purpose-built fireboat to protect the docks and the many waterside and maritime risks inherent in a seaport city. This was the *Cissie Brock*, originally the 'Iris'. Built in 1942 by Taylors of Chertsey, on the Surrey Thames, 'Iris' had a traditional wooden hull with a long fore-cabin and a wheelhouse aft. The powerful fire pump could supply shore-

The first post-war TL at Greenbank was also originally a wartime appliance, a 1941 100-foot Leyland-Merryweather registered CDR 287, and this was replaced in 1961 with YJY 44, a Merryweather 'Marquis' series 100-foot power-operated TL – the last word in aerial appliances at that time. The Merryweather hydraulic TL had a console on the turntable, which rotated with the ladders ensuring a clear view for the operator. In 1981, these ladders were put onto a new Shelvoke chassis for further service, being finally replaced by a hydraulic platform in 1994.

based appliances as well as the monitor gun mounted on the foredeck. The fireboat was originally named after the daughter of the wartime Fire Force Commander, Mr Drury. She became *Cissie Brock* when that lady acceded to the chair of the Plymouth Fire Brigades Authority. The Plymouth City Brigade kept the fireboat in the navy's Royal William Yard, where she is reputed to have sunk at her moorings at least twice. At times of neap tide, the fireboat could not get out of her berth except at high water, so she was manned by a crew from Camel's Head and sent out into the Sound for the duration of low tide conditions – a duty that proved popular with the sea-angling members of the Camel's Head watches!

Although, like the Exeter and Devon County brigades, Plymouth had started out with a heterogeneous mixture of pre-war and wartime Utility appliances – see fleet list in Appendix 2 – modernisation was quicker in this brigade than elsewhere in Devon. Most of the old pre-war open-bodied machines had been replaced with modern enclosed appliances by the mid 1950s, the replacements including a Dennis F12 pump-escape and several Dennis F8 pumps. As was usually the case, the brigade's two open TLs, both 100' Merryweather ladders on Leyland chassis, soldiered on for rather longer, lasting into the 1960s. The 1940 Utility Leyland at Greenbank was replaced with a new AEC 'Marquis'/Merryweather 100-foot hydraulic TL in 1961, while the very handsome half-cab 1942 Leyland – which had been

Here is a broadside view of a Plymouth multi at Plymstock in the early 1970s. Carmichael appliances always had wonderful paint jobs, and these machines had a real 'coachbuilders shine'. Note how long the machine is – the Bayley 35-ft secondary ladder doesn't even come over the cab.

*This is, strictly, a Devon Fire Brigade shot, but it's pure Plymouth so finds its place here. This is the fire that occurred at the 'Unity' public house in Eastlake Street in the city centre in September 1978, which involved three rescues from the roof of the building. The appliance in the foreground is LJY 999H as 501, one of Greenbank's two multi-purpose appliances. The 35-foot Bayley wooden ladder has been slipped and pitched to the second floor parapet of the pub, while the Greenbank TL behind is pitched to the roof for rescue purposes. Note the superb quality of the bodywork on the Multi, and the American-style 'wailer' siren, another Plymouth feature.*

loaded to the city by the navy – served at Camel's Head until 1967. It was replaced by a 70-foot Simon hydraulic platform, or 'Snorkel', one of the first such appliances to see service in Britain.

During the later 1960s, when the 1950s Dennis appliances became due for renewal, Plymouth was the first brigade in the country to develop a new 'multi-purpose appliance', the progenitor of the modern water/ladder/rescue vehicle. After experimenting with a prototype converted from an old Dennis, Plymouth's first production multi-purpose appliances appeared in 1967. These were massive machines on Leyland 'Beaver' chassis, incorporating almost all the functions of a pump-water-tender, a PE, a salvage tender and an ET/rescue tender. They carried one of the new all-alloy '464' rescue ladders, a 35-foot Bayley wooden ladder, roof and short extension ladders, together with hand-pumped hydraulic rescue equipment, power cutting equipment and powerful electric lighting. These machines were intended to replace either pump-water-tenders or pump-escapes and to take on much of the work of the 'specials', with the idea that much greater flexibility in mobilising and operations would result if every pumping appliance in the city could do every routine job. In this concept Plymouth was well ahead of most of the rest of the country.

*Below right: Another unique Crownhill appliance was the hose/foam tender, built in 1965 to replace a wartime combination of a 1941 7V Ford hoselaying lorry and a foam tender converted from a 1943 Austin K4 ATV and stationed at Greenbank (See 1950 Plymouth Allocation in Appendix 2).*

*Below: This is Crownhill's 'Equipment Tender', an ET in all but name. Built on a Bedford/Hawson chassis in 1970, MDR 999H was a 'one-off' and remained in service until 1986. It carried heavy lifting gear, lighting, a wide range of tools and some specialist items connected with incidents in the Naval Dockyard. Like all Plymouth appliances, it had a first-class paint job and plenty of chrome.*

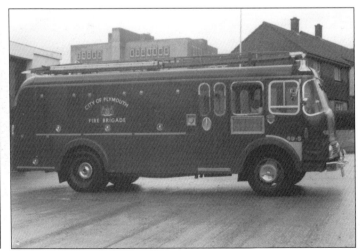

Although the Plymouth brigade, with its greater resources of men and machinery, was more self-contained in operational terms than Exeter, there was still a need for 'section 12' arrangements, not only with the surrounding Devon stations like Ivybridge, Yelverton and Bere Alston, but also with the Cornwall County Fire Brigade at Saltash, just across the river – especially after the Tamar road bridge opened in 1961. Like Exeter, Plymouth was independent for its engineering requirements, and determined to be so for training. There were extensive and well-equipped workshops at the new Crownhill fire station, where all the brigade's equipment could be maintained. The NFS 19 area had established a training camp at Lee Mill, between Plymouth and Ivybridge, but this closed with the disbanding of the NFS. Although initially sending its recruits off to London for training at the LFB school at Southwark, Plymouth later opened its own training centre at Camel's Head, and started work on a project for a new fire station and training establishment at Plympton, which would be commissioned by the Devon Fire Brigade after 1973. This complex later became the main fire service training facility for much of south-west England.

*The 'Gang of Seven' – the senior officers of the City of Plymouth Fire Brigade photographed just before the 1973 amalgamation into the Devon Fire Brigade. Back row, left to right: ADO Donaldson, ADO Harvey and ADO Watson. Front row: DO Corbett, DCFO Dawe, CFO Havery and DO Fiddaman.*

*Last word on the Plymouth City brigade – the line-up at Station 'A' Greenbank just after the Devon Fire Brigade took over. At far left is the Emergency/Salvage tender TJY 999, built on a TK Bedford chassis; next is the 1961 Merryweather turntable ladder YJY 44, then the two 'multis' LJY 999H and KJY 999G*

*The spirit of the Devon County Fire Service: the old wartime Merryweather 60-foot manually operated TL allocated to North Devon was stationed at Ilfracombe and was kept in immaculate condition, as witnessed by this 1960s photo of TL drills at the new Ilfracombe station. This vehicle was re-chassised in 1965 into a special Bedford TL/pump combination unique to Ilfracombe.*

# THE DEVON COUNTY FIRE SERVICE

With Plymouth and Exeter looking after their own affairs in what was more or less a continuation of the pre-war status quo, the rest of Devon was the remit of the new Devon County Fire Service. This was a large brigade with more than fifty stations, being an amalgamation of around seventy or so pre-existing brigades. As such, Devon County had a far more mixed heritage than either of the two city brigades. There was an initial period of upheaval and consolidation, with some brigades being disbanded and others being re-equipped. An interesting document that surfaced during the research for this book was an NFS 'blueprint' for the proposed Devon County Fire Brigade (sic), which shows a different disposition to that which finally emerged. A number of towns or villages without fire stations under the NFS were to get them, presumably to meet the twenty-minute attendance time. These locations included Beaworthy, Bradworthy, High Bickington and Up-Ottery. Chagford and Clovelly stations, having been closed by the NFS in 1946, were missed off the list. In the event, the new brigade chose to build on existing foundations, and the proposed extra stations were never opened, while Chagford was re-instated as a retained station and Clovelly as volunteer. The Devon County brigade was organised in three divisions, A (East Devon), B (North Devon) & C (South Devon) and one sub-division, D (West Devon), which was administratively a part of C division. The make up of the divisions and the identities of the stations, together with the appliances they were operating in 1957, are given in Appendix 3. The new brigade's administrative headquarters was at 'The Knowle', at Clyst St George near Exeter. This country house was bought in 1948, and as well as being the home of the CFO, it housed the 'A' division control room. As this was situated directly beneath the CFO's living quarters, the control staff were asked to wear plimsolls and to talk quietly! The Knowle was also the operations base for the AFS in Devon, with a separate control room situated in the basement. It was from this AFS control that the emergency response to the *Torrey Canyon* oil tanker disaster was co-ordinated in 1964.

For control purposes, each Division was mobilised separately. There was initially no county-wide radio scheme due to the size and topography of the area, so all communication was by telephone. One man on a fire appliance crew was appointed as 'runner' to convey messages to and from the nearest phone – some stations had a push-bike to aid the 'runner' in this arduous task. This was obviously an unsatisfactory arrangement, especially when a large incident occurred near the border of two divisions, thus involving two control-rooms and a welter of phone messages. Only with the coming of universal radio communications was it possible to set up a single central control; this was created from the old A division control room beneath the chief's bedroom – and plimsolls were still regulation wear for the operators!

*Below: Typical of the older machines still in service in the 1950s was this elegant Leyland 'Cub' pump with traditional Braidwood bodywork, but carrying a 35-ft Bayley ladder, used for some years at Ottery St Mary and now preserved.*

*Below: A similar machine but with more modern bodywork was this 1940 Leyland FKT turbine pump stationed at Kingsbridge. While most of the extra fire appliances supplied during the war were the Home Office 'Utility' designs, the regular fire engine builders were still producing normal machines, and this 'semi-limousine' appliance with cross-bench seating is an example. The machine in the background is the Dennis F8 that replaced it.*

*Above: Ford 7V water tender converted from a wartime Utility Escape Carrier unit. This is the most basic 'conversion', fitted with a 400-gallon cylindrical steel water-tank of the type fitted to the later wartime 'water carriers'. A Coventry-Climax light 250-g.p.m. portable pump fitted crosswise behind the tank feeding a hosereel and twin deliveries. A utilty 25-ft extension ladder was carried, and hose and fittings were stowed in the existing lockers below load-bed level. A medium trailer pump could be towed on the long A-frame hitch fitted to clear the escape. This type of appliance formed the backbone of the rural retained service in Devon until the early 1960s; this example was at Moretonhampstead, with sister machine GXM 822 at neighbouring Chagford.*

*Top Right: By contrast to the older and Utility machines, here is a new post-war 'Type A' water tender built in 1950 on the underfloor-engined Commer truck chassis. These machines did not have an integral pump driven by the road engine, but a self-contained demountable pump unuit carried across the rear of the appliance – in essence, a 350-g.p.m. trailer pump shorn of the trailer and mounted direct onto the chassis. This supplied a hosereel each side and two deliveries at the rear. The commodious bodywork had room for a six-man crew and carried a wide range of equipment, with a 400-gallon water tank in the centre of the chassis. These were popular and competent machines that served Devon well. This example, photographed in the 1960s, is on the reserve fleet.*

## The Devon Inheritance and Early Advances

Much of the Devon County heritage was antiquated, ill-equipped and geographically ill-placed. The fire stations that existed were located by historical accident rather than placed to meet the new statutory fire-cover requirements, as the NFS had proposed. Many of the actual buildings were also too small to house modern appliances or to provide the necessary accommodation. Most of the stations were equipped either with pre-war appliances, many comparatively little-used and in good order, or with converted NFS Utility types. Initially, the policy had to be one of 'make do and mend' in respect of both stations and machines, and until about 1965 Devon was a fire-engine buff's delight, where one might come across anything from an immaculate pre-war classic through a variety of conversions of wartime Utility appliances to brand-new machines.

Two Devon appliances improvised from ex-NFS Utility appliances deserve particular mention, as they formed the backbone of the rural retained service throughout the 1950s. These were the Type A Water-Tender (WrT) and the Pump/Hose-Reel Tender (HrT). The first of these was based on the Utility 'large chassis' – forward-control 30-h.p. Ford V-8 '7V' or normal-control 27-h.p. Austin 'K3' – used for wartime Self-Propelled Pumps and Escape Carriers. The original Utility bodywork fitted for both these types was similar – a rearward-facing crew shelter behind the cab and lockers on the lower bodysides. The SP pump had a large petrol-driven pump on the load bed, whereas the Escape Carrier had mountings for a wheeled escape and towed a trailer pump with an A-frame hitch. The second Devon type, the HrT was converted from the sturdy wartime Austin Auxiliary Towing Vehicle (ATV), which had a roomy van-type body.

For the Devon WrT conversions – mostly on the 30-h.p. 7V Ford chassis – the pump or escape of the wartime appliances were removed and replaced by a rectangular steel 400-gallon water tank fitted in the centre of the bodywork. Behind the tank, a Coventry-Climax 150 or 250 g.p.m. self-contained fire pump of the type supplied trailer-mounted during the war was mounted crosswise on the chassis, with permanent connections to the tank and to a hosereel mounted at the rear of the body. A two-section extension ladder was carried on gantries above the tank and cab, with a short ladder mounted on the tank-top. The bodywork was 'tidied up' by the addition of extended side panels

*Drill competitions continued to be popular after the war, and here is a crew from Braunton victorious after a Water Tender Drill Competion in the 1950s. They are standing in front of a somewhat-more-accomplished water-tender conversion of a Ford 30-h.p. V-8 heavy pump unit, which has the crew shelter elegantly fared-in to new bodysides to conceal the decidedly inelegant rectangular rivetted 400-gallon tank and the demountable Coventy-Climax pump. The usual Utility ladder sits on brackets atop tank and cab, and the suction is also at tanktop level. Extemporised they may have been, but these appliances gave good service.*

Winners of the Devon County Water Tender Drill competition held at Exeter.

Okehampton Firemen – left to right are D J Kelly, A Welham, Sub Officer T Heale, F Mason and H Bevan

*Another year, it was the turn of a crew from Okehampton to bring home the drill prize. This is a good view of the rear of one of the water-tender conversions of the type illustrated in the Braunton picture, showing the rectangular water tank and the engine casing of the Coventry-Climax 250-g.p.m. fire pump. These pumps were originally carried on light two-wheel trailers, but were always demountable. They had all-alloy OHC engines and could (just!) be carried by four men. Note the suction hose and wicker basket pump strainer on the tank-top. The men are wearing NFS tunics with belt-lines.*

faired-in to the crew shelter and lockers and swept down at the rear. Stowage for suction hose and other gear was provided within the new bodysides, while hose and small gear was carried in the original lockers. Those WrTs converted from Escape Carriers retained their A-frame hitches and usually operated with a medium trailer pump as WrT + TP. A few such WrTs later gained inbuilt 500-g.p.m. pumps mounted to the nose of the crankshaft in front of the radiator, thus becoming pump-water-tenders under the new Home Office specification.

The HrT was an altogether simpler conversion. The main modifications were the installation of a 150-gallon water tank within the front part of the ATV body and the fitment of a PTO-driven first-aid pump which gave about 50 g.p.m. at 75 lb. sq. in. pressure through a hosereel mounted on top of the body. A pump control panel and tank inlet were recessed into the nearside bodywork. The tank took the place of most of the ATV's extensive hose-racking, but enough space was left for some twenty lengths with nozzles and branchpipes plus a section of small gear. Simple wooden extension ladders and a short ladder were carried on the appliance roof. Many of the HrT conversions

*Devon County fire stations were extemporised out of all sorts of structures, mostly of a rather bucolic nature. An exception was Brixham, modified from one of the old Torbay Borough Electricity sub-station buildings; this looks almost as if it was meant to be a fire station!*

*Somewhat more basic was Princetown, a crude edificice in concrete block with a tin roof. It was originally a store shed associated with the goods depot of the old Princetown railway station. Headroom was so restricted that in order to house a Commer 'multi-purpose' in 1979, two 'wheel tracks' had to be excavated in the floor. This station was finally replaced in 1995.*

retained their towing frames and operated with a medium trailer pump. All these WrT and HrT conversions were repainted from NFS grey to traditional red, receiving coachlining in old gold with reversed corners and lettered 'Devon County Fire Service' on two lines, with the county shield between them.

The fire stations in which these machines were housed were a very mixed lot, as almost none of them were purpose-built. Pre-war or during the wartime NFS period of 'sub stations', many brigades made arrangements with the local garage to house the fire appliance, while others were operating out of buildings dating from the days of a manual pump and a few buckets. The new county fire authority had to improvise and many fire stations were created out of a variety of pre-existing buildings; Braunton from a school, Moretonhampstead from a pound-house, Brixham from an electricity sub-station, Budleigh Salterton from a chapel, Chulmleigh from part of a house and Chagford from a piggery. Princetown had a store-shed and Yelverton a recyled military barrack hut, while Bovey occupied the town hall basement. Only one or two stations were modern and dated from the 'motor age' but for the most part the story was one of inadequate or unsuitable accommodation.

A programme of modernisation initiated by Devon's first CFO, W. H. Barker, soon got under way. The most unsuitable fire stations were replaced first with economical modern buildings of simple design evolved by the county architect. There was more-or-less standard design of one-pump station for the rural

The opening of Holsworthy's new fire station in 1955, showing the roomy appliance bay and simple outline with low-pitched roof. The flat-roofed watchroom and lecture room are to the left, and there was a small drill tower. The appliance is one of the handsome Dodge/HCB water tenders and was also new at about this time.

Bere Alston fire station is an example of the later Devon County design which was built to replace less suitable accommodation. A simple building with a generous appliance bay, watchroom, lecture room and kitchen. The hard-surfaced drill yard has a 3-storey drill tower.

Torquay's old Market Street station was of an altogether earlier age, with the appliance sheds and stabling for horses grouped around a cramped yard behind 'Corporation Buildings', a block of flats and shops with only a narrow arch to give access out onto the street. This may have sufficed for horse-drawn fire engines, but it was a decidedly tight fit for motor appliances. Here, the unique Torquay short five-section TL turns out for a Home Office drill (hence the generous crew).

*Even the modest dimensions of a Dennis F12 were a tight squeeze in the arch. There was no way this station could have accommodated modern machines, and even with the smaller vehicles of 40 years ago there were problems with clearance.*

areas which had a good-sized appliance bay, an office-cum-watchroom-cum lecture room, a toilet and washroom and primitive kitchen facilities. The buildings were in rendered concrete block with Critall metal windows, and many started out with asbestos roofs. This basic structure was built in many places throughout rural Devon, starting at Hatherleigh in 1950 and continuing right through the Devon County Brigade's independent existence until 1972, the last DCFS station being Dawlish, built that final year. In all fifteen new one pump stations were built in this period, as well as the new large divisional stations at Torquay (1955) and Barnstaple (1964), together with stations for two or three pumps at Crediton, Honiton, Ilfracombe, Lynton, Newton Abbot, Okehampton, Paignton, Sidmouth, Tiverton and Totnes.

The largest of these Devon County buildings was the new Torquay fire station, opened in 1957 to replace the cramped Market Street station. There were many problems with this former location, not least of which was the narrowness of Market Street itself and the arched access to the station yard by which all machines had to turn out; the dimensions of this arch determined the size of Torbay machines, and even a narrow-bodied Dennis F8 was a tight fit. The spacious new building on Newton Road at the northern edge of the town had none of these problems, and housed the area administrative HQ and a well-equipped workshop as well as having space for six front-line fire appliances. Its siting was in accordance with the post-war thinking that it was better for the fire brigade to go into a conurbation from the edge rather than trying to fight its way out from the centre.

## NEW DEVON FIRE APPLIANCES

On the appliance front, Devon's new post-war Dennis appliances had initially been allocated to the busier fire stations like Torquay and Barnstaple, with most retained stations soldiering on with old machines. As the role of the fire service continued to expand, the small Dennis proved to be rather *too* small to carry the increasing range of equipment needed in the urban areas, while the next generation of Dennis appliances, designed for the needs of major city brigades like London or Manchester, were too large and too costly for brigades like Devon. Since the war, a number of modern commercial-vehicle chassis had come onto the market that were to prove highly suitable for fire-service purposes, and these formed an alternative to purpose-built machines.

*Newton Abbot crew in the early 1950s with their new Commer water tender. Newton Abbot has a reputation as the busiest retained station in Devon and has usually been allocated modern appliances. Note that even this new appliance carries only a basic Utility 25-foot extension, later replaced with a 35-ft trussed Bayley ladder.*

*Above: In time, the machines on even the remotest stations were upgraded. Hartland was still a volunteer station when it received this Dennis F8 water-tender, photographed here in the late 1960s with a blue light tacked on top of the bell bracket. Most Devon country-area F8's had all-silver aluminium bodywork as shown in the Dartmouth picture, but this 'town' example – almost certainly relocated from Torquay or Barnstaple – is fully painted (and beautifully kept). These narrow-bodied machines, with their flat sides and short wheelbase, were well-suited to Devon's narrow lanes*

*Left: The old and the new at Dartmouth in the 1950s, with a new 1955 Dennis F8 water-tender joining the Dartmouth brigade's pre-war Leyland Cub pump which, unusually, is carrying a lightweight 3-section 45-foot ladder. This is the old Dartmouth station in Flavell Street, replaced in 1983.*

*Top Left: Torquay's Dennis F12 pump-escape is an example of the state of the art in 1955 – a purpose-built PE on a long chassis with a midships mounted pump with controls and deliveries on the nearside (often duplicated both sides). This overcame the main drawback of the older pump-escapes – namely, the need to slip and remove the escape before the pump could be got to work. These Dennis machines had Rolls-Royce B6 or B8 petrol engines, which sounded magnificent. The wooden escape ladders were usually by Morris.*

Devon bought some new type-A water-tenders based on Dodge 'Kew' and Commer chassis during the early 1950s for the busier retained stations, but otherwise those retained stations that were fortunate enough to be re-equipped received 'passed-down' Dennis F8's after about 1955. Such machines went, amongst other places, to Moretonhampstead, Ottery, Hartland, Kingsbridge and Dartmouth, (replacing a pre-war appliance). Throughout the later 1950s, six-cylinder Bedford 'S' and 'T' series chassis became a popular basis for fire appliances so, in conjunction with Hampshire Car Bodies at Southampton, Devon County Fire Service developed a series of highly-successful machines on this running gear. These included TK series PWTs and PEs, together with the famous 'J' series country-area water-tenders for the rural retained stations. The HCB bodies were most distinctive, and a few were built onto Dodge chassis as well as the more usual Bedford.

The HCB-bodied Bedford and Dodge machines of 1960/67 rapidly became the standard Devon rural-area appliance and proved a most successful design. The bodywork, on a short wheelbase chassis fitted with a powerful 3.3 litre 6-cylinder petrol engine, combined a fibreglass cab and an all-alloy body with roller-shutter lockers. These compact and manoeuvrable lightweight machines had good accommodation with room for breathing apparatus and generous locker space. They were full Home Office type 'B' water-tenders carrying 400 gallons of water, a 500-g.p.m. major pump with a 250-g.p.m. portable pump and 35-

*Above: To succeed the F series Dennis machines and the various converted wartime appliances, Devon County Fire Service turned to Hampshire Car Bodies (HCB) of Southampton. For the rural stations, HCB came up with the 'country' water tender, based on Bedford or Dodge chassis but with an all-HCB body using a moulded fibreglass cab and alloy-over-ash bodywork. The sides were unpainted alloy, and rubber wings were fitted. At only 6ft 9ins wide, with excellent ground clearance and a short wheelbase for manoeuverability, there were very few places in in Devon that one of these vehicles could not reach. This is a Dodge example, stationed at Yelverton.*

*Right: For retained stations that did not warrant a full water-tender appliance, Devon developed the pump/hosereel tender, a 'mini' appliance with a first-aid water tank of around 150-gallon capacity feeding rear-mounted hosereels, but also fitted with a 350-g.p.m. major pump and carrying a 35-foot Bayley ladder. These were built on the lighter Bedford 'medium' AS chassis and did not require the driver to hold an HGV licence as they were below 7 1/2 tons weight. This austere example, popularly known as 'The Bread Van', has more than a touch of the 'utility' about it; it was stationed at Ashburton.*

*Top right: This later 1966 P/HrT is a little more comely than the Ashburton example. It was stationed at Princetown, being replaced by a J series Bedford WrT about 1974–5.*

foot Bayley wooden ladder. Small gear included powerful propane-powered arc lighting, many small tools and a limited foam capability, plus roof and short extension ladders. Most retained stations received these Bedfords to replace their old WWII Utility appliances – and what an enormous step forward they were at the time! Some 'J's were later adapted to WrT/L with light-alloy '464' three-section escape ladders on a rather lethal swinging gantry mounting. For a few smaller retained stations, Devon County also perpetuated the pump/hose-reel tender. These were again on Bedford chassis fitted with rather basic bodywork by HCB. It must be admitted that these machines were as ugly as the 'Devon Js' were comely, but they fulfilled their role. Amongst other stations to operate P/HrTs were Ashburton and Princetown.

## TECHNICAL ADVANCES – BA AND RADIO

Other technical developments were also in hand in breathing apparatus and radio communications. BA, which had initially been considered an 'add-on' even within urban brigades, gradually assumed a greater and greater importance as the widespread introduction of synthetic materials into the home and industry made the products of combustion of fires

*Above: By the time Bedford 'J series' 206 TTA was photographed in Devon Fire Brigade Days in the mid-1970s it was on the reserve fleet as SR-3 (South Reserve 3) and had been upgraded to water-tender/ladder with a 135 alloy ladder on a swinging gantry.*

*Left: This is the standard Bedford TK/HCB water tender, a very popular type of appliance throughout Britain in the 1960s and early 1970s. 31–3 is allocated to Totnes and is here seen in Devon Fire Brigade days. The alloy bodysides with roller-shutter doors and flush-fitted rubber wings of these appliances were very practical in Devon, being less prone to damage on narrow roads.*

*Top Left: For the towns, HCB had a PE design on the Bedford TK chassis. These machines had a rear-mounted pump but with side controls and deliveries, hence the cut-out in the rear bodysides. Exeter City purchased a similar machine at about the same time, 1968. Here, the machine is photographed as 17-8 at Torquay in Devon Fire Brigade days. This was the PE involved in the Hotel Florence rescues in 1974, about the time this picture was taken. The last four Bedfords had Rolls-Royce B6 petrol engines with twin carburettors and five-speed gearboxes, and went like the wind.*

more hazardous. By the mid-1960s most Devon fire appliances carried a pair of short-duration (20 minutes working time) compressed-air Draeger Normalair self-contained BA sets, and at least a proportion of firefighters were trained in basic BA procedures. The major BA provision was, however, still on the Emergency Tenders, which carried six long-duration Proto sets and were crewed by men who were specialist BA wearers.

The other great advance of the 1960–1970 era was radio. Although the city brigades, with their compact operational areas, had this almost from the outset it was a problem for the county service, with its extensive area spread over topography difficult for radio communications. To overcome this, powerful AM sets were needed which were not suitable for fitting to fire appliances. Initially, the sets were fitted into vans which were crewed by the outposted whole-time supervisory officers, so messages in outlying areas still had to be passed by public telephone until the 'radio car' turned up. The eventual answer to the radio problem proved to be the construction of a number of 'hilltop repeater' stations on high points across the county during the 1960s, and once these were in service low-powered transistorised FM radios could be fitted on the fire appliances.

*Above: The first self-contained breathing apparatus was the Proto set seen being worn here by fireman E. Shepherd of Exeter. Oxygen contained in a small cylinder was discharged into a 'breathing bag' and breathed by the wearer. The expired carbon dioxide was 'reclaimed' by special oxygenating crystals allowing the oxygen to be re-breathed several times. Consequently the Proto set had a working duration of up to two hours using a single cylinder of oxygen. The set was introduced in 1937 and remained in use until long-duration compressed-air sets became available around 1970.*

*Above Centre: The Proto oxygen breathing apparatus was replaced by a compressed air set known as the Normalair throughout most of Devon in the early 1960s. A compressed air cylinder carried on the back allowed a firefighter to work for some 25 minutes with a ten-minute safety margin.*

*Above Right: Firefighters enter a smoke chamber for a breathing apparatus exercise. The bag being carried on the shoulder of the man opening the door contains a guide-line to allow the crew to retrace their steps from the building. The man on the right is the BA Entry Control Officer (BACO) whose job it is to ensure the safety of any crews wearing breathing apparatus in the building. The board he is holding contains details of the amount of air in the cylinders and the estimated duration of the sets along with the location of the team.*

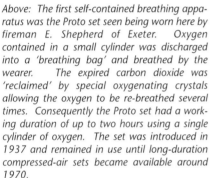

# DEVON'S RETAINED FIREFIGHTERS

As Devon was predominantly a rural county, the vast majority of the service was staffed by retained firefighters. Whole-time men were confined to Torbay, Exmouth, Barnstaple and, from the mid-1960s, Ilfracombe. Whole-time officers also served as outposted supervisory officers overseeing retained crews. There were also four volunteer stations – Clovelly, Hartland, Kingston and Modbury. Here, the county provided an appliance and some training, but the firefighters were unpaid. Clovelly was phased out but the other volunteer stations remained open. Devon was – and still is – one of the largest employers of retained firefighters in Britain, and the training, equipping and organisation of the retained service was improved steadily throughout the life of the Devon County Fire Service. The backbone of fire provision in rural Devon is the one-pump retained or volunteer station, of which there are no less than 33 in the county, each with a complement of twelve men commanded by a sub-officer assisted by two leading firefighters. The larger country towns – Bideford, Crediton, Dartmouth, Honiton, Newton Abbot, Okehampton, Sidmouth, Tavistock, Teignmouth, Tiverton and Totnes – had larger retained establishments with two pumping appliances and 20–24 men. Lynton also became a two-pump station, by virtue of its relative isolation rather than from size or population.

The more important seaside towns such as Paignton, Exmouth and Ilfracombe, with their greater densities of hotels, high life-risk and difficult access, had a two-pump establishment with one pump at least day-crewed by whole-time firefighters. Ilfracombe, where there is a combination of large hotels, narrow streets and geographical isolation, has always been something of a special case within Devon and came to have an establishment of two pumps and an ex-NFS wartime 60-foot TL, with a core of whole-time firefighters. Barnstaple, too, had a core of whole-time men manning one of the two pumps. In both cases, retained men manned the second pump. Even in Torbay, the largest station, there were still retained firefighters working alongside whole-time men to crew a third pump.

The Devon County Fire Service control room at 'The Knowle' at the end of 1967 when, for the first time, the whole brigade was being controlled from a single point. This first view shows the magnetic map with metal tallies to show appliance locations and status. To the right of the map is the Fire Situation board for use in logging and controlling individual incidents (note the AFS section at the bottom of the board), while across the corner is the Group Fire Control Officer's position for overseeing the control room functions.

The communications side of the 1967 control room, showing the radio operator seated at the main radio panel. To his right is the status board for officers, while in front of the curtained windows are the telephones and address directories for call handling. The long desk in the centre is for logging and recording and holds all the risk information in a manual filing system. This room is now the Chief Fire Officer's office.

Here is the new purpose-built control room in the grounds of 'The Knowle' in the early 1970s, showing the much clearer layout. Above the main consol is the status board, displaying all the stations in geographical groups of five; the duty principal officers' names are prominent at the left, and the 'live' incidents are shown below by division – the left-most one reads 'Park Road, Exmouth' and shows two appliances and an officer in attendance. Each operator's console has radio communication, while the retained stations are still being alerted by the DX system (sirens and call-bells), actuated by the large knobs at the top left of each panel); VFA equipment is just starting to be installed in preparation to the move to radio-alerting. This control room was in use until 1986.

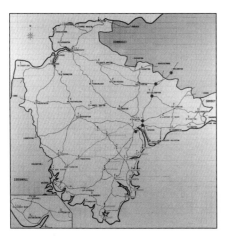

*Control room map*

The conditions of service for the retained service were set out under the 1947 act, and initially read rather like one of the old brigade 'scales of charges' in reverse. There was a retaining fee of £30 a year, plus a list of fixed payments for different types of attendance: 7/- for a chimney fire or other call under one hour, 5/6d for a standby, 12/- for a fire up to two hours, and 5/- per hour thereafter. There was a compulsory two-hour training period each week, included in the retaining fee! About 1960, these conditions were extensively revised. The retainer was still annual but was paid for a specified level of fire cover. 'Full cover' was for the entire 168 hours of every week while 'part cover' was for 126 hours a week, or 75% of the time; part-cover men thus only received 75% of the retainer. For attending weekly training a 'drill night payment' was introduced together with payments for attending longer courses. And there were also a range of operational payments – a 'turnout', an 'hourly rate' and an 'attendance allowance'.

The retained men were called out by a mixture of means. During the day, air-raid type sirens were used to alert the crews with a one-minute continuous blast. At night, the siren was switched off and call-bells were used. These were loud electric bells fitted in each firefighter's home and actuated over special telephone lines; they usually roused the firefighter, his wife and children and most of his neighbours. The first man to reach the fire station had to unlock the door and answer the 'red phone', a direct line to service control. He took down the turnout message on a special pad, hopefully legibly. Once a crew (minimum four men, maximum six) had assembled, the appliance could turn out. With most of Devon being 'D' risk, attendance time was 20 minutes – five minutes to turn out and fifteen for travelling time. The speed and times were calculated at 30m.p.h., which theoretically allowed an appliance to reach an incident $7\frac{1}{2}$ miles from the station. However, with the predominance of single-track lanes and the relatively poor performance of older machines, this often proved a little optimistic. Only with better roads and more powerful fire engines was a universal twenty-minute attendance possible.

*The joys of Drill Night on a retained station – in this case, Crediton. Firefighters are practising tying the rolling hitch on a length of GP line strung across the drill yard. Notice the traditional bright-metal shoulder rank markings (leading fireman) still in use, and the tarpaulin 'wet-legs' being warn by the crew. The lines being used to practise the knots are belt-lines, lengths of strong cord about four feet long carried by every firefighter.*

All retained firefighters attended initial training on their station followed by a 'recruits' course'. They then attended 'specialist courses' to increase their skills: driving, breathing apparatus wearing, pump operation and first aid. The emphasis of the training was on the old NFS 'standard drills' contained in the Home Office's *Fire Service Drill Book*. These were intended to teach basic equipment-handling skills in a somewhat regimented manner – all done by numbers – but the basic skills, suitably updated, still form the basis of modern-day training. Much of this basic NFS-type training was highly relevant to the job at this period, and the sort of calls that a rural retained station might normally expect to attend included chimney fires, house fires of all sorts, thatched roofs, barns and ricks, grassland or hedgerows, farm implements or hay and straw in transit. 'Special services' still lay in the future throughout most of Devon.

## THE AFS IN DEVON

The AFS was a national organisation controlled by central government – who also owned all of the equipment with which it was provided. When originally founded under the 1938 Fire Brigades Act the AFS was simply a way of increasing the general operational strength of local fire brigades by making available to them 'trained' men and some basic equipment. The 'training' was 60 hours, at least half of which was theoretical, and the period of the blitzes showed up many deficiencies in the auxiliary service. In the 1948 reorganisation, the AFS was reinstated, but with a rather different relationship to the regular brigades. It was realised that a few hours basic training in simple pump and hose drills did not make a skilled fireman, but that by creating a voluntary part-time force with an ongoing training programme, regular exercises and the appropriate equipment, it was quite possible to build up an auxiliary service that could take over some of the more basic fire-fighting functions such as water relaying, exposed risk protection and 'deluge' fire attack, thus releasing the more qualified men for the more skilled aspects of the job.

The post-war AFS embraced the NFS concept of the 'fire column' - the self-contained mobile firefighting force that could be moved swiftly around the country to wherever it might be needed. The structure of the new AFS was based on these 'columns', which were in turn made up of NFS-style

*An AFS 'Fire Company' assembled for practice in the 1950s. This is believed to be the North Devon detachment based at Barnstaple and surrounding stations, and the locaton of this shot is probably Torrington. The 'Company' had ten trailer pump units with wartime ATVs, of which five are visible here. The vehicle at the rear with the chequered design is a Control Unit, based on a wartime Ford 7V Radio Van and manned by the firewomen seen in the foreground. An AFS 'Company' was 100 men with officers and support staff including cooks, mechanics, despatch riders and wireless operators – a total of around 140 personnel.*

'Companies' of ten pumping appliances under a Company Officer. Six such companies made a column, commanded by a Column Officer. Each company had two five-pump sections directed by Section Leaders, while each pump and its ten-man crew were the responsibility of a Leading Firefighter. The companies, sections and crews were based at normal civilian fire stations according to the size of the station; as most Devon stations were small then they mostly had an AFS attachment of one or two pumps and their crews. Most of the Devon AFS pumps were the wartime 'medium trailer pump' of 350–500 g.p.m. capacity with their ATVs (Auxiliary Towing Vehicles), although later some AFS crews received 'Green Goddess' self-propelled pumps; these are still regarded by many firemen as a very good fire engine indeed. Many Devon retained crews, still riding pre-war open pumps or converted wartime Utility units, envied the AFS boys these comfortable, powerful machines.

The Devon AFS units joined together regularly in large-scale exercises to practice their mobilising procedures and firefighting techniques. The AFS crews became very proficient at certain tasks, notably in setting up huge water relays of a type that would have been invaluable in the Plymouth blitz. But they suffered, inevitably, from a lack of any real operational experience. With the escalation of the nuclear threat beyond any realistic hope of firefighting or other civil defence measures, the AFS entered a period of decline. Much of the more specialised equipment was sold off towards the end of the 1950s, concentrating on the core unit of the pump and its crew. Nevertheless, in the disastrous floods that affected Exeter and many other parts of Devon in 1960, the AFS men and their powerful pumps were of great assistance to the Exeter City and Devon County brigades, putting in many hours of tiring, uncomfortable work at the thankless task of flood-pumping.

The AFS also had the beneficial effect of introducing firefighting to many people and the interest thus aroused produced a steady stream of recruits for the retained and whole-time service. The whole AFS organisation was finally abandoned in March 1968, although a core fleet of 'Green Goddesses' remains in Home Office hands against times of need. They see still occasional use at major flooding calls, on large and protracted forest fires and at times when industrial disputes affect regular fire service provision.

## THE DEVON SITUATION IN 1972

On the eve of the 1973 Local Government Reorganisation, firefighting provision in Devon had made enormous strides since the return to local authority control. The County Fire Service, in particular, had made great progress in moulding a modern, unified fire service out of the hodge-podge of small independent brigades it had inherited. By 1972 it had a central control and county-wide radio communications, most of its stations – retained and whole-time – were operating modern, purpose-built appliances from purpose-designed buildings and the attendance times for the various risk categories were being met. As one of the largest 'shire' brigades, Devon became a model of the economic management of modest resources to cover a large area.

The two city brigades were rather more contrasted. Plymouth, with five busy stations, a large urban area with a wide range of category A and B risks, plus special risks like the naval dockyard, the commercial port and several oil storage complexes, had of necessity become a very progressive city brigade, operating the latest appliances and equipment, with its own training facilities and a large staff of fire prevention and other specialist officers. The city was enjoying something of a post-war boom and the fire brigade was well-resourced, to the point where the CFO could indulge such whims as acquiring number plates including the figures '999' for the fire engines, and fitting them with fancy chrome wheel trims. Exeter, by contrast, was a much smaller and more constricted brigade. True, the provision had improved by the acquisition of modern appliances, notably the Rolls-Royce-engined Dennis 'F' that was generally reckoned the fastest fire engine in the county in 1972. But its small size told against it, and the cost of the section-12 arrangements with Devon was a constant drain due to the imbalance in mutual aid.

All three services had their strengths and weaknesses, but it was becoming increasingly apparent in the economic and political climate of the time that much could be gained from merging them into a single county-wide unit. The time was right for the birth of the Devon Fire Brigade.

*Devon County Fire Service developed a number of solutions to particular problems, but none was more unusual than this appliance designed to meet the particular needs of Ilfracombe, which has a difficult combination of steep, narrow streets and tall buildings. To meet this situation, the brigades designers came up with the idea of mounting the ladder from the old war time TL at the rear of a new appliance which could also function as a pump-water tender and carry a full crew.*

*Smoke and flames issuing from Bridgetown Church, Totnes, on Friday the 9th of July 1976. The ex-Devon J series Bedford WrT/L in the foreground is from Paignton. Altogether nine pumps and a turntable ladder fought this blaze, which unfortunately completely gutted this lovely church. One of the problems initially was the lack of water until firefighters pumped up water from the River Dart some 200 yards down the road. A Mr Woodbine was later arrested and subsequently convicted of setting fire to the Church.*

# THE DEVON FIRE BRIGADE
# 1973–1987

The 1973 amalgamation of the three Devon brigades created one of the largest 'shire' brigades in Britain, with 58 stations and over 80 front-line pumping appliances. The risks covered ranged from 'Special risks within A risk' in parts of Plymouth to 'remote rural' in the depths of Dartmoor and Exmoor. But, at the time the Devon Fire Brigade was formed, Devon was about to enter an era of rapid change, and the new county-wide fire service would soon need to adapt to new challenges.

*Blue Watch at Greenbank in 1974, smartly turned out in their Lancer tunics and standing in front of three Plymouth City appliances – a Leyland Beaver 'multi', the 1961 Merryweather TL and Bedford Emergency Tender.*

*Opposite page: Baptism of fire! Early in the life of the Devon Fire Brigade a serious fire occurred at Nicholls builder's merchants in Valletort Road, Plymouth. The fire broke out on the afternoon of 26 June 1973 and escalated to a protracted 15-pump incident – the brigade was in attendance for just over 19 hours. Extensive damage was caused and the story goes that the discount previously enjoyed at these premises by Plymouth firefighters engaged on a spot of D-I-Y was translated into a surcharge! Greenbank's ex-Plymouth City 1961 Merryweather turntable ladder is being used as a water tower at the height of the blaze.*

*Top left: January 1979 brought heavy snow to Devon. As luck would have it a fire call was received to the village of Dunsford deep in the Teign Valley between Exeter and Moretonhampstead on the night of the worst snow storm. Appliances from Moretonhampstead, Bovey Tracey and Exeter were mobilised due to the conditions on the roads. One of the Exeter appliances, the ex-Exeter City Bedford/HCB pump escape, became trapped in a snowdrift at Longdown and – despite heroic efforts by the crew – was unable to proceed. The firefighters were given shelter at the Lamb Inn before being rescued nearly 24 hours later by Land Rover – just in time for their second night shift! The intrepid crew were, left to right, firefighters Bill Tremlett and Gerry Holmes, Station Officer Mick Munroe, and firefighters David Youngs and Rod Ousley. Note the American Metro helmets.*

*Centre Left: Cullompton's crew about 1980, a typical retained establishment of the Devon Fire Brigade period. The station itself is of the standard Devon County design while the crew are wearing the short Melton tunic that replaced the double-breasted 'Lancer' design, together with yellow overtrousers and yellow 'Cromwell' helmets. The signage on the station has been altered to read 'Devon Fire Brigade'. The appliance is an ex-Plymouth City early Dennis D-series equipped as a multi-purpose.*

*Left: The first DFB purpose-built control room in the grounds of The Knowle about 1980. Mobilisation of retained stations is now by means of VFA (Voice Frequency Activated) alerter equipment using both private and PST (Public Switched Telephone) circuits. Risk and chemical information is stored on Microfiche, viewed by Microfiche Readers on the control consoles, and each operator has full radio communications.*

## THE NEW STRUCTURE IS FORGED

The first task facing Devon County Council's new 'Public Protection Committee' was to appoint a Chief Officer to oversee the Devon Fire Brigade. The obvious front-runners were the existing chiefs of the Exeter, Plymouth and Devon brigades, CFOs Varnfield, Havery and Drake respectively. In the event, it was CFO Ralph Havery who got the job, bringing with him his progressive ideas from Plymouth. The first task that faced the new CFO was to unify the three brigades under a single command, with a single county-wide radio scheme and mobilising structure. This was not easy, as not only were the three existing radio schemes organised on different lines, but in trying to come up with shorthand code descriptions for the different types of appliance in use problems were encountered due to a lack of equivalence between machines of ostensibly the same type. It was, for instance, important to distinguish the type of ladder carried, whether a pump had RTA rescue gear, or whether it was a true water tender carrying 400 gallons or a pump-hosereel tender carrying far less.

The Devon Fire Brigade was organised in four geographical divisions, logically, North, South, East and West. Each station was numbered in sequences that put the divisional HQ station first followed by any whole-time, day-manned or core-manned stations, then the retained stations in alphabetical order. These station identities are given in table form as Appendix 4, together with the manning status and appliance allocations in 1973. The new station numbers formed the basis of the radio scheme callsigns, which added a code that indicated the type of appliance. Thus, station number plus 1 was a multi-purpose appliance with 135 ladder, plus 2 was a multi-purpose with 105 ladder, plus 3 was a water tender, plus 4 was a turntable ladder or hydraulic platform, plus 5 was a hose-laying-lorry or hose/foam tender, plus 6 was the fireboat, plus 7 was an emergency tender or equipment tender, plus 8 was a pump-escape or pump-ladder carrying only limited water, and plus 9 was a pump converted from a hose-reel tender. Stations having more than one of the same type of appliance used letter suffixes. Thus, 171 would be the first multi-purpose from station 17 Torquay, 171A (one-seven-one alpha) the second with 171B (bravo) the third. 484 would be the Camel's Head HP and 497 Crownhill's ET. 441A would be Tiverton's second appliance, 015 Barnstaple's hose-laying lorry and 199 Ashburton's pump/hose reel tender.

The new service had a much larger staff, split between the various divisional headquarters and the central Brigade HQ still at The Knowle. The control for the new brigade was based here, too, although soon relocated to a new purpose-built structure in the grounds, leaving the CFO to slumber undisturbed. Many other operational support, management and training facilities have been now located on the headquarters site, while the whole of The Knowle was turned over to office space and a new CFO's residence built in the grounds. With the county now on a common radio network, it was necessary to integrate the various officers. Headquarters staff took 'H' (hotel) call-signs, from H1 – the CFO – down to H16 (the spare car). Each division had around eight operational staff officers and these men used the initial of the division plus a number in order of descending rank. Thus 'S1' (sierra one) was the South Divisional commander, with N8 (November eight) being an out-posted station officer in North Division, in charge of a group of retained stations.

Having integrated the command and mobilising structure, Mr Havery then turned his attention to the question of fire appliances. With the spread of major trunk roads into and through the county road traffic levels were escalating rapidly, bringing with them a substantial increase in calls to road traffic accidents (RTAs). The old policy had been to attend with a pumping appliance plus the nearest Emergency Tender, on which was carried the equipment needed to rescue trapped motorists. However, there were only four front-line ETs in the county, and these resources soon proved inadequate to meet the increasing workload; it was evident that more RTA equipment was needed. There were a number of possibilities, including more ETs or specialised 'Rapid Intervention Vehicles', small appliances equipped solely for RTA work.

Ralph Havery had, however, been greatly pleased with the success of his 'Multi-Purpose Appliances' in Plymouth, with their wide range of operational capabilities including RTA rescue. He reasoned that the best approach to achieving the necessary RTA provision would be to make it universal and he thus decided that every station in Devon, whole-time or retained, should have at least one 'Multi-Purpose Appliance'. This decision was taken at a time when many of the older Devon County machines were nearing the end of their service lives, which was normally around 15 years. So the Plymouth 'multi' design was dusted off and adapted to the needs of the wider County brigade.

## THE DEVON MULTI-PURPOSE FIRE APPLIANCE

The Plymouth 'multis' were huge machines on 16-ton Leyland 'Beaver' chassis. They weighed some twelve tons fully laden, were around eight feet wide even without their fancy chrome hubcaps, and were more than twenty-six feet long. It was realised that such machines, fine in a modern city like Plymouth, would be far too unwieldy in many parts of rural Devon. So smaller, lighter appliances capable of carrying the 'multi-purpose' range of equipment were sought, and two types were eventually procured. These were the Commer 'Commando' with HCB or Carmichael bodywork, and the Dennis 'D' series with Dennis' own bodies. These machines started to arrive in 1976, and were a complete revelation to most Devon crews – as they would have been to most fire crews anywhere in the country.

The Devon multi-purpose was based on a Home Office type B water-tender, but was extensively equipped over this basic requirement. Two 25-minute Aga '219' compressed-air BA sets were stowed in a side locker and the appliance carried the new triple-extension '135' 13.5 metre alloy escape ladder with props, a design which was replacing the traditional wheeled escape throughout the British fire service as the standard rescue ladder. That made the new Devon machine officially a 'water-tender/ladder', a new category of general purpose appliance replacing the old 'dual-purpose' water-tender/escape carrier. But the Devon 'multi' also carried a 35-foot Bayley wooden ladder, a wooden roof ladder and an alloy short extension, plus rescue gear that included a collapsible 'Paraguard' rescue stretcher, a 'Minuteman' oxygen resuscitator, a 'Tirfor' hand-operated winch, 'Epco' hydraulic lifting and spreading gear and a petrol-powered 'Partner' disc-cutting saw. The new machines also had full foam fire-fighting capability and carried six 5-gallon drums of foam concentrate. Amazingly, all this extra equipment was stowed within a normal-sized body and resulted in an overall vehicle weight of 10.5 tons. The Commer Commando 'multi' was 7ft 3ins wide, and the Dennis 7ft 1ins – still small enough to get to most places.

A Commer 'Commando' multi-purpose with HCB/Angus bodywork, built in 1975/6. They had a 600-g.p.m. major pump with inbuilt foam proportioner and carried alloy 135 and wooden Bayley 105 ladders, plus a short alloy extension and a wooden roof ladder. Portable pumps were initially lightweight Honda 150 g.p.m. units, later replaced with Hathaway 250-g.p.m. versions. Rescue equipment included Epco hydraulic spreading and jacking gear, a Partner petrol disc cutter and a Tirfor winch. 'Minuteman' oxygen resuscitators and a Paraguard rescue stretcher were also carried. LTT201P was one of the first batch, allocated to Station 29 Salcombe.

The Dennis D Series multi arrived in 1977, and TTT 564R was one of the second batch, allocated to Station 05 Braunton and here seen leading the town's carnival procession. The equipment was identical to the Commer version. Both types had manual transmissions and non-power-assisted steering. The Dennis had servo hydraulic brakes, the Commer air-assisted hydraulics. The main difference was the pump; the Commers had Godiva pumps with automatic water-ring primers, while the Dennis machines used Dennis' own pump with a manual piston primer.

In the mid-1970s, the DFB was still essentially a 'greater Plymouth' brigade, and the new multi-purpose machines were delivered with the famous Plymouth 'Sabrina' chrome hubcaps. These may have been fine on Plymouth's broad boulevards, but they were a decided liability in a narrow, sunken lane hedged with granite-faced Devon banks. As denting a 'Sabrina' was a near-capital offence, preserving an unblemished set was a case of a little crafty swappery at a nice, dark multi-pump shout! LTT 207P as 40-1 was new at Honiton in 1976, with hubcaps unsullied.

The 'multi' rapidly became the universal appliance in Devon, allocated to whole-time and retained crews alike. Here is a later D series, SJY 846T, on the run as Torquay's 17-1B, the retained third pump. This offside stowage shot shows canvas fire hose still in use, but stowed flaked in wire containers rather than traditionally rolled. The front upper locker contains two Ago Spiro 219 BA sets and the Minuteman resucitator, while the rear upper locker is stowed with salvage sheets, protective gloves and rescue and GP (general purpose) lines. The light pump shown here is the later Hathaway type.

Another departure was the use of 165 h.p. Perkins turbocharged six-cylinder diesel engines, in combination with air over hydraulic or hydraulic servo brakes, manual gearboxes and non-power-assisted steering. The bodies were of traditional aluminium-over-ash coachbuilt construction and a retrograde step – in practical terms – was the abandonment of the Devon County policy of unpainted aluminium-alloy sides, 'unbendable' rubber mudguards and roller-shutter locker doors in favour of painted sides, metal wings and, worse still, top-hinged lockers. These features betrayed the Plymouth City origins of the type – things that prove no problem in wide city streets are a different matter in a close-hedged or 'sunk' Devon lane a scant few inches wider than the appliance! It was often impossible to open those hinged lockers properly. The 'multis' were also the first appliances supplied from new with blue beacons and two-tone horns built-in rather than 'tacked on', as had been the case previously. But they still carried a traditional fire-bell – electrically operated, thankfully – as a back-up warning.

The arrival of these new machines on rural retained stations was nothing short of revolutionary, and at a single stroke the capability of a large part of the Devon Fire Brigade was enormously enhanced. There was, of course, a lot of training associated with the new equipment, and retained firefighters soon found themselves spending considerably more time than the basic two hours a week assimilating all these developments. There was a marked shift among Devon's retained personnel at this time toward a far more professional attitude – no longer did they have to wait for whole-time appliances or 'specials' to come on to an RTA or other specialised incident before they could take action; they now had the tools and the training to tackle almost anything.

Subsequent Devon CFO's have carried on with the basic Havery policy of equipping every station to tackle all routine incidents – and RTA rescues have increasingly become 'routine', to the point where they form a very substantial proportion of the brigade workload. As well as the new Devon multi-purpose appliances, a few older machines, particularly the larger Bedford 'TK' series water tender/ladders that formed the last of the Devon County purchases, were upgraded to multi-purpose status, and even a few of the J5's were upgraded to Wrt/L status as reserves, although in this case not everything could be fitted in and a J5 Wrt/L conversion could barely pull itself up a steep hill under the additional load! The 'multis' anyway arrived rapidly from 1976–1980, so that by the beginning of the latter decade most Devon stations were equipped with at least one of the new appliances, with the large TK-type Bedfords as reserves.

On the two-pump retained stations, only one 'multi' was supplied, with a water-tender/ladder as the second appliance. The original 'multi' design also underwent development, resulting in newer machines which had 'Blackhawk' air/hydraulic pincer cutters replacing the Partner disc saws, with air-operated chisels and the 'Cengar' air-saw also now being carried. All Devon fire appliances were also upgraded to carry 4 BA sets – at least two of them cab-mounted – over this period. The last of the Devon 'multi-purpose' machines were six Carmichael-bodied Dodges G13s (similar to the Commer Commandos) that arrived in late 1980. These final machines had 4-speed Allinson automatic gearboxes, full air brakes, power steering, an integral compressed-air supply for air tools, chemical protection suits, 4 cab-stowed BA sets, light-alloy two-section 105 and roof ladders, a two-stage pump and high-pressure hosereels. As virtually all 'first away' (the first or only appliance to be mobilised from any station) Devon appliances became 'multi-purpose' the term gradually fell into disuse, and the classification went back to 'water-tender-ladder'; it was assumed that all such first-away machines had the full range of capabilities.

*Two generations of emergency tenders at Torquay; top is the old Devon County Bedford class 'A' and below it the replacement machine with control unit of 1983.*

With this re-classification and the subsequent arrival of other new appliances, the numbering system for appliance type identity was revised. '1' remained a full multi-purpose with RTA capability, but the A and B suffixes were swept away and were replaced with numerals 2 and 3. These signified appliances carrying 135 ladders but not necessarily full 'multi' gear. 4 was still an aerial appliance – a TL or hydraulic platform – and 5 was a hose-layer. These were built on Ford A series or Dodge light truck chassis with a 4 x 4 conversion and each carries one mile of $2^{3/4}$-inch hose flaked for twinning together with two 250-g.p.m. light portable pumps for relay purposes. The odd-man-out here is the hose/foam tender at Crownhill – kept to cover Stonehouse oil depot. This is also a '5' appliance. The fireboat 'Cissie Brock' was now stationed at Plymstock and manned by the crew from that station as 516, while the four Dodge Emergency-tender-cum-control units introduced in 1979 and 1983 still went under the '7' suffix. These machines had a control compartment forward but only a relatively small emergency tender section aft. The advent of the 'multis' meant that these new ETs did not need to carry as much equipment: Six BA sets, gas-tight suits, high-expansion foam, emergency lighting with generators, air bags, air-powered disc cutters and smoke extraction gear. One of these machines each went to Barnstaple, Torquay, Greenbank and Exeter.

## NEW FIRE STATIONS

With the appliance replacement programme in place and the extended radio scheme operating satisfactorily, attention could now turn to the legacy of old, unsatisfactory fire stations that were by now in drastic need of upgrading. With the arrival of the multi-purpose appliances, which were generally somewhat larger than the old Devon County machines they were replacing, several fire stations proved simply unable to accept them, and various extemporised arrangements had to be made. At Moretonhampstead, the floor was lowered and the roof and doorway raised to admit a new Dennis 'D', while when Princetown's new Commer Commando arrived in 1979 the

only way to get it into the station was to excavate 'wheel tracks' in the floor. Chagford, where the station exit was at an acute angle, could now only turn right with their new Commer, while Modbury's old volunteer station was simply too short and had to be replaced . Similar problems were encountered elsewhere as new machines arrived on the remoter stations.

Many rural stations had been replaced by the Devon County Brigade during their modernisation programme, but the state of the remaining stations was becoming critical and a further programme of building work was initiated. A more-or-less standard design of one-pump station had been evolved in Devon County days and although somewhat lacking in refinements most of these possessed an appliance bay of reasonable size, a watchroom, a drill yard with tower, a lecture/recreation room, a small kitchen and full washroom facilities. Under the Devon Fire Brigade, the new buildings followed the same basic plan but had a somewhat higher specification. The programme was pushed forward as rapidly as possible as, until new buildings were provided, some appliances could not be replaced. Ivybridge was the first DFB station, opened in 1975 on the far side of the A38 and connected to the town by a special tunnel beneath the road. Tavistock got a new two-pump station in 1976, and in 1978 Bovey Tracey and Moretonhampstead both got new stations and new 'Dennis D' multi-purpose appliances. The process continued into the 1980s, with Modbury going from volunteer to retained status with a new Commer 'multi' in 1980, Dartmouth gaining a fine new 2-pump station on an edge-of-town location in 1983, and Ottery St Mary getting the last DFB-built station in 1986.

*The last batch of seven Dodges were built by Carmichael in 1980 on G13A chassis fitted with Allinson 4-speed automatic transmissions, power steering and air brakes. The rescue cutter was now the 'Blackhawk' air-powered hydraulic shear, and air-powered Cengar saws and 'Zip Gun' metal-cutting chisels were also carried. The rescue stretcher was the 'Chance' and the 4 BA sets were cab-stowed. The wooden 105 ladder was replaced by a lightweight alloy version. These machines reverted to the old classification of WrT/L. Like all Carmichael appliances, these machines were beautifully finished and very solid; but they were rather slow.*

*Ex-AFS 'Green Goddess' fire appliances crewed by military firefighters on the streets of Plymouth during the 1977 whole-time firefighter's strike. These are the 4 x 4 versions of the AFS 'SP Pump' – basic fire engines, but very capable.*

## THE 1977 STRIKE

Operationally, the Devon Fire Brigade had hardly settled down to its new regime of county-wide working when matters were thrown into disarray by the difficult period of the 1977 Fireman's Strike. This was a national dispute involving men belonging to the Fire Brigades Union (FBU), the representative body for most whole-time firefighters in Britain. The dispute in Devon was particularly divisive because of the 'split' nature of the service, with whole-time and retained crews working alongside each other. The terms under which whole-time and retained firefighters are employed derive from 'Conditions of Service', documents issued nationally by the National Joint Council, the fire service's negotiating forum. The FBU action concerned those conditions affecting their whole-time membership, and had little to do with the terms for retained firefighters. The majority of retained firecrews were either non-union or were members of the Retained Firefighters Union (RFU), which was not in any dispute.

In areas such as Plymouth, where the fire cover was provided entirely by whole-time crews, the situation was analogous to that elsewhere in the country. Military firefighters and ex-AFS 'Green Goddess' fire appliances replaced the normal provision on whole-time stations or the whole-time watches on core-manned stations. This inevitably created a difficult situation for the retained crews operating out of these same stations, who had to face picket lines on responding to calls and an inevitable degree of friction with their whole-time colleagues. Although many retained men had sympathy for the aims of the dispute, most felt that they had to remain at work throughout the strike – which inevitably soured relations once the industrial action was over.

Even in areas where the fire cover was entirely provided by retained crews, difficulties were encountered, especially where the retained station adjoined a whole-time one. There was considerable resistance among the retained personnel to the idea of redeploying retained pumps to cover the risks in the whole-time areas, although retained crews did agree to respond to any life-threatening incidents. In the purely retained area – most of the county – there was far less effect on the service except that there was no back-up from the whole-time divisional stations, and the specialised appliances such as TLs and Emergency Tenders were often unavailable. Supplies of consumable stores and things like BA servicing were also affected, while in order to conserve resources the initial attendance to virtually all incidents was reduced to one pump. On a lighter note, one retained crew were somewhat nonplussed early in the strike when, on arriving at a chimney fire at a cottage in a small mid-Devon village, they were greeted by the elderly female inhabitant with the words: 'Oo be yew lot, then? Oi thort oi was gonna git th'army. I likes to see a soldier, so I do... If oi'd a-knowed t'were only gonna be yew boggers oi wouldna' bothered tu call 'ee.'

## COMPUTERISED MOBILISATION

Local knowledge has always been a great weapon in the fire services' armoury, especially in a county as geographically complex as Devon. The tangled road network is a maze and the several thousands of farms often have the same names repeated in almost every parish. It is difficult to speculate how many 'Coombe', 'Bowden', 'Chapel' or 'Barton' farms there are in Devon – but ensuring that attendance is made to the right one is essential.

*In September 1986 the Remsdaq computerised mobilising system went 'live', and this is the revised control room showing this first generation of computerised equipment. A pair of mainframe computers in an adjacent air-condition room fed mobilising information to monitor screens on the control consoles, while the operators now had headsets rather than handsets for the main scheme radio and telephone communications. But the VFA panels for mobilising were still in use, and the Microfiche readers for chemical and risk information had yet to be dispensed with.*

With the centralisation of the mobilising function for the whole county, the problem became acute and it was necessary to find a system that could store and present information on locations throughout the county. Devon at the time was – and still is – lucky to have some experienced and long-serving Fire Control Operators (notably Peter Reagan and David Honeywell) whose geographic knowledge of Devon bounds on the miraculous; but with the increasing rate of development and change, it was apparent that a system that did not rely on individual knowledge was becoming vital.

Fortunately, at this time various firms were developing computer-based emergency service mobilising systems that stored all the requisite information on a database. Devon, in common with several other large brigades, opted for the Remsdaq system, and work started in the early 1980s on a new control room complex at the Clyst St George HQ site. At the same time, the requisite database was being compiled. The new system went 'live' in September 1986, with details of over 58,000 individual addresses stored. The locations were pinpointed using Ordnance Survey 6-figure map references and the system could search on any address field within the database, including premises or street name, parish or district name, map reference or postcode. To simplify mobilisation, each 1km square on the revised 1:25000 OS map was allocated to the appropriate fire station, although initially this resulted in a few anomalies where the kilometre-square boundaries fell in the middle of a risk. The control suite has been refined and updated constantly over the intervening 15 years or so, with a new computer system being installed in 1995, and it is telling that what initially required the memory capacity of a pair of mainframe computers can now be stored on a standard laptop! Each of the new Incident Command Vehicles can boast substantially more onboard computer power than the main control could muster back in 1986.

With the new computerised mobilising scheme came a change in the alerting of retained fire crews. Gone were the old sirens and night-call bells, replaced by radio-activated personal alerters. Calls were transmitted from control to fire station by any one of three systems – dedicated phone line, public phone line or radio. On being received by the fire station system, the station alerter transmitter was activated, the station lights came on, and the details of the call were printed out by a desktop teleprinter. It was popularly suggested at the time that the system was not quite complete – it should have started the appliance engine and made the tea! However, after some initial teething problems the new equipment proved itself, and the role of computers has gradually expanded as further databases were built up. These replaced the old flip-card registers for detailed risk and hazardous materials information. In parallel with these developments in control room facilities came further improvements in communications. The main radio scheme was replaced with a new AM system which for the first time enabled Devon appliances to 'talk through' with the neighbouring county controls, as well as providing 'Multiplex' appliance-to-appliance direct channels. Fireground hand-held radios were also introduced.

## TRAINING FOR THE NEW BRIGADE

The Plymouth City Fire Brigade had laid the groundwork for a new purpose-built training centre on a site at Glen Road, on the edge of Plympton, and this ambitious scheme was brought to fruition under the new management when the Devon Fire Brigade Training Centre opened on 23rd June, 1976. The new Glen Road complex included a headquarters building for the brigade's West Division and a new Plympton fire station as well as the training school. The training facilities are extensive: as well as a full suite of lecture rooms and workshops, there is domestic accommodation for trainees, an administration section that runs courses right across the brigade, a school for fire appliance drivers and, of course, the extensive drill yard with its sophisticated firehouse complex. This last enables firefighting in different types of structures, from normal domestic dwellings through multi-storey structures to industrial premises, to be replicated for training. The structure also incorporates a drill tower for ladder work and a domestic dwelling to teach basic techniques like window entry and chimney fire attack.

In addition to this main facility, the Devon Fire Brigade set up two further training complexes. The first of these took over the older Plymouth City training ground at Camel's Head to provide a specialist training facility for ship fire-fighting, including a realistic replica of a substantial section of a typical ship complete with all the difficult accessways, vertical ladders, watertight doors and confined spaces encountered on board. This structure can be used for 'live fire' training and reproduces with uncomfortable accuracy the punishing environment encountered in shipboard fires. It has not only been used to train a substantial proportion of Devon's fire crews in shipboard firefighting, but also large numbers of merchant navy seamen and officers; it is one of only a handful of such facilities in Britain. With the growth in the role of breathing apparatus in modern firefighting, there was also seen to be a need for a specialist BA training school, and this was established on the headquarters site at Clyst St George in 1974. It was an early policy of the new brigade that all operational firefighters should be trained in the full range of BA techniques including search and rescue, landmarking and navigation in smoke-filled buildings, the use of guide-lines and BA operations in confined spaces such as sewers. The BA school complex includes a special structure, the smoke chamber, which can be heated and filled with artificial smoke to reproduce fire conditions. Internally, the smoke chamber can be configured to reproduce all manner of building environments, while different types of doorway

The Devon Fire Brigade Training Centre at Plympton was opened in 1976. It was soon established as the premier training establishment in the South West and catered for an extensive range of initial recruit training for whole-time and retained personnel, as well as offering more specialised fire service and industrial fire training courses. The high-quality teaching is supported by excellent facilities and equipment. Since the Centre opened over 18,000 students have been trained. Here, whole-time recruits bring to a spectacular conclusion 16 weeks of gruelling training, using the purpose-built firehouse and tower complex to demonstrate various forms of rescue.

Training facilities at Camel's Head Fire Station in Plymouth include a purpose built steel 'ship' to enable firefighters to gain experience of maritime incidents. The station ground includes the Royal Naval Dockyard and over the years Plymouth firefighters have attended many serious incidents involving sea-going vessels. Here, a maritime course is in full swing with a crew cooling the sides of the ship's superstructure while their colleagues enter a hatchway to fight the blaze.

and other access points enable most of the practical problems encountered on the fireground to be simulated. Also included in the BA training complex are sewer pipes going down to only 18-inches in diameter, complete with vertical access shafts and ladders. Lecture rooms and a control room to monitor the interior of the smoke chamber are also provided.

While the technical and theoretical skills needed for firefighting broadened dramatically during the span of the Devon Fire Brigade, these new disciplines had to overlaid on the basic competence gained at the local, practical level. Here, the learning process may have been less formal, often amounting to no more than the natural assimilation resulting from working alongside experienced firefighters who knew both the job, the risks and the locality. But this on-station and on-the-job training is perhaps the most enduring of all. No 'artificial' training, however well-contrived and realistic, can equal the experience of actually entering a burning room, of crawling beneath the layers of heat and smoke to locate and extinguish the seat of fire, or to find and rescue a casualty. And no amount of cutting up scrap cars in the drill-yard will teach half much as being there, 'for real', in the pouring rain with the vehicle upside down in a ditch, making cuts overhead or at some awkward angle to release a trapped occupant. The training counts, of course; but nothing is more real than the knowledge that upon the success of your efforts hinges someone else's future.

*The Torquay hose-laying lorry was built on a Dodge chassis with a 4x4 conversion.*

## THE GROWTH OF THE FIRE PREVENTION ROLE

British fire brigades have had a fire prevention/fire inspection branch since the 1947 Act made these roles statutory. But with the growth of legislation and advances in the science of fire prevention, these aspects of the job have progressively assumed greater and greater importance. During the earlier period of the Devon Fire Brigade's existence, the pivotal task was that of inspection of premises to ensure conformance with building construction fire codes and the proper management of fire risk. New legislative measures had been driven by a series of disastrous fires over this period – the Dublin and Paris night-club blazes which killed scores of young people, the Summerland disaster involving a seaside leisure complex, the Keighthly cotton-mill fire, some lethal hotel fires and several alarming incidents in new high-rise buildings. All these fires pointed to the need for proper passive fire safety design in structures, especially public buildings where large numbers of people might gather in unfamiliar surroundings. It was also realised that proper policing of the active component of fire safety – the way in which such buildings were managed – was of equal importance. A locked or obstructed fire exit was soon seen as potentially more lethal than no fire exit at all.

These growing legal responsibilities led to far greater emphasis being attached to this less-glamorous but potentially more-productive aspect of the fire service. The firefighter who – by advising, cajoling, informing or enforcing – prevents a fire occurring in the first place was increasingly seen as a combatant in the fight against fire every bit as vital as the crew member riding an appliance. Most firefighters aspiring to senior rank became students of the Institute of Fire Engineers and served at least part of their careers in the fire prevention role. Even the regular on-the-watch whole-time firefighter had his role to play in risk visits and fire prevention duties, while retained crews were expected to familiarise themselves with any premises in their area carrying substantial life risk or hazards that might affect the safety of the public, or of firefighters responding to an incident.

As well as a headquarters fire prevention staff, each Devon division had a fire prevention department staffed by specialist officers. These personnel had a far wider-ranging role than was generally realised. As well as the task of inspecting all premises classified as coming under the aegis of the Fire Precautions Acts of 1971 and 1974 – which included public buildings of all sorts, but particularly hotels, hostels, residential homes and hospitals – the fire prevention arm also assumed responsibility for petroleum installations, for running public advice helplines, for regular spot-checks on known risks to ensure that good housekeeping practices were being observed, and for advising council planning officers, building inspectors and others involved in the overseeing of new developments. The fire prevention officer's job rapidly became more complex as new legislation was heaped onto his head, as the scope and sophistication of the measures he had to inspect grew ever more complex, and as the cost of implementing the new levels of fire safety began to impact on the profitability of many types of business. The job has always demanded tact and firmness in addition to a keen eye for detail and a sound knowledge of what is required.

Over this period, the science of fire investigation also made great strides, much of it arising from the same studies of fire behaviour that had given rise to the new codes of building design and the important legislation as to fire precautions. Investigating fires calls for a combination of the skills and knowledge of the operational firefighter tackling a blaze and the fire prevention officer aware of the way that a building and its systems are constructed. The mass of data resulting from fire inspections was added to the Devon fire control computer databases, enabling often-vital information to be swiftly retrieved and transmitted direct to the fireground. The process came full circle when the fire prevention department found itself on the fireground advising the officers commanding major fires, and undertaking the recording and analysis of data while the fire was still in progress to assist in subsequent investigations. The work of Devon's fire prevention department over the period up to the later 1980s when both their title and the role of the department changed laid the foundations for two of the most important developments within the contemporary Devon Fire & Rescue Service: firefighting strategies based on detailed tactical information, and the development of fire safety in the community on a far broader basis.

*Originally bought by the Exeter City Fire Brigade to deal with fires in the new multi-storey car parks, this Land Rover L4P was stationed at Dane's Castle and Topsham.*

## THE RS APPLIANCE, HYDRAULIC RESCUE EQUIPMENT, NEW BREATHING APPARATUS

By the early 1980s, the type of multi-purpose fire appliance pioneered in Plymouth in 1967 was becoming widely adopted as the standard vehicle across much of the British fire service under the old description of 'dual-purpose appliance' or the newer (but less wieldy) title of water/rescue ladder. The traditional wheeled fire escape had by now universally been replaced by the light-alloy three-section 13.5 metre escape ladder of the type that had been standard in Devon since the inception of the DFB, and many items of more specialised equipment that had characterised the Devon multis of 1976 were now being widely carried elsewhere. In 1980, Dennis had introduced a new standard appliance, the RS, and this vehicle rapidly became the preferred choice across much of the British fire service. The RS had a 'universal stowage' system that could be configured to accommodate a very wide range of equipment and applications, and this proved to be well-suited to Devon's wide-ranging requirements. By 1983, RS appliances were replacing the older Dodge and Dennis 'multis' on

The Dennis RS Wr/l or WrL/Rescue became Devon's new front-line appliance from 1982 onwards. The Dennis chassis was equipped with a Perkins V8 non-turbo diesel engine and 4-speed Allinson automatic transmission, anti-lock braking and low-profile tyres to give excellent handling. The original machines had Dennis standard bodywork with traditional top-hinged lockers, and carried all-alloy ladders. The commodious lockers provided stowage for the Hurst powered rescue equipment.

whole-time stations and on the busier retained stations such as Newton Abbot, Bideford or Crediton. With their Perkins V8 diesel engines, commodious boxy bodies, effective anti-lock brakes and excellent handling characteristics, the RS soon proved a valuable addition to the Devon fleet.

At roughly same time as the RS was emerging as the new standard appliance, the business of road accident rescue was also undergoing a substantial advance in equipment and techniques. This came about with the introduction of powered hydraulic rescue sets to replace the older types of hand-pumped or air-actuated equipment. Devon's technical services staff soon evaluated this advance, and initially purchased the Hurst hydraulic rescue system, which had a large alligator-jaw spreader and separate shear cutter, plus powerful hydraulic rams and chains for forcing open crushed and deformed vehicles swiftly. This equipment was powered by a small petrol motor driving a hydraulic pump and proved a great advance operationally, being quick to set up and far more powerful than the previous 'Epco' or 'Blackhawk' systems. However, it was both heavy and quite bulky, and was not compatible with the stowage lockers on the older appliances. The RS, however, had been designed to accept this type of equipment from the outset, and new Devon RS appliances used as 'first away' machines were configured to carry the full range of Hurst equipment.

The rapid arrival in service of the readily-available 'off the peg' RS machines with their hydraulic rescue equipment on the whole-time stations enabled the existing fleet of custom-built Devon multi-purpose appliances – many of which were still relatively new – to be re-assigned to the more rural retained stations. This reflected the policy of the new Devon CFO, John Killoran, who took over from CFO Havery on the latter's retirement in 1977. In the face of a tighter financial regime, CFO Killoran wished to maximise the use and life of all fire appliances in the Devon fleet by placing them on the busiest stations when new, then moving them onto less-busy stations for the second part of their service life at around five years old, before retiring them to reserve or training roles at twelve years. This policy had been made possible due to the standardisation by CFO Havery of the multi-purpose type, with its common stowage.

However, with the arrival of the RS, the practice soon ran into difficulties. While the 'cascading' idea was fine in theory, the relatively large dimensions of the RS meant that they were less than ideally-suited to the more rural areas, especially to Dartmoor and Exmoor. With narrow stone-banked lanes overhung by low trees, the 7-foot 6-inch wide, 11-foot tall Dennis was especially vulnerable, while the high driving position and relatively large turning circle also made them more difficult to manoeuvre in such confined locations.

Also concurrent with the arrival of the RS machines in the early 1980s, the Devon Fire Brigade upgraded its breathing apparatus from the Aga Spiro 219 type to the newer Aga 'Spiromatic' sets. The 'Spiromatic' was an automatic positive-pressure set; that is, it automatically maintained a slightly-above-atmospheric pressure in the facemask to ensure that any leakage of the sealing system would result in air seeping outwards and not smoke or fumes seeping in. The old 219 sets had to manually configured into this mode. With the replacement programme came a welcome increase in BA carried to four sets per appliance, the new RS machines having stowage for all four sets to be cab-mounted. The older appliances, which had their BA stowed in side lockers, were modified to carry the two additional sets in the cab, although this was made more difficult be the rearward-facing crew seats on the Devon multi-purpose design. With the new BA sets also came a move away from the old 9-litre air cylinders which, at a modest 132 bar, had a working duration of only twenty minutes or so. Higher-capacity 9 litre cylinders capable of holding 200 bar pressure for a working duration of 35 minutes were adopted, these in turn being replaced with lighter 11 litre alloy-steel cylinders with a 45-minute duration.

By the time that John Killoran retired as CFO in 1987, the Devon Fire Brigade had gone from being a proficient but traditional organisation to a leading-edge and innovative service with wide-ranging capabilities. The appliance fleet was now entirely equipped for rescue work, the computerised mobilising system was up and working, and technical progress was being made on firefighting kit and BA. One of the last acts of John Killoran as CFO before he handed over to his successor Neil Wallington was to change the name of the organisation to reflect its new, broader role: out went the Devon Fire Brigade, and in came the Devon Fire and Rescue Service. The modern era in public fire service had truly arrived.

*Devon's aerial appliance fleet was upgraded in the early 1980s, when the Merryweather 100-foot TLs from Greenbank and Torquay were modernised and mounted on new Shelvoke and Drewry chassis. In this view of the Torquay TL VDV 143X, the operator's console on the ladder turret platform is clearly visible, as is the powerful monitor at the ladder head. TLs generally have a long life, with periodic overhauls and safety checks, and may well be mounted on two or more different vehicles during their in-service life.*

*Another aerial appliance to receive a new chassis in 1981 was the ex-Plymouth City 'Snorkel' from Camel's Head, which was also re-mounted on Shelvoke and Drewry running gear. This 2-section hydraulic boom had a 75-foot reach and was originally fitted to a Leyland 'Beaver' chassis similar to that used for the Plymouth multi-purpose. It was eventually replaced by the first of the 'Bronto' aerial ladder platforms.*

*Right: Devon Fire and Rescue Ceremonial Unit pause for this picture during their display at the Wrigley factory in Plymouth in 1996. The Unit was formed during the latter part of 1983 when a small group of volunteers serving within the Devon Fire Brigade decided to form a Corps of Drums. Following a very successful initial first year, which included a visit to Ypres in Belgium to take part in the Remembrance Day Parade march to the Menin Gate, the Corps has gone from strength to strength.*

*Every day at 8pm, buglers of the Belgian Fire Service sound the 'Last Post' and 'Reveille' beneath the Menin gate – which is dedicated to 'Soldiers of the Commonwealth who laid down their lives in and around the Ypres Peninsula during the great war and have no known grave'. In 1987 the Devon Ceremonial Unit, which had by then added buglers and trumpeters to its ranks, was accorded the very high honour and privilege of sounding the 'Last Post' at the Menin Gate during the evening ceremony on Remembrance Day. This honour continues to be enjoyed to this day, now with the added privilege of leading the main Poppy Parade from the Town Square of Ypres up to the Menin Gate.*

*1990 saw the addition of the fifes to the Corps and in 1993 it further expanded with the formation of a bagpipe section. 1995 saw the proud debut of a full military band. The unit has performed throughout the County of Devon, the United Kingdom, in Belguim and in France. It has been invited to perform in Germany, has performed before Royalty and both for and with the Military.*

*The Devon Fire Brigade Headquarters remained at The Knowle, Clyst St George, the building acquired in 1948 by the Devon County Fire Service. The Headquarters staff pose for a photograph in front of the main building in the mid 80's with Chief Fire Officer John Killoran (1977-1987) and his two principal officers, Deputy Chief Officer Peter Whitehouse on his right and Assistant Chief Officer Les Smith on his left.*

*The Devon Fire Brigade era came to a close in 1987, and to reflect the changes the brigade had undergone over that 14-year span, here is the Torquay line-up of 1986. The pumping appliances are all new Dennis RS types, with the first-away 171 and retained pump 173 being WrL/Rescue and 172 a WrL. The TL seen here is the 1980-re-chassised ex-Devon County 100-foot Merryweather, and next to this is the 1983 Dodge/HCB Emergency Tender-Control Unit. At the far right is the 4 x 4 Dodge hose-laying Lorry.*

# THE DEVON FIRE
# & RESCUE SERVICE
# 1987–TO DATE

In July 1987 the title of the Devon Fire Brigade was changed to Devon Fire & Rescue Service, to better reflect the wider role of the modern fire service. It was strongly felt within Devon that, with the universal equipping of the brigade's front-line appliances for a whole range of rescue roles, the change was well-rooted in capability rather than reflecting the politics of self-justification.

## FIRE AND RESCUE – THE CHANGING ROLE

Throughout the decade of the 1980s, the role of the fire service had continued to change substantially. The statutory fire safety initiatives introduced in the 1970s – notably the 1971 Act – had by now taken effect, and along with demographic changes and the introduction of local authority grants for housing improvements, were dramatically improving fire safety in many homes. New, tighter regulations concerning domestic furniture construction, wiring in the home and other safety-related matters were now in force, while the 1974 Health and Safety at Work Act had revolutionised many aspects of the workplace, including fire safety. Sophisticated fire detection systems had also come onto the market, along with the first generation of domestic smoke alarms, and the insurance industry started to demand far better fire precautions from the industrial and retail sectors. Farming methods, too, were undergoing fundamental change; silage was taking over from hay as the preferred winter feed, and silage does not represent anything like the fire risk of hay. Straw, too, was less common in baled form stored in barns; it was likely to be large-baled, sheeted and kept outside. Newer designs of farm machinery were better-designed and less fire-prone than had been the older combine harvesters or grain-dryers.

*The history of firefighting in Devon started with burning thatch, and nearly two hundred years later the Devon Fire and Rescue Service still tackles a good number of thatched roof fires each year. And, although the equipment has changed beyond all recognition, the technique hasn't: make a break ahead of the fire, and strip the thatch as quickly as possible.*

*The part of the job that has changed the most is probably the wider civil rescue role, especially in relation to RTAs. Here, an Exeter crew work to free the driver of a car after a high-speed impact, working closely with the ambulance crew to ensure the best quality of patient care.*

*There are many occasions when the modern fire and rescue service is called because of its ability to improvise and use a great deal of ingenuity and initiative. Here crews from Modbury and Kingston test the special 'sea tractor' – which takes passengers from Bigbury-on-Sea to Burgh Island at high tide – for use in an emergency.*

Severe domestic, farm and industrial fires of the type experienced in the earlier post-war period became far less frequent, although they have certainly not died out. Thatched roofs, so common throughout Devon, still pose substantial risks, and the fashion for wood burning stoves during the later 1980s brought a new problem in the form of chimney fires of previously-unknown ferocity, due to extensive tar-build up in the flues of these stoves. A wood-stove inside and a thatched roof outside proved a disastrous combination on a good number of occasions. But it was the rapid – almost exponential – growth of road traffic and road-related incidents that was the most significant factor in the changing workload. RTA rescues became commonplace, and incidents like car fires, making vehicles safe after accident damage, and dealing with spilt petrol or chemicals became an increasing feature of the service workload, especially on those stations that now found themselves with a new high-speed trunk road on their 'patch'. To reflect these new priorities the title of the brigade was changed and new appliances now carried the words 'FIRE–RESCUE' in large reflective lettering across their cabfronts.

*One of the last generation of Dennis RS appliances in service at Torquay as a Wrl/Rescue. These machines had a more powerful Cummins 6-cylinder turbodiesel, and were fitted with bodywork by John Dennis Coachworks Ltd – Dennis Bros. now build chassis only, relying on outside builders to complete the appliance. The John Dennis bodywork is of lightweight construction in alloy over a steel frame, with Robinson roller-shutter lockers.*

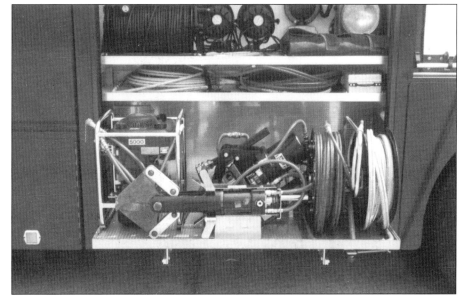

*Second-generation Hurst powered hydraulic rescue equipment on an RS appliance. The lightweight petrol-driven power unit is on the left, with the shear-cutting jaws in the front and the spreader behind. At the right are drums of high-pressure hydraulic hose for connecting the tools to the power unit, with extra hose stowed above. Not seen are long and short hydraulic rams for spreading wider openings. On the top shelf is lighting gear – two 'Haldane' quartz-iodine floodlights, a traffic warning lamp and the versatile 'box-lamp', a portable high-power halogen light source.*

With the changes in the operational workload of the Service came additional requirements for new equipment and new skills. The increasing speed of traffic, the introduction of heavier lorries and the stronger construction of modern cars all presented greater challenges in RTA rescue work, where it was soon found that some of the existing techniques and equipment were no longer up to the job. Firefighting, too, was becoming more technical in the wake of new research, while the sort of materials often involved even in simple domestic fires could pose grave new hazards. Video-tape cassettes, for instance, burn fiercely and produce a lot of heat and large volumes of toxic smoke. The increasing use of plastics in many types of furniture and domestic appliances also posed problems, while the legislation banning older foams from carpets and furnishings did not mean that all such materials had vanished from the environment overnight. The car fire, too, became an increasing hazard, with pressurised suspension systems, new electronic components, silastomer sealing compounds (which can form a potent corrosive when heated in fires), the use of composite plastics materials in bodywork, and new high-pressure fuel injection systems all adding to the dangers. Breathing apparatus wearing now assumed a central importance in many aspects of operational fire-fighting, as did protection from chemical hazards. Increasing awareness of the environmental consequences of fire or spillage also placed a new responsibility on the fire service to mitigate as far as possible the impact of incidents on the surroundings.

## TECHNICAL DEVELOPMENTS – MOBILISATION AND BA

To meet these new challenges and to keep abreast of the operational work-load, a number of technical initiatives were put in place under the new CFO, Robin Currie, who succeeded Neil Wallington in 1991. First area to be tackled was that of control and the control room facilities. With the advent of the second-generation Remsdaq mobilising system and its asso-ciated computerised data handling capability, a new control room was seen as necessary, and this was installed in 1991–92 within the same com-plex as the existing control facilities. The new system did away with much of the bulky equipment previously required for the control function, using modern PCs linked in a network to provide each control operator with a work station from which they could fulfil all the call-handling, information retrieval and mobilisation tasks. This swept away the last vestiges of the old VFA (voice frequency activated) direct phone links, replacing them with multiplexed signals over normal phone lines and direct radio links. Each station now had a in-station computerised mobil-ising system addressed directly by the control, speeding communication and allowing a lot of information to be included on turnout message slips.

*The new computerised control room dating from 1992, using a PC-based system arranged as a network of individual work stations. Each operator can work independently and several calls can be handled simultaneously. The calls are logged onto the computer network which will search for the address and present a list of the nearest available appliances, together with the PDA (pre-determined attendance, which is set according to the degree of risk) and any additional risk information. The operator can simply select the required appliances and trans-mit alert signals to the stations. The details of the call are currently printed out by on-station high-speed printers, but onboard data handling is being trialled on some fire appliances.*

One major advantage of the new installation was that it was easy to upgrade each aspect of the system without the need to replace the funda-mental framework, and the Devon fire control network has been steadily improved both in terms of the speed and reliability of the hardware and the quantity and quality of the information that can be accessed and transmitted to stations. New software has added a number of sophisticat-ed facilities, such as the powerful GRS mapping system that allows opera-tors to 'zoom in' from a map of the entire south-west region to the ground plan of an individual building. With the arrival of the cellular phone network in the Devon area in the early 1990s, it also proved possible to provide an alternative channel of communications independent of the main radio scheme. This has been a great benefit, as with independent communications between officers, control and the service and divisional headquarters, a lot of pressure could be taken off the main scheme network, which was getting increasingly busy as call numbers rose throughout the period. The cellular network also allowed fax machines to be installed in the mobile control units, enabling the main control to transmit information such as hazardous chemicals action cards or detailed building plans direct to the fireground.

The DFRS has continued to invest heavily in IT, not just for the control functions but also for administration. The installation of PCs on all fire stations allows fire service personnel to access technical and training information via the service's own internal 'Intranet', while most routine instructions, course details and equipment returns are now made by e-mail, saving time and paper. Virtually all the internal communications in the service are now electronic, and work progresses to get more and more of the record-keeping and routine reporting into this form. Computerised fire report forms that can be transmitted straight to the Home Office and electronic ordering of stores and equipment are the next stages in this process.

The latest round of operational IT development has seen the introduction of on-board computer systems in vehicles, initially on the Incident Command Vehicles that are in the process of replacing the old Control Unit/ETs. A trial is also being conducted with cab-mounted computers on

*Incident command, twenty-first century style. Devon's new ICVs have powerful onboard computers and sophisticated communications. They carry onboard generators and lighting, an air-supported structure and equipment to set up a command facility for the largest incident.*

fire appliances, a facility that allows accurate topographical information, route maps and risk details to be transmitted to appliances whilst they are responding to an incident. One of the key advances made possible through computerisation has been the advent of the Tactical Information Plan (TIP), a system for bringing together all the known and recorded information on a particular risk in one simple-to-access database which can be quickly interrogated give a wealth of operational data to crews and officers in the event of a call. The TIP contains address and access details, floor plans of all floors and structures, site plans, number of people normally on the site at different times, escape routes or emergency access points, location of gas and electricity supplies, any on-site special hazards, location and capacity of water supplies, the pre-determined attendance, details of keyholders or specialist advisers, any pre-determined Fire Attack Plan, the location of specialist resources – such as foam or dry agent – that might be needed and even details of previous incidents at that address. This degree of foreknowledge can cut out confusion and make fire service action – especially initial action – far more effective. It can, in the ultimate analysis, save lives.

The other main area of technical progress has concerned BA, which has seen considerable change since 1987. The longer duration Aga Spiromatic set introduced by the DFB was proving somewhat demanding to wear in service due to the weight of the actual air cylinders. To contain pressures of 200 bars (3000 p.s.i.) and above, these of necessity were of substantial construction and even the light-alloy-steel type were proving uncomfortably heavy. With the quest now on for a 300 bar 1-hour duration set, the first problem was to find a better (ie, lighter) form of cylinder. The answer proved to be a spin-off from the US space programme, where lightweight pressure vessels made from thin aluminium reinforced with carbon-fibre had proved successful. A US firm, Efic, developed a 300-bar aqualung/BA cylinder made using this technique which was very significantly lighter than the alloy steel type, and Devon Fire & Rescue Service became the first UK brigade to trial and subsequently purchase this type of BA cylinder, which became universal throughout Devon by 1996. This represented a major step forward in BA capability, and was a long stride from the old Draeger and Aga 20-minute cylinders.

Not content with extending the duration of the sets, Devon also decided to replace the life-expired Spiromatics with the latest evolution of the Aga-Spiro BA set, the computerised Spirotronic. These incorporated a number of major advances, the most significant of which were the computerised monitoring of the set which identified and gave warning of faults and kept the firefighter constantly informed of the functioning and air reserve of his set via a mask-mounted display. The sets are self-diagnostic on testing, and have the facility to interface with new radio-location and communications systems still being developed. They can also be adapted for 'buddy-breathing', which allows a firefighter to share an air supply with a colleague in cases of emergency, are easier and quicker to don and start-up, and have a fresh-air breathing facility that allows firefighters to stand by fully-rigged in BA without using up vital air supplies. The rescue teams that are always on standby during difficult BA operations can now go from fresh-air to firefighting status in less than a second simply by snapping shut an air hatch, giving them instant availability rather than the 30 seconds or so previously needed to don a facemask and start up a set.

## FIREFIGHTER PROTECTION

By the mid 1980s, the traditional firefighting uniform of the Melton wool tunic, tarpaulin or plastic overtrousers and high-peaked helmet was being called into question. The tunic itself had been simplified from the double-breasted many-buttoned type familiar since the days of brass helmets and steam pumps to a shorter single-breasted design with many fewer buttons, and velcro-fastened over-flap and insulated lining. With the arrival of the newer tunics, the old axe-belt had gone, and the traditional high-crowned cork-covered helmet with its prominent comb had been succeeded by lightweight composite helmets, first the American 'Metro' style and then the Bristol 'Cromwell' helmet, now in yellow for firefighters and junior officers, white for officers above Station Officer rank.

New standards for certificated firefighting gear were introduced in 1988 (British Standard) and 1992 (European Standard) in response to fires that, while less frequent, tended to be more severe and far hotter when they did occur. The older uniform no longer offered anything like the required degree of protection, while the advent of new space-age materials that had far greater fire-resistance and much-improved thermal insulation qualities made more effective fire fighting uniforms technically possible. The new Bristol fire tunic appeared in 1988, manufactured from Nomex – the material that was protecting racing drivers and fighter pilots from fierce fuel fires. The first Nomex fire tunics and overtrousers were introduced into Devon in 1989 to Home Office specification A26; these tunics had detachable linings and no sleeve restraining system, and thus did not conform to the Europe-wide EN469 requirements. Bristol introduced a modified version of the tunic with an integral quilted lining and thumb-loops to ensure sleeves would not ride up during operations.

These tunics were a stop-gap, as the chief officers of the various West Country brigades collaborated on the design and procurement of the 'Wessex' tunic, a basic design suited to rural-area firefighting that could be adapted to the equipment-carrying needs of the various brigades in the region. The Wessex has been made in various versions, with the latest being a joint Cornwall/Devon design that meets all the detail requirements of both brigades; being able to order fire kit on a combined basis makes obvious sense on economic grounds. The 'new Wessex' has attachment points for personal radios and torches and stowage for all the smaller items of PPE now carried, which include firefighting gloves and safety spectacles for eye protection. More recently, flash-hoods or 'snoods' – fire- and heat-resistant Balaclavas – have been issued to further increase the modern firefighter's personal protection.

As with the fire tunic, so with the remaining firefighting uniform; the high-waisted Nomex overtrouser replaced the yellow plastic Bata type, and rubber boots with steel inserts gave way to a leather fireboot with a composition sole. These still had steel toe and sole protection, but were much better-insulated and, being leather, could 'breathe' and were far more supple, making them comfortable to wear over a protracted period. Although more expensive initially than the rubber boot, the new leather design had a far greater life and could be repaired and re-soled if damaged or worn, thus making them a good long-term proposition. Gloves have always been a problem for firefighters, with the need to balance adequate hand protection with enough 'feel' to perform complex tasks. The current pigskin Bristol glove is the best compromise yet found, and gives excellent wrist protection when worn with a thumb-looped tunic.

The old 'Cromwell' helmet, more compact and lighter than the traditional designs, still fell some way short of the new EU requirements, and was been replaced in 1994 by the American Cairns Metro 660 helmet, which combines a lightweight shell with a shock-absorbing lining, fully-adjustable head harness, heat- and shatter-proof polycarbonate visor and a Nomex neck curtain. The combination of all this modern uniform with the Spirotronic BA set means that the Devon firefighter of today is completely protected from his environment and can operate in conditions that would not have been tolerable with the fire kit of only a decade ago.

## REORGANISATION AS THE PURSE-STRINGS TIGHTEN

Robin Currie, Devon's CFO from 1991–1997, was overseeing the Devon Fire & Rescue Service through a period when central government was taking a long, harsh look at all elements of public expenditure – the fire service included. The 1995 Audit Commission Report on Britain's Fire Services 'In the Line of Fire' made uncomfortable reading in places, and the pressures for reforms and economies were growing. With Devon's Standard Spending Assessment effectively being cut from 1993-on, and with the amount of money that the county council could raise locally being capped, the fire service found itself looking at real-term budget cuts of a substantial order; it was evident that something fairly drastic would have to be done to reduce costs. A wide range of possibilities was examined, ranging from draconian measures like closing stations or reducing the number of fire engines deployed to contracting-out some brigade operations, replacing firefighters with civilian non-uniformed employees who would fall outside the rigid fire service Conditions of Employment. Many senior and middle-ranking management posts were not filled when they became vacant, and several important projects had to be put on 'hold'

In the end, it was decided that the best approach was to try and improve efficiency at all levels of the service. Devon is a large county and lines of communication have always been long and somewhat unwieldy. So the service was divided up into a series of self-contained 'Districts', each under the command of a District Officer, and each with its own discreet budget. The idea was that solutions appropriate to the very different areas of the county would be better devised and secured locally rather than through a central administration. The 'District' system also enshrined the then-current doctrine of the 'internal market', with District Officers 'buying in' training, equipment maintenance and other services from the core provision of the Devon Fire & Rescue Service. Originally, there were 13 districts each with around 4–6 stations. The geographical size of the districts varied enormously, from compact urban areas like Plymouth or Torbay to the sprawling vastness of 'Torridge & West Devon' (popularly known at the time as the 'Wilderness District') which ranged from Moretonhampstead to Holsworthy and down to the Cornish border.

Unfortunately, emergency services such as the fire brigade do not lend themselves readily to such a structure, and the savings achieved by devolving administration and budget-handling were more than outweighed by additional expenses incurred trying to co-ordinate and provide for all the different requirements and systems of working thrown up by the different districts. Some districts did evolve a very high degree of self-sufficiency and efficiency in many areas, but many – especially in the more populous parts of the county – soon found that complex arrangements were needed with adjoining districts to meet operational needs. In an attempt to address these problems, the number of Districts was reduced from thirteen to seven, coinciding with the various District Council boundaries. This made the 'Wilderness' of Torridge and West Devon even bigger, and these new bigger districts proved even more problematic than the original small units, as the lines of communication once again became over-extended. It was realised that high-quality communication was the key to efficient management, and with the rapid advances in IT then taking place the answer was to be found in taking advantage of these new capabilities.

When Paul Young – a Devon veteran, having been commander of the old East Division before going to Somerset Fire Brigade as Deputy Chief and subsequently CFO – took over the Devon CFO's chair in 1997, sufficient progress had been made on the IT front to permit a return to the old four-divisional framework, although the divisional boundaries were re-drawn to take account of the vastly improved trunk road network in the county. The flexibility made possible by the brigade-wide IT network has radically improved communications throughout the service and is leading to real economies in the efficient utilisation of resources. Furthermore, there is still a vast potential for further improvement and for more aspects of the brigade's work to be brought onto the new systems.

The economic stringencies of the past few years have seen the senior management of the DFRS take a long, hard look at all aspects of the brigade's operations and its purchasing strategies. However, these reviews have had to be undertaken against a background, not just of fiscal restraint, but also of the legal obligations of the service. A particular problem is that much fire brigade equipment – such as firefighting garments and other personal protective equipment, BA sets, ladders, hydraulic rams and pipework – has a certificated life, and once these certificates have expired the equipment must either be re-certificated (a costly process in itself) or replaced. In recent years, the acquisition policy of many fire brigades – including Devon – has moved from outright purchase to leasing equipment over the currency of the certificates. However, the areas in which substantial savings can be made on frontline equipment are very limited. The Devon strategy has been to identify the areas where economies can be made without in any way compromising operational capability. And one area where this approach has proved beneficial is in the design and procurement of fire appliances.

*Five brand-new Dennis DS appliances photographed on Plymouth Hoe before being put 'on the run' at stations with difficult fire-grounds requiring a narrow-bodied appliance. Currently, there are twelve of these small Dennis appliances in the fleet, based at Bampton, Bovey Tracey, Brixham, Dartmouth, Lynton, Moretonhampstead, North Tawton, Ottery St Mary and Woolacombe, with two as reserves.*

*Dartmouth's DS 241 shows the similarity to the larger RS and also displays the full-width light bar and the compact triple-extension 7m ladder that has replaced the 105 on new appliances.*

## The Devon Country-Area Appliance Arrives

As the original multi-purpose machines on many retained stations became due for renewal in the early 1990s, it was necessary to find a new, smaller appliance to meet the needs of those stations that could not accommodate an RS-sized vehicle on their firegrounds. Due to the growing size of modern commercial vehicles and the phasing-out of traditional medium-weight trucks like the Bedford TK, it became more of a problem to identify suitable chassis on which to base new fire appliances. With the need becoming urgent as older 'multis' reached the end of – and, in many cases, exceeded – their service lives, it proved necessary to look for a readily-available appliance. The initial answer proved to be another Dennis type, the DS. This was effectively a 'mini' version of the RS that was only seven feet wide. These compact machines did not have stowage space for the full range of equipment then being carried by the RS, especially for the bulky Hurst rescue set, which was anyway proving over-large in some operational situations. The DS appliance was therefore equipped with the newer, more compact Zumro rescue tools and at the same time dispensed with items of gear carried on the older multi-purpose machines that had now become outmoded.

The DS appliance departed a little from the previous water-tender standard by carrying 350 rather than 400 gallons of water, and in dispensing with the 10.5 metre '105' ladder in favour of a new type of ultra-light-weight aluminium alloy triple-extension ladder with a 7-metre reach. This new ladder was much handier and more flexible in deployment, needing only one or two men to pitch it as against a minimum of three for the 105. The DS introduced some other innovations for Devon fire appliances, including computer-controlled pumps and hosereels having quick-release couplings and American Akron 'Marauder' guns suited to high-pressure operation, but also having foam-making capability. They were also the first machines to have American-style full-width 'light bars' in place of individual blue beacons, and 'wail and yelp' sirens as well as two-tone horns. However, very few other brigades bought the Dennis DS appliance, which made the machine very costly due to the low production runs; Dennis discontinued the type in 1994.

With the introduction of the DS type to Devon there had been a move away from the concept of procuring a 'universal' fire appliance and following the Killoran strategy of placing all new machines on busy stations then 'cascading' them down to rural stations after a few years. It was realised that the needs of the urban and rural areas of Devon were growing ever more divergent, and that it simply was not possible to design one fire appliance suited to the whole county, especially given the nature of much of the road network. The new policy was to continue to buy standard 'urban' machines from Dennis for the whole-time stations and the busiest urban retained or core-manned stations, but to develop a dedicated rural-area appliance for the rest of the county. A shortfall in the availability of Dennis appliances in some years during the early 1990s had already led to the purchase of a small fleet of other machines, notably a batch of seven Volvo FL6 chassis with bodywork by Saxon-Sandbech and a smaller batch of Mercedes with Carmichael bodywork. But these were still large machines, comparable in size to the RS; there was still a need for a compact, manoeuvrable appliance to replace the remaining Dennis D and Dodge 'multis'.

A working party was set up to evolve a specification for a new Devon appliance. The brief was a demanding one, as the new vehicles had not only to meet the operational requirements but to be substantially more economical to buy and operate. With the price of a new Dennis now soaring to well over the £100,000 mark, a saving of at least 20% was called for. After considerable research, a suitable chassis was identified in the MAN light truck range from Germany. For fire appliance purposes, the 10-ton chassis was selected, but specified with a more powerful 224-bhp turbo-diesel engine and a six-speed Eaton air-operated manual gearbox. Although a little wider than the DS appliance, the MAN chassis boasted a very tight turning circle with quick-acting power steering and had very powerful anti-lock disk brakes. It also had a low centre of gravity promising excellent handling, and sat on wide-rim sixteen-inch wheels fitted with low-profile tyres. The pay-off for this excellent on-road performance was relatively poor ground clearance, making these vehicles somewhat vulnerable if taken off-road.

*First series Saxon-MAN country area appliance-this is 531 based at Ivybridge, and hence one of the machines equipped for co-responder ambulance duties.*

During the design process, great attention was paid to keeping the weight as low as possible and every piece of equipment was carefully weighed and assessed before being specified. Bodywork was to be of lightweight aluminium and alloy steel construction, with GRP mouldings in the cab area, while roller-shutter doors and plain aluminium sides for the bodywork returned, although the cabs were fully painted. With the low-loading chassis and compact bodywork, the resulting appliance had an overall height more than a foot less than an RS. The new country-area vehicles were shorn of all fripperies, and have a rather plain appearance with very little brightwork. As many standard fittings and components as possible are incorporated to ease the need for extensive spares stocks, while the use of a popular and newly-introduced chassis from a major manufacturer has ensured ready and economical spares availability over the life of the appliances.

The first MAN country-appliances were delivered in late 1994 and had bodywork by Saxon Sandbech. They were to full water tender/ladder specification with 1800-litre (395-gallon) water tanks, a 2750 litre/min (600-g.p.m.) two stage main pump with a high-pressure stage giving up to 30 bar on the hosereels, and round-pump foam-making capability. The ladder equipment, as on the DS, consisted of a 135 main ladder together with the triple-extension 7-metre, a short extension and a folding lightweight alloy long-reach roof ladder. Successive generations of appliance had carried less and less traditional fire hose, and the DS and MAN machines are both stowed with only five 75-foot lengths of 45mm firefighting hose and fifteen lengths of 70mm delivery hose. Modern firefighting techniques and the advent of the high-pressure hosereel gun have lessened the need for large volumes of water in most firefighting applications, while the availability of the high-speed hoselayers means that pumped water supplies can be speedily established where they are needed.

*Nearside stowage on a MAN country-area appliance showing the Zumro 'Kombi-tool', a combined cutter and spreader popularly known as 'The Jaws of Life'. Also seen is a ram used for spreading wider openings.*

On the rescue front, the MAN country-area appliance is equipped with a new and more compact version of the Zumro powered hydraulic rescue equipment, the 'Kombi'. This combines a powerful spreader and shear-cutter into one tool, reducing stowage requirements and also proving easier to manage in use. Other rescue gear includes a hydraulic ram, the 'Tirfor' winch, a 'Chance' cliff-rescue stretcher with helicopter harness, rescue lines and a wide range of hand tools. Four Spirotronic computerised BA sets are stowed in the spacious crew cab, along with MARS

*The latest batch of MAN appliances have JDC body work and improved conspicuity aids and a folding rather than air-operated lighting mast. This is 251, Dawlish's appliance, also equipped for co-responder duties.*

oxygen resuscitator sets. Other innovations on these machines include air-operated lighting masts – invaluable in the largely-unlit rural areas – hose-reel based foam capabilities and environmental protection equipment.

The new country-area appliance has proved largely successful. The road performance in terms of both speed and handling is excellent, and the two-stage pumps are very effective. The roomy crew cab is comfortable and quiet, and the range of equipment carried has proved well up to the roles these machines are called upon to play. The Achilles heel has been the low ground clearance and general lack of off-road capability, and where this has been felt to be a basic requirement, as on moorland stations like Princetown and Lynton, special versions of the country-area vehicle have been built on 4 x 4 Mercedes chassis. More recently, a small fleet of light 4 x 4 auxilliary vehicles have been purchased for off-road work where needed, and these are used to back up the MAN appliances operationally. More recent deliveries of the MAN appliance have John Dennis bodywork, while one machine – stationed at Cullompton – is on a heavier and more powerful MAN chassis and carries a full set of hydraulic rescue equipment for motorway work on the M5.

*The current standard appliance for the busiest urban stations is the Dennis 'Sabre', equipped here as a rescue appliance with a front-mounted power winch. A 135 ladder is normally carried. This is 322, stationed at Exeter.*

## UPDATING THE DEVON FLEET

Although Devon's cities do not yet have the type of ultra-high-rise structure seen elsewhere in the country, there is still a need for aerial appliances able to operate at around the 30-metre/100 ft mark. The old hydraulically-operated Merryweather TLs from Plymouth, Torbay and Exeter – dating from the 1960s – initially filled this role, with the unique 60-ft Wrt/TL built in Devon County days for Ilfracombe's tall hotels serving the north of the county. By the later 1970s, thought was given to replacing these machines. Exeter received a new Shelvoke/Metz 100ft TL in 1980, while two Magirus 100ft ladders were purchased for Plymouth to replace the existing re-chassied Merryweather at Greenbank and to provide a spare/training machine, usually kept at the Service Training Centre in Plympton. This left Torquay's re-chassised Merryweather TL and the Ilfracombe Wrt/TL hybrid. For Torquay, a French Camiva 30m TL on a low-loading Dennis F127 chassis

*Above: The second last TL bought by Devon was this French built Camiva 30 metre appliance, mounted on a Dennis low loading chassis. The appliance is seen here when new, allocated to Torquay. It is now stationed at Barnstaple.*

*Above right: Current policy in aerial appliances favours the hydraulic ladder platform. This is the appliance that replaced the Camiva TL at Torquay, a Swedish designed Bronto 'Skylift' of twenty-eight metres reach. When in operation, the vehicle stabilisers lift the whole appliance clear of the ground.*

was purchased and the Merryweather sold to Suffolk. The new TL had computer-controlled actuation and incorporated a rescue cage, but the sophisticated control system did suffer a number of initial problems.

However, it was becoming apparent that the latest generation of hydraulic-boom 'Aerial Ladder Platforms' could now achieve the height and reach attainable with the TLs, while offering far greater flexibility, greater load-carrying and swifter deployment. It was therefore decided that future aerial appliances would be of the hydraulic platform type, and after evaluation the Bronto 'Skylift' 28-metre (91-foot) three-section platform was selected, built onto six-wheeled Volvo chassis. With their six-person rescue cage, fully-computerised actuation, enormous stability, integral scene lighting and powerful monitor jets, these are state-of-the-art aerial appliances that will see the Devon service well into the twenty-first century. Three of these machines were purchased, for Camel's Head in Plymouth, Torquay and Exeter. With the arrival of the Exeter Bronto, the Metz TL was re-allocated to Ilfracombe but was unfortunately written-off in a road accident a short while afterwards. The ex-Torquay Camiva, now fully sorted, was at Greenbank for a while before going north to replace the wrecked Metz at Ilfracombe. It is now stationed at Barnstaple, while the ex-Greenbank Magirus ladder went to Crownhill. The service thus now has six aerial appliances: Bronto skylifts at Exeter, Torquay and Camel's Head, a Magirus TL at Crownhill and the Camiva at Barnstaple, with the second Magirus as a reserve/training ladder.

Other older front-line urban appliances – almost exclusively Dennis RS machines – were coming up for replacement. The decision was taken to stick with the mainstream Dennis products, initially the 'Rapier' that had replaced the RS in the early 1990s and subsequently the 'Sabre' that succeeded the Rapier in 1995. These machines are, again, 'state of the art', with air-suspended chassis and a full rescue/water ladder specification. They have a powerful 265-bhp turbocharged diesel engine driving through a 5-speed automatic gearbox, disc/drum brakes with third-generation anti-lock brakes and traction control for excellent road performance, and use similar lightweight construction techniques to the country-area MAN appliances to reduce weight. They come in two versions, as water tenders and as full rescue/pump-ladders, which last also carry power winches and a full range of new-generation Hurst hydraulic rescue equipment. All the Sabres have multi-stage pumps for high-pressure and foam capability, and can deploy the latest environmental protection measures. Their aerodynamic bodywork improves high-speed stability and reduces fuel consumption, while advanced structural design offers a high level of crew protection.

*The stowage on a WrL/Rescue Sabre is comprehensive: On the nearside, the powered hydraulic rescue equipment and tools occupy the foremost locker, with lighting and rescue stretcher in the centre locker and fire and delivery hose, hosereels, branches and foam gear at the rear. On the offside, the light portable pump occupies the lower front locker, with chimney fire kit and digging tools above. In the centre locker are GP and rescue lines, the BA fireground cleaning kit, first aid kit, Tirfor Winch and salvage sheets. At the rear is the environmental spill kit, delivery hose, hose reel and more foam. BA and chemical protection gear is stowed in the crew cab, and additional hose fittings are located in the pump bay.*

## DEMOUNTABLE SYSTEMS

With the front-line pumping appliances – both in the cities and on the rural stations – having such substantial rescue and environmental protection capabilities, the role of the traditional emergency tenders was now called into question. It was decided not to replace these vehicles with new ETs, but to approach the provision of in-depth back-up to the regular front-line pumping appliances in a different way. The basis of this new approach was the use of the demountable body system originally developed for the army by Devon-based Reynolds-Boughton Specialist Vehicles for the rapid mobilisation and deployment of battleground stores. The key feature of the Reynolds-Boughton system was its robustness, speed of use and substantial weight-carrying capability. It is based around a prime-mover vehicle chassis fitted with a large hydraulically-operated hook and a runner system that enables hefty containers – pods – to be speedily lifted into place or positioned for operations, the whole process requiring only one man.

It was obvious that this system had a wide range of possibilities for fire service use, offering flexibility, economy of initial cost, versatility and efficiency. So the ETs were initially supplemented by, and later replaced by, prime movers with demountable body lift gear, and a programme of pod commissioning was put in hand. The first pods to be introduced were for training purposes, two breathing apparatus training units. These were followed by a fire education unit for use by the Community Fire Safety department, and a large Control Unit for use at major incidents. These initial units were used to evaluate the system, and once a number of improvements and modifications had been made, work commenced on commissioning the two key operational pod designs, for Incident Support and Environmental Protection.

The first of these, the Incident Support Unit (ISU), is designed to provide a wide-ranging back-up to front-line appliances at larger or protracted incidents. It carries a varied range of lighting, portable generators, propping and shoring gear, salvage sheets, hi-expansion foam gear, smoke extraction and ventilation fans, a BA main control and extra BA cylinder stocks. The actual pod, which is much the same size as a portable site

*The basis for the DFRS demountable system is a sixteen tonne MAN prime mover which can accommodate a standard container, known as a pod. Currently, there are three main types of pod in use; the Environmental Unit, the Incident Support Unit, and the Mobile BA Training Unit. This is 490, the unit based at Crownhill, Plymouth.*

building, incorporates washing and toilet facilities, a kitchen area capable of providing hot meals and drinks, and an under-cover operations area. It can be linked to an air-supported structure to provide further shelter for rest and recuperation, crew feeding and other operational purposes. These units replace the ETs operationally and also fulfil the functions of a canteen vehicle.

The Environmental Unit is largely an expansion of the service's capabilities rather than a replacement for functions previously carried out by the ETs. These pods have been specified and equipped in conduction with the Environment Agency, and all the equipment and procedures used are full compatible with the measures taken by the EA. The pod carries a wide range of absorbent materials, special protective clothing, containers for contaminated waste, vacuum units to remove hazardous powders, portable dam units to store liquids, special pumps and large-capacity hose, floating oil-containment booms, decontamination equipment and a wide range of scene lighting with generators.

One ISU and one Environmental pod is allocated to each division, and normally carries a crew of three on the prime mover to speed pod deployment on arrival. It can be mobilised in a few minutes, and a 'pod' can reach most locations in the county in around half an hour. The MAN prime movers are of 16 tons capacity, fitted with 224-bhp turbo-diesel engines, and are front-line 'blue light' vehicles. One prime mover is allocated to each division, being stationed at Exeter, Torquay, Barnstaple and Crownhill. A further prime mover is kept at Service HQ to move the training and education pods and to act as a back-up to the front-line vehicles. Future pods planned include one for foam equipment and a marine/flooding rescue unit. The great virtue of the pod concept is its capability to permit a swift alteration or increase in capability to be made in the face of a new risk.

*The equipment carried on the environmental unit includes floating booms to contain spillages on water, special absorbant materials to deal with oil and chemical spills, vaccum equipment to remove powder spills, pumps and holding tanks to cope with leaking vehicles or storage tanks, lighting equipment and decontamination showers.*

*The DFRS specialist rescue team based in Plymouth can deploy a number of rescue techniques. Here they are operating in 'high-line' mode some two hundred feet above the ground on the brigade's main radio mast. They can also work in confined spaces and operate on marshy ground for rescues from bogs and esturial mud.*

## SPECIALIST RESCUE

With the division of the non-fire rescue functions between the front-line pumping appliances and the back-up provided by the pod units, there was felt to be a gap in the Devon service's capabilities in some more specialised areas – in particular, in rescue from a height or from confined spaces, from hazardous environments such as loose particulate materials, mud, bog or quicksand, and from predicaments difficult of access by traditional means. To meet this need, a specialist Line Rescue Unit was formed, based at Camel's Head fire station in Plymouth and equipped with a dedicated vehicle. Initially, this was a secondhand long-wheelbase Land Rover, but this has now been replaced by a brand new four-wheel-drive Mercedes-Benz 'Unimog' vehicle with special low-ground-pressure tyres, enabling it to cross the most difficult terrain in safety.

As well as the line rescue equipment, rescue stretcher with helicopter gear, extra first-aid equipment, digging and stabilising tools and a powerful winch, the new vehicles carry inflatable mud-matting for rescue work on boggy or unstable ground. A second Line Rescue Unit, with members trained in all aspects of line-work including abseiling, cliff rescue, high-line access and helicopter rescue, is being prepared for the North Devon area, using a new specially-built Land-Rover based vehicle. As the civil rescue function of the fire service assumes ever-greater importance, it will doubtless be necessary to devise, train and equip more specialist units within the Devon Fire and Rescue Service.

## INCIDENT COMMAND SYSTEM

In the wake of a number of major incidents in Britain, notably the Bristol supermarket fire that claimed the life of Fleur Lombard, the Gillender Street fire in London and the Sun Valley Chickens blaze in Herefordshire (both incidents also having fatal consequences for firefighters), the traditional structure of fireground command was subjected to a new examination by the Health and Safety Executive, as a result of which stringent new requirements for a much more structured, risk-assessed and informed command procedure were introduced. These procedures have now been fully implemented in Devon, and have revolutionised the manner in which officers-in-charge assess fires and deploy their resources, as well as much more clearly defining the role of each level of command at larger incidents.

As part of the new command system, a far more sophisticated type of fire-ground control unit was required, and this need has been met by the new Incident Command Vehicles. Based on turbo-diesel Mercedes-Benz Vito light vans, carrying a crew of two and capable of very rapid deployment anywhere within the county, these new command units are very different from the old ET-based mobile controls. With a powerful onboard computer system incorporating updatable databases for all the geographical location, chemical, and TIPs (Tactical Incident Plans), the control operators on the ICV have the capability to inform the officer commanding an incident on all aspects of the risk with which he is dealing. Backed up with powerful communications tools including a sophisticated fireground radio scheme, cell-phone compatibility giving fax and voice links to the main control, all the control functions with the exception of mobilising can now be carried out on the fireground of a large incident, greatly reducing the load on both the central control operators (who still have the rest of Devon to worry about) and reducing to a minimum extra traffic on the main radio scheme.

As well as the computers and communications gear, each ICV carries an air-supported structure, lighting, a generator and lightweight collapsible furniture to provide a command post/briefing room. This structure can also be linked with the operations space on the Incident Support Unit to give an integrated BA main control and fireground control capability capable of handling the largest type of incident. Again, there is one ICV on each division, based at Exmouth, Ilfracombe, Torquay and Plymouth. They are automatically mobilised to any incident with either a pre-determined attendance of three or more pumps or where the initially-attending pumps have requested assistance.

## FIREBOAT *VIGILES*

The old 1942-vintage Plymouth fireboat *Cissie Brock* came to the end of its operational life in the early 1990s when it developed faults that put it beyond economic repair. As a stopgap it was replaced by a naval 'Rigid Raider' dory with onboard firepump and other firefighting capability while a project was initiated to specify and source a new fireboat for Plymouth. As can be imagined, there have been very considerable advances in marine design since 1942, and the new fireboat *Vigiles* is totally different to a traditional vessel like the *Cissie Brock*.

Developed and built by the same firm that built London's two new fireboats, the welded-aluminium vessel is of a unique catamaran hull configuration and was built by Alnmaritec of Alnwick, Northumberland. The design was specified by a small DFRS development team led by Station Officer Colin Rockey, and has resulted in an appliance with a great deal of capability not just as a fireboat, but as a high-speed, high-stability general rescue craft. *Vigiles* has a water jet propulsion system powered by two Cummins 315 hp diesel engines which give it a service speed of 25 knots and the capability to operate in water only half a metre deep. The engines are the same type as are used in some of the heavier Devon fire appliances, allowing commonality of spares.

*The new Devon Fire and Rescue fireboat Vigiles arrived in Devon at the close of the twentieth century, being accepted for trials in the final months of 1999. This unique craft, with it's catamaran hulls and all-alloy construction, has a far wider range of capability than any previous fire boat. It is fully equipped to carry out a wide range of firefighting, environmental protection and rescue tasks.*

The fire pump on *Vigiles* is powered by a seperate 84 hp marine diesel engine, and incorporates an Italian Tamini turbine pump feeding a number of deliveries fore and aft, as well as monitor mounting positions. *Vigiles* can operate in the Plymouth Sound area north of a line from Rame Head to Bolt Tail, and has satellite navigation, radar and echo sounding equipment. Communications are possible on both the marine band and the Devon Fire and Rescue Service main radio scheme.

At the stern of the craft is a water level rescue platform, while the commodious pilot-house has accommodation for the five-man crew as well as stretcher-borne casualties. All fireboat crew members are trained as coxwains and hold RYA power boat handling certificates. As part of their additional training, firefighters from Plymstock who man *Vigiles* are receiving co-responder training, and the boat will also be equipped for this role. *Vigiles* was both the last technical development project of the twentieth century for the Devon Fire and Rescue Service and the first major new piece of equipment to be commissioned in the twenty-first.

## COMMUNITY FIRE SAFETY – THE NEW PRIORITY

Fire brigades have been charged with the tasks of fire prevention and fire education since the 1947 Act, but since the 1989 Audit Commission Report these activities have assumed a far more central role in the operation of the fire service. In particular, the task of ensuring and promoting fire safety in the community at large has become particularly significant, and the development of a really effective Community Fire Safety (CFS) programme has become a central preoccupation of the modern fire service. The problems of implementing such a programme in a large rural county like Devon are considerable, but over the last few years the retained fire service has started to play a major role in delivering fire safety advice and more formal fire education in their areas to back up the community work that has long formed a key part of the whole-time firefighter's workload.

Devon's Community Fire Safety programme operates over a wide range of levels and delivery methods. There is a formal schools programme that extends from Key Stage One infant children right through the secondary education system, delivered by specially-trained firefighters working in conjunction with class teachers. This scheme is supported with videos and with written resources, and has a proper evaluation element. The messages delivered range from the most basic fire safety for young children to sophisticated fire prevention and social responsibility programmes designed to counter malicious fires and false 999 calls in the teenaged groups. There is also the FireEd programme aimed at youngsters who have been involved in fire-raising or other offences involving fire or abuse of the emergency call system. In many parts of the county, the Life Skills Programme for young people also operates. This covers a wide range of hazards facing youngsters, from drugs and domestic emergencies through farm accidents, beach and water safety, danger from strangers, road safety, unexploded munitions, solvent abuse, fist aid and, of course, fire safety. The Devon Fire and Rescue Service has participated in these schemes since their inception, both by use of the mobile fire education pod and by the involvement of many fire service personnel, whole-time and retained.

Community Fire Safety officers are appointed on every fire station in the county to co-ordinate and carry out all of this formal education-based work, as well as organising visits or talks to community groups of all types in their area, from crèches through playgroups and youth clubs to over-60s or disabled organisations. Firefighters also visit individual homes under the CFS scheme, particularly those housing families with young children or inhabited by elderly people or those suffering from disabilities, to assess the risks and advise on appropriate fire safety measures. Getting smoke alarms in as many Devon homes as possible is a central plank of the CFS strategy, and firefighters offer advice on correct alarm location and in many cases actually install the equipment. As part of the CFS scheme, sponsored by South West Water and other local business partners, the DFRS can arrange the free supply and fitting of smoke alarms in cases of need. These in-home aspects of the fire safety programme are often linked to community action schemes run by Devon Social Services, local GP surgeries, district nursing/midwifery or health visitors and local welfare organisations such as the WVS and Age Concern. All the fire safety messages are backed by up-to-date and informative leaflets, and fire stations maintain leaflet dispensers in public venues throughout their area.

*Community Fire Safety in action: the chip pan demonstration unit shows graphically what happens when water is poured onto burning cooking oil! This demonstration is being staged by Ilfracombe firefighters at an open day.*

On a less formal note, most fire stations – particularly those in smaller rural communities – have very strong traditional community links that have now been built on to carry the fire safety message at local level. Many fire stations have a regular slot in their village newsletter or local newspaper for 'fire news' and fire safety messages, and the co-operation of the local press in the CFS programme has been a major plus throughout. Schools, youth and other community groups frequently visit fire stations to learn how the service operates and to discuss fire safety concerns and receive advice (as well as enjoying the chance to put on a helmet, squirt some water and operate the siren!). Almost every fire station has at least one open day during the year when the community at large is invited into the station, while fire appliances and firefighters happy to give advice are to be found at fêtes, carnivals, school open days, agricultural shows and many other local events. The CFS department has a fleet of mobile display units, including trailer-mounted displays and the spectacular chip pan fire demonstration unit, and these are available to the individual fire stations to support their own fire safety displays. In short, the Devon Fire and Rescue Service seeks to spread the fire safety message and the use of life-saving equipment such as smoke alarms throughout the community by whatever means are available to it.

*The first new fire station to be built by Devon Fire and Rescue service was at Chagford on the edge of Dartmoor, a structure that had to be carefully designed to meet the requirements of the Dartmoor National Park. The station went into service in October 1989.*

## BUILDING FOR THE FUTURE

The programme of fire station replacement and development instituted by the old Devon County Fire Service has been continued under the Devon Fire and Rescue Service, although with most stations now being purpose-built the pace of building has slowed somewhat in recent years. Chagford was the first new fire station opened under the DFRS, in 1989, followed by Princetown in 1995. Both these stations are within the Dartmoor National Park, and entailed careful design and siting to fit in with the planning requirements of the Park. A number of older stations still await replacement, including Teignmouth and Exmouth, while the one-pump stations at Chulmleigh, Hartland and Braunton are in need of upgrading. And, as the century draws to a close, several proposed reorganisation schemes have implications for the building programme, including a major change in the Exeter area that might well see the city served by two stations, one to the south-west at Marsh Barton and a second close to the M5 at Sowton, better reflecting both the pattern of risk and road links in the modern city and the preferred philosophy of going into the city centre from the outskirts when needed rather than having to come out from a central location for every call. The current Exeter proposal would amalgamate part of the Exeter whole-time provision with the existing retained provision at Topsham, eliminating the need to replace Topsham fire station.

*Most recent of Devon's fire stations is also on Dartmoor, one of the highest fire stations in Britain at fifteen hundred feet above sea level. Princetown fire station opened in 1995, and in common with other moorland stations such as Moretonhampstead, Ivybridge and Chagford operates a co-responder scheme.*

Training and administration facilities are a further aspect of the Devon service that have seen new building works. As well as the Fire Attack complex at Exeter airport, which is still being developed, the BA training has now been concentrated at the Training School Annex on the Clyst St George headquarters site, with the original BA complex being modernised and extended to provide the necessary facilities. A new East Division headquarters building has also opened on the HQ site, while outposted training facilities have been created at Okehampton, where there is a mini-firehouse and a lecture suite.

## THE CO-RESPONSE SCHEME

Firefighters have always received at least basic training in first-aid, but in recent years this topic has gradually assumed greater and greater importance. The Health and Safety at Work Act had anyway required a greater degree of basic first-aid training so that firefighters could treat colleagues injured in the course of duty as well as members of the public, but even this level of skill was soon falling short of operational needs. The DFRS introduced a Casualty Care Course in the mid-1980s, mainly aimed at treating and handling the victims of road traffic accidents (RTAs), but obviously also having relevance in other spheres of work where traumatic injury might be encountered. Since the introduction of the multi-purpose machines in the mid 1970s, Devon fire appliances had carried oxygen resuscitators and rescue stretchers in addition to the basic first aid kit, but in recent years this provision has been further augmented with burns kits containing water-gel anti-burn agents and immobilisation kits with stiffneck collars. However, it was the extension of the 19-minute 'first response' requirement for the ambulance service from urban areas to the whole country in 1995 that triggered the next development. Ambulance policy over the previous years had tended towards greater flexibility in utilisation of the ambulance fleet, which produced efficiency savings and made better use of vehicles and crews, but also made it more difficult to guarantee attendance anywhere in Devon in the required time. The fire service, however, was already meeting a universal twenty-minute attendance over the whole of Devon except the most remote areas of moorland, so they were well-placed to help the ambulance service by providing a 'first response' in the remoter rural areas. Hence, the 'Co-responder' scheme was initiated.

'Co-responders' are individuals – firefighters in this case, but coastguards, National Park wardens or other people working in and familiar with the remoter areas in other schemes – who are trained in basic trauma care and life support skills. In the case of the fire service, the scheme initially involved the rural retained stations, being trialled at Moretonhampstead on Dartmoor. Co-responding firefighters must first have the basic first aid and the more advanced casualty care qualification as a basis. They then attend a specialist course run by West Country Ambulance Service at the end of which they take a practical and theoretical examination, as well as spending time working on front-line ambulances to gain practical experience. Co-responding stations have a number of such trained co-responders and the appliances carry a range of additional first-aid equipment including extra oxygen, Entonox pain relief, a trauma bag with dressings and additional resuscitation equipment, a burns kit, an immobilisation kit and an automatic defibrillator. Co-responders wear distinctive uniform and are alerted by a special tone over the normal alert network. Co-responding fire appliances make an initial response but do not preclude ambulance attendance – an ambulance always follows up the first responders.

Initially, the scheme was voluntary, with the stations themselves raising funds to buy equipment and training, but following the success of the pilot scheme and backing from the British Heart Foundation, who provided defibrillators, it has now become more formally established. Most co-responding stations are rural retained stations, but the scheme is now being extended to larger towns like Crediton and Plymstock – the latter being the first whole-time station to commence co-responder training. Following on from the pilot at Moretonhampstead, co-responder crews operate at Axminster, Chagford, Dawlish, Hatherleigh, Holsworthy, Ivybridge, Princetown, Seaton and Woolacombe, and the scheme is being steadily extended, with North Tawton the latest station to join. To date, the co-responder scheme has saved several lives, and participating fire crews have found the additional first aid training of immense value in their day-to-day work.

## FIRE VICTIM SUPPORT

Firefighters have always been aware of the effects of fires and other similarly-traumatic incidents on those unfortunate enough to suffer them, and there is a tradition in the fire service of endeavouring to help beyond the point of the immediate emergency. However, this is a role for which the fire service is neither resourced nor trained, so such efforts in the past have relied on goodwill and voluntary action. This was obviously an unsatisfactory state of affairs, and it was long felt that there was a need to provide some organised form of 'first help' in the wake of an incident before the formal agencies such as local housing offices and Social Services were able to act – particularly 'out of hours', when such agencies do not operate. In other words, what was needed was a support service that would arrive while the incident was still in progress and assist those affected to organise basics like food, shelter and clothing, as well as offering comfort, practical advice and help in dealing with problems like insurers or distraught relatives.

Such a service now exists in Devon and Cornwall, an initiative between the British Red Cross and the fire brigades. The Fire Victim Support Units are staffed by specially-trained Red Cross volunteers experienced in counselling as well as being versed in the practicalities of dealing with the aftermath of fire, flooding, storm damage and accidents of all kinds. The support units themselves consist of specially adapted motorhomes fitted out with communications equipment, stocked with blankets, hot drinks, foodstuffs and other necessities, and carrying a wide range of information sources covering everything from insurance to emergency accomodation, security services, salvage specialists and emergency repair or environmental clean-up contractors. Fire Victim Support Units are mobilised by the respective fire controls to all incidents where people have suffered loss of their homes or injury to someone they are close to. The firefighters are always glad to see the Support Unit arrive – a piece of the jigsaw that has long been missing.

## WHAT DOES THE FUTURE HOLD ?

It seems certain that the Devon Fire and Rescue Service will continue to place growing emphasis on community fire safety. It now seems obvious that trying to prevent fires, and therefore deaths and injuries from fire, should be the primary task of a humane fire service. However, this pro-active approach is relatively new and will doubtless become the focus of more attention in the future resulting in a gradual reduction in the number of destructive fires that occur in the home.

The long term future of the fire service, not only in Devon but throughout Britain, is likely to be one of declining workloads in terms of property fires. For Devon, however, fires in the rural environment make up a significant proportion of the total workload and this may be a more difficult problem to address. Dartmoor, Exmoor, Woodbury Common and general farmland present significant fire risks. In fact, the three moors together equal an area bigger than many English counties.

Preventing and extinguishing fires has become only part of the role of the modern fire service. Devon Fire and Rescue Service already attends numerous special service calls including road traffic accidents, flooding, water rescues, chemical spillages, rescue from heights or confined spaces. These calls now account for 20% of the operational workload and that is likely to increase as a proportion of a growing overall call total. The fire service has already recognised that it has a broader role to play in community safety generally and it is likely that the future will see it contributing to such things as road safety education campaigns.

The traditional approach to dealing with special service calls was for the fire brigade to utilise the equipment provided for firefighting at such incidents. That improvisatory approach demanded innovation and flexibility – but it has become increasingly unable to meet the demands of Health and Safety legislation. The future is already clear. Devon Fire and Rescue Service will in future train firefighters to deal with such incidents through many more specialised training courses. In addition, Devon will seek to acquire more specialist equipment designed for the task. One example of such dedicated capability is the newly-obtained mudmat – an inflatable walkway that can be laid over unstable surfaces such as soft mud thus enabling firefighters to safely reach trapped victims.

Of course all of these developments in the future depend upon adequate funding being provided for the Service and the last 20 years have seen continuously tight financial constraints. The Fire Authority and the Chief Fire Officer are constantly having to balance the available funds against the spending needs of the Service. The long term future on this front is anyone's guess! However, as this book goes to print at the end of the year 2000, the indications on spending are slightly more encouraging than has been the case in the preceeding decade.

So what will the Devon Fire and Rescue Service look like in in the future? Will it continue to be run by local government and will Devon continue to keep its own discreet service? The answer is that we simply do not know. However, this book is about Devon's firefighting services throughout the twentieth century – and we can learn a lot from the last 100 years. During that time, fire brigades in the United Kingdom have become far fewer in number and, as a consequence, much larger in size. In fact the numbers have shrunk from over 1,600 in 1939 to less than 60 in 1999. In Devon , we have likewise moved from a situation where almost every town had its own brigade to one single service for the whole of the county. The obvious question is – will that process of amalgamation continue in this new century? Will Devon Fire and Rescue Service be absorbed into some larger organisation? History suggests that it will. If there is to be continued change, it seems most likely that either Devon and Cornwall will combine or there will perhaps be one unified fire service for the whole of the south-west England. When will this happen? That is anyone's guess!

*In 1999 a new recruit was introduced into the DFRS. 'Cappa' a two-year-old black labrador is the latest weapon in the fight in the detection of arson. Sponsored by Zurich Services, Cappa and his handler, Firefighter Nick Miles, underwent training at Karenswood International Ltd in Worcester.*

*The dog's sense of smell is more than 400 times more sensitive than that of a human and is far better than any man-made detection equipment. Consequently minute traces of hydrocarbon accelerant can be indicatd with pin-point accuracy. Cappa and his handler are on call 24 hours a day and are regularly mobilised to incidents where arson is suspected.*

*Cappa (left) is pictured with Nick Miles along with another labrador, William, who accompanies Nick on visits as part of the community Fire Safety Initiative. The dogs are particularly popular on school visits.*

## EPILOGUE

The close of the twentieth century finds Devon with one of the most progressive and best-equipped of 'Shire' fire services. The appliance fleet is modern and well-fitted to the particular risks and tasks it faces. In particular, the 'punch' of the front-line appliances throughout the county, both in terms of equipment carried and crew capability, represents a huge advance on what was possible when the Devon Fire Brigade was formed in 1973, and Devon crews, whole-time and retained, routinely deal with incidents and hazards that would have lain well outside the scope of their forebears. Those of us who are nearing the end of our fire service careers have seen enormous changes in working practices, equipment, command and management and, not least, the incidence of fire and the suffering it causes. We may well wax nostalgic over the memory of a 'good going job', but we must own that the comparative rarity of serious fires causing injury and death are the greatest achievement of the modern fire service.

In the twenty-first century, the Devon Fire and Rescue Service will work to reduce still further the incidence and consequences of fire, while meeting the new challenges posed by road and other civil accidents, flooding and the effects of climate change, and the protection of our priceless environment from pollution of all types, however caused. That it has the experience, dedication and equipment to accomplish these tasks is more than evident from the evolution described in these pages.

*Fifteen years of progress – one of the last Devon Fire Brigade traditional appliances is replaced by a brand new MAN country area machine at Chagford in September 1995. The vehicles are much the same size but a world apart in technology, performance and capability.*

# A DEVON FIREFIGHTER'S ALBUM

## INCIDENTS

The image of a fire brigade is often seen as glamorous – never more so than in the days of fine brass helmets, many-buttoned tunics and broad belts with gleaming axes. The truth is that the firefighter's job has usually been hard and dirty, often distressing and occasionally comic. This selection of fires and 'special services' over the last century will give an idea of what Devon firefighting has been all about throughout the evolution of the modern Fire and Rescue Service.

*Damping down at the fire which gutted the premises of the West of England Sack Company in Exeter in 1936. Plenty of sacks seem to have survived but, as was so often the case in the days before BA and interior fire fighting, the building is severley damaged. In the background is the Merryweather sliding-carriage escape from the 1932 Exeter City pump escape, here with a line of hose taken aloft in the approved manner over the levers.*

# FIRES

*Right: Crowds flock to watch Hatherleigh fire-fighters at work on a thatch fire involving the New Inn (now the 'Tally Ho!') in 1926. This picture shows the traditional method of thatch fire-fighting; cut a break in the thatch ahead of the fire (at the left of the picture) and strip the burning thatch back from this as quickly as possible. More of a problem, of course, if there had been thatch on both sides of the outbreak. In fire service terms, this is a 'good stop'; the crew have been successful in containing the fire and limiting damage.*

*Left: Fire severely damages the Lion Inn, Colyton during the 1930s – a classic thatched roof fire that has spread into a slated lean-to extension and has a good hold. Note non-fire brigade personnel assisting operations, and the way the fire is being tackled from the outside. Today, BA crews would fight such a fire internally as well.*

*Right: Colyton again, with a fire in the roof severely damaging the town's fine parish church. A jet held by two firefighters is working inside the building.*

Above: In July 1952 a devastating fire ripped through Waycotts House Agents in Victoria Street, Paignton. The blaze was thought to have started in a shop adjoining and at one point threatened the whole of the main street. Crews from Paignton, Torquay, Brixham, Totnes and Newton Abbot prevented the blaze from spreading. A number of firefighters were injured including one who was blown down the stairs when a flashover occurred and another who suffered a cut tendon in his hand when he was struck by a falling slate.

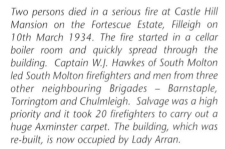

Two persons died in a serious fire at Castle Hill Mansion on the Fortescue Estate, Filleigh on 10th March 1934. The fire started in a cellar boiler room and quickly spread through the building. Captain W.J. Hawkes of South Molton led South Molton firefighters and men from three other neighbouring Brigades – Barnstaple, Torringtom and Chulmleigh. Salvage was a high priority and it took 20 firefighters to carry out a huge Axminster carpet. The building, which was re-built, is now occupied by Lady Arran.

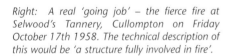

Right: A real 'going job' – the fierce fire at Selwood's Tannery, Cullompton on Friday October 17th 1958. The technical description of this would be 'a structure fully involved in fire'.

Severe flooding always stretches both the resources and the resourcefulness of the fire service. One of the worst flooding incidents in Devon occurred in the autumn of 1960 when heavy rains over Exmoor had the River Exe and its tributaries in full flood. Here, Crediton firefighters bring a boat into use for rescue work at Fordton, where the River Creedy has burst its banks; all the cottages here were severely damaged by the incident.

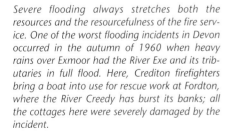

### The John Colley rescues

This is the fire at the Hotel Florence, Tor Vale, Torquay at quarter past one in the morning of Saturday 25th May, 1974 at which Torquay's Leading Fireman John Colley gained the George Medal for his actions. The 'Honours and Awards' printed in The London Gazette of Monday, 16th December 1974 outlined the circumstances of this award:

'In the early hours of the morning the Devon Fire Brigade answered a call to a fire at a three-storey guesthouse where it was reported that a number of people were trapped on the top floor. The ground floor and the first floor were on fire and the flames were licking at the face of the building. A wheeled escape ladder was pitched immediately to the second floor and a breathing apparatus team made an attempt to gain access to the upper floor by the main staircase, but was unsuccessful.

A covering jet of water was played over the first and second floor windows to protect the ladder from the flames and as the ladder was pitched to a top-storey bedroom window, cries for help were heard from the trapped people. By this time the head of the escape ladder was enveloped in thick smoke and threatened by flames but Leading Fireman Colley, without breathing apparatus, reached the level of a narrow window to the room and assisted a man to escape. Although by this time the fire was spreading rapidly and the heat and smoke were intensifying, he returned to the head of the ladder and rescued a girl. Leading Fireman Colley then went back again to rescue the third person who was known to be trapped in the room.

By this time the whole of the first floor of the building was incandescent and the floor of the top-storey was seen to be glowing with heat and cracking. The Officer managed to locate the man who was unconscious and trapped. After releasing the man he tried to drag him towards the window, but was overcome by heat and smoke and forced to leave the room. Personnel equipped with breathing apparatus then tried to gain access, but were unsuccessful because of the narrowness of the window.

Despite the deteriorating situation and in full knowledge of the dangers that awaited him, Leading Fireman Colley decided to make yet another attempt to rescue the man. After persistent and determined efforts, he managed to drag the victim towards the window and to manoeuvre him on to the back of another fireman waiting at the head of the wheeled escape. The Leading Fireman did not leave the building until after the carry-down had begun.

With a complete disregard for his own safety, Leading Fireman Colley displayed courage of the highest order in an extremely hazardous situation. He played a vital role in the rescue of two persons and was solely responsible for saving a third at great risk to his own life.'

This dramatic sequence of pictures shows the rescue of the man found unconscious and brought to safety to the head of the ladder by John Colley. The first picture shows the man at the moment he was passed out of the window onto the shoulders of the fireman at the head of the ladder; another fireman (ff Les Morris) mounts the ladder to assist. In the second picture the firefighter at the ladder head secures the victim for a carry-down. In the third picture the carry-down is in progress, with the firefighter carrying the unconcious man being aided by colleagues as John Colley climbs out of the window. The last photo shows an exhausted John Colley being helped to an ambulance by colleagues after carrying out rescue work in the finest traditions of the fire service.

*Right: A severe fire engulfed the Islander Bar on the end of Princess Pier, Torquay on the 16th of April 1974, the fire already having taken a hold on the structure before the crews arrived due to the timber construction and a stiff onshore breeze. The fire was thought to have started by a painter using a blowlamp to burn off the old paint.*

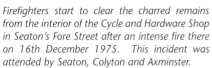

*Firefighters start to clear the charred remains from the interior of the Cycle and Hardware Shop in Seaton's Fore Street after an intense fire there on 16th December 1975. This incident was attended by Seaton, Colyton and Axminster.*

*Right centre: The fire thar ripped through the Tiverton Motel in the mid-1970's. Station Officer Percy Sowden of Tiverton was trapped beneath the front balcony when it collapsed a few minutes after this picture was taken. He fortunately escaped with only minor injuries. The appliance is an ex-Devon County Bedford/HCB WrT converted to a WrT/L by the Devon Fire Brigade, with a 135 ladder on a swing-down gantry.*

*Right: Budleigh Salterton's crew damping down after tackling a fierce blaze in an upholsterer's workshop at the rear of the Rolle Arms on 28th May 1977. This shows the tradional style of fire-fighting uniform still in use – black, cork-covered helmet, heavy double-breasted Melton wool tunic with belt and axe, Bata waterproof overtrousers and steel-reinforced rubber fire-boots, just replacing the original all-leather pattern at this time. Yellow helmets and short tunics were only a year or two away.*

A tangled web of hose at a 10-pump fire involving propane cylinders which occurred on Saturday 4th February 1978 at Lockyers Quay, Coxside, Plymouth. The fire was reported at 7:58 a.m. and involved a large stock of cylinders, many of which exploded and others of which discharged gas through rupture plates when they overheated. There were numerous explosions and fireballs as the gas ignited, and the incident threatened to escalate out of hand. Eventually, firefighters led by well-known Devon DO's Dibble and Fiddaman managed – at considerable risk – to start removing cylinders from the fire area so that it was possible to contain the fire. Even so, the incident kept crews busy for most of the day.

On 25th October 1981, this major fire devastated Maristow House, the former home of Lord Roborough and the Lopes family. The three-storey house on the banks of the Tavy near Milton Combe was empty at the time but was used as an adventure and study centre. A total of twelve appliances from all over the Plymouth and West Devon area were called to the blaze and Devon CFO John Killoran took personal charge of the fire-fighting effort. The South wing of the house had been gutted once before by fire, in 1952.

*Above & opposite top: Ilfracombe – Candar Hotel: One of the biggest fires to occur in Devon in recent years was the fatal outbreak involving the Victoria Arcade and Candar hotel in Ilfracombe, in some respects a re-run of the 1896 'Great Fire'. The blaze started on the night of 1st September 1983 in the arcade, and was already a severe fire when the first Ilfracombe pump commanded by SubO Ray Woofe arrived. At an early point in the incident a calor gas cylinder exploded, unfortunately killing the occupant of a flat and spreading the fire dramatically to other properties in the arcade and to the nearby Candar Hotel, from which many people had to escape or be led to safety by fire crews.*

*Ilfracombe has more than its fair share of major fires, owing mainly to the unusual mix of older property with intensive Victorian development. Large hotels, particularly ones past their prime, seem particularly susceptible to fire, and this blaze at the disused Beacon Castle Hotel in Granville Road occurred only three years after the Candar fire, although fortunately with less serious consequences. The call came at 2 a.m. and the fire was already through the roof when the first Ilfracombe pump arrived a few minutes later. The incident went to 10 pumps, and water had to be pumped from the sea over several hundred yards. Here, Ilfracombe's Metz TL is in use as a water tower at the height of the fire.*

*Crews were still in attendance and damping down well into the following day, when the building was declared unsafe and demolished. Note the steepness of the roads in both these pictures; Ilfracombe presents many operational problems for firefighters needing to access premises and pitch ladders.*

The Candar Hotel fire escalated rapidly to a twenty-pump attendance with two turntable ladders; appliances from as far away as Exeter were called in. It was two full days before the last pocket of fire was extinguished, and the protracted firefighting operations involved crews from all over North and Mid-Devon, with the Cornwall Fire Brigade also being called on for assistance in maintaining fire cover. Here at the height of the blaze, a turntable ladder is used as a water tower to direct a main firefighting stream into the upper storeys of the hotel.

Early on the morning of the General Election in May, 1989, officials arriving to set up the polling station in North Bovey found that the Glebe House Hotel, the largest building in the village, was well alight. The fire was 'persons reported' as, although the hotel was closed, staff were thought to be sleeping on the premises.

Initial attendance was made by retained crews from Moretonhampstead and Chagford, who arrived to find the three-storey main hotel building alight on all floors and a large two-storey annex threatened. BA teams entered the first and second floors to search for any sleeping staff and had a close call when the timberwork supporting a 150-gallon galvanised iron water tank in the roof gave way – the tank smashed straight down through all three floors into the basement and brought part of the roof with it! Fortunately, no one was seriously hurt, but the fire became an 8-pump incident and extensively damaged the main building; the annex was saved.

*This fire in April 1989 involved a former hotel on The Plains, Totnes, that had been converted into a shopping arcade containing craft units and small retail outlets. The fire took hold in the early hours of the morning and severely damaged the historic building. In this scene, taken at first light by brigade photographer Mark Wilkins, the Metz TL then stationed at Torquay is being used as a water tower, with Ff Les Morris on the head of the ladders.*

*This is a rear view of the fire at the derelict Northcliffe Hotel, Brixham. Due to the dangerous state of the building, an external attack only was mounted using hose reels and two turntable ladder monitors. Unfortunately for crews working at the rear of the building, the roof of the hotel was a flat span covered in tarmac and gravel, which meant that when the monitor jets struck the roof they were peppered with flying stones. To fight this fire water had to be relayed from Brixham Harbour some two hundred feet lower than the hotel.*

One of the largest thatched-roof fires ever to occur in Devon was on 15th June 1994 and involved an important historic property, Langford Court at Clyst Hydon near Cullompton – a house mentioned in the Domesday Book. The fire crews from Cullompton, Tiverton, Topsham, Exeter and Honiton were able to salvage most of the contents, but it was impossible to prevent the fire damaging much of the interior and destroying the large roof. This photograph, taken at the height of the fire, required a lengthy time exposure, hence the lack of firefighters in the picture; none of them stayed still long enough to register on film!

Over 30 calls were received to this spectacular blaze at the Buckleigh Laundry in Bideford on 7th February 1994. Firefighters from Bideford, Appledore, Torrington and Barnstaple used six jets and eight sets of breathing apparatus to get the fire under control. At the height of the blaze, temperatures of over 800°C caused glass in the roof to melt around the steel trusses and girders.

A famous Devon pub in trouble – the newly-thatched Cott Inn at Dartington, near Totnes, which suffered a serious roof fire in the early hours of the morning of 30th August 1989. Here, early in the incident, crews from Totnes and Buckfastleigh start the backbreaking job of stripping the burning thatch. The fire went to 8 pumps and was attended by crews from Totnes, Ashburton, Newton Abbot, Torquay and Paignton.

Redhayes House was a listed building on the outskirts of Exeter, which had been a fine stately home in its heyday. It was almost derelict when a disastrous fire broke out around midnight on August 1996. First crews on scene from 32 Blue Watch found the building well alight and no water nearby. Sub Officer Eric Smith made pump 6 and requested the hose-laying lorry, as the nearest supply proved to be a mile away. The incident was attended by pumps from Exeter, Topsham and Ottery St Mary.

In August 1998 a large fire ripped through a group of historic thatched properties at Kingsteignton, Newton Abbot. This was a major and protracted incident involving crews from Newton Abbot, Teignmouth, Torquay, Bovey Tracey and Moretonhampstead. Here, a hydraulic platform is being used to reach over properties bordering the road to attack fires involving outbuildings in a rear courtyard.

Firefighters tackle a blazing speedboat on Meadfoot Beach, Torquay, on 10th May 1990. Here, Torquay's Green Watch are using a light portable pump and a branch. No shortage of water on this occasion! The fire followed a blast at sea after the boat had been refuelled at Torquay harbour – a young woman received burns when she was blown into the sea as fuel vapour exploded.

The long, dry spell of weather in March and April of 1997 followed several wet springs when little controlled burning could take place on Dartmoor, Exmoor and Woodbury Common. This led to large areas of dead vegetation accumulating, representing a far greater fuel load than usual so that when fires occurred in the dry, windy conditions they frequently reached severe proportions. There were a large number of multi-pump incidents throughout the county, culminating in the huge fire at Trendlebere Down near Bovey Tracey on the afternoon of 7 April. The initial attendance, crews from Bovey Tracey, Moretonhampstead and Chagford, were completely overwhelmed by the rapid fire spread, fanned by a strong south-easterly wind.

The main means of tackling heath fires is still the traditional beater, and crews of moorland stations become very adept at using these every spring! A fit and willing crew so equipped can tackle a surprisingly large fire, but the work requires a high degree of stamina.

In a rural county like Devon, incidents involving animals are relatively commonplace, and this rescue of a bullock from boggy ground near Cullompton by crews from Cullompton and Exeter is typical. Exeter Station Officer Mark Wilkins is 'comforting' the stricken animal (keeping well away from the end that kicks!) while other crew members position lines and strops to allow the beast to be winched to safety using a tractor.

'Well alight' is the only possible description for this hapless motor coach, which caught fire on the 'banjo' of the approach ramp to the Dartmouth ferry at Kingswear. The photograph was taken a few moments after a crew from Brixham arrived in their brand-new Dennis DS appliance to find the vehicle completely engulfed in flames. November 1992.

A sad sight – a historic Devon longhouse heavily involved in fire at Newton St Cyres. Once again, the thatched roof is the villain of the piece, and when it is as well-alight as this there is little even the best-equipped crews can do other that attempt to salvage furniture and other household goods. With historic properties like this, the local crew will usually have made a risk visit so that they will be aware of the location of any particularly important architectural features or valuable antiques and paintings. This enables firefighting and salvage efforts to be concentrated on the most important items.

A motorist had a lucky escape when he ploughed beneath the back of a lorry that had broken down on the A30. It took crews from Okehampton, Exeter and Chagford over an hour to free him; the Okehampton appliance seen here was used as an anchor point to winch the car out from beneath the lorry once this had been jacked up.

Far more serious was the crash of a British Airways (ex-Brymon) De Havilland 'Dash 7' four-engined turboprop airliner near Ashburton in 1999. The plane, on a test flight, apparently went into an irrecoverable stall at low altitude and ploughed into farmland just east of the town, killing both pilots and presenting the Ashburton retained crew with a major fire situation. This was a very difficult incident, with the wreckage of the plane strewn over the upper slopes of a steep field inaccessible to normal fire appliances. Even the purpose-built all-terrain crash tender from Exeter Airport had difficulty in reaching the incident, and it was some hours before everything was made safe for the ensuing investigation. Here, firefighters in BA are tackling a fire involving one of the engines.

A Cessna four-seater light aircraft was forced to crash-land shortly after take off in a field near Torrington. The four people on board suffered serious injuries but all survived. Firefighters from Torrington, Barnstaple and Bideford dealt with the incident in December 1999.

The last major fire of the twentieth century in Devon was the 20-pump blaze that occurred in the Paignton plastics factory of Wilton Bradley on Thursday 9th December 1999. The fire, which broke out late in the evening, led to parts of Paignton being evacuated due to the poisonous fumes given off by tons of burning rubber and plastic footwear. This protracted incident lasted for more than three days and involved crews from all over South Devon as well as Exeter and Plymouth. Here, as the fire develops in high winds, two hydraulic platforms, from Torquay and Exeter, are used as water towers.

The factory was totally destroyed in the fire and subsequently had to be demolished. In these two views taken by the Devon fire investigating officer StnO Doug Smith, the extent of the damage can be seen. The first view was taken from the head of the Bronto hydraulic platform on the Saturday morning more than 36 hours after the fire broke out, and shows the main building still smouldering as SWEB engineers and relief crews work on the incident. The second view shows the utter devastation resulting from this intense fire, with building, contents and external services reduced to a jumbled pile of wreckage resembling a war zone. The sad thing is that a simple sprinkler system would almost certainly have contained the initial fire and prevented this substantial loss.

*St Peter's School in Budleigh Salterton suffered a serious roof fire on 17th. August 1987, fortunately during the school holidays. Budleigh Salterton's crew faced a well-developed fire on arrival.*

*Thatch roof fires are still a regular occurence in Devon, as here in Kenton near Exeter on 12th October 1987. As in the previous century, thatched terraces are particularly vulnerable, and it is rarely possible to confine a fire to one cottage. This entire row was affected, in spite of the best efforts of crews from Exeter and Topsham.*

*Firefighting in foul weather can be pretty miserable as here when, in the teeth of February gale in 1991, crews from Paignton and Torquay tackle a blaze which gutted a disused warehouse in the goods yard of Paignton railway station. High winds and torrential rain hampered operations, while the fire had to be fought from outside as the threat of collapse made it too dangerous to enter the building.*

This fire at the Chase Webb factory in Plymouth in 1986 claimed the lives of three employees and taxed the resources of the Devon Fire Brigade to the utmost – it became a 25-pump incident involving virtually every station in West and South Devon. Here, a Plymouth RS appliance stands in front of the huge factory, which is totally involved in fire, while a BA team wearing sets fitted with long-duration 'yellow' cylinders (the colour code of the cylinder jackets) enter a side door. BA crews were beaten back by the severity of the fire and it was many hours before the bodies of the victims could be located and recovered. The incident stripped the City of Plymouth and surrounding area of fire cover, requiring back-up moves from all over Devon and Cornwall, and took many hours to bring under control.

A major incident of an earlier era was this fire at Lawsons the ironmongers in Plymouth city centre in 1968. Most of the Plymouth City Brigade is in attendance with the Dennis F8 PE and turntable ladder from Green Bank in the foreground. The emergency tender and a further pair of Dennis F series are parked further up the street. There seems to be a lack of crowd control with spectators pressing close about the appliances and well within the danger zone.

One of the best-known fires in Devon was that which destroyed the Dingles department store in Royal Parade, Plymouth, just before Christmas in 1988. Greenbank's appliances responded to a routine 'fire alarms sounding' at the premises at 22.03 on Monday, 19th. December. WrLs 501, 502 and TL 504 with Station Officer Sallis in charge arrived at 22.07 to find a serious fire developing in the upper levels of the store following an incendiary attack by animal rights terrorists. At 22.09 the first assistance message 'Make pumps 4' was sent, and the senior West Division officer, DO Ross Durbin, was sent on.

The fire spread rapidly and soon reached major incident status; pumps were made up throughout the first hour, with 'Make pumps 12' being sent at 23.02. By 23.30 there were 90 personnel on scene, and the Chief Officer was en route to take charge. At 00.20 he arrived and pumps were made 15, TLs 3; by 00.31 there were 25 BA wearers committed. The situation continued to deteriorate; at 01.32, there was a collapse at a BA entry point, followed by a flashover on the fourth floor. All BA crews were withdrawn as the building was now unsafe, and the external attack was stepped up. TLs were made 4, HP's 1. By 02.28 there were 110 firefighters attacking the fire using 10 jets with 5 aerials being used as water towers. At 04.27 the CFO was able to send a 'fire surrounded' message (meaning that further spread had now been prevented) and the 'Stop' message (no further increase in current level of attendance) was sent at 05.01.

With some crews having been involved for more than six hours, reliefs were implemented, and in all some 25 pumps from all over south and west Devon were in attendance, as well as numerous 'specials' including the emergency tenders from Crownhill and Torquay and five of Devon's six aerials – the Greenbank TL and Camel's Head HP plus Exeter and Torquay's TLs and the 'spare' TL from the training school. With the necessary back-up moves to preserve fire cover and a large number of reliefs required during the protracted incident, there were very few stations in south and west Devon or East Cornwall that did not have some involvement.

Short-lived 'Aspirations' gone up in smoke; this fire on Paignton's ground occurred at 22.10 on the evening of 6th February 1989. The shop – which was brand new – sold bedding and furniture, and there were occupied flats above. Thirty per cent of the premises was badly damaged, and several people were led to safety.

Firefighters from Hatherleigh, Torrington, Holsworthy, Barnstaple, Bideford and South Molton were called to a thatch roof on fire at the Bull and Dragon pub in Meeth. As can be seen here, the crews saved much of the roof by making fire breaks in the thatch ahead of the spreading fire using the traditional tactic. However, in comparison with the historical thatch fires illustrated earlier in this book, which usually resulted in the total loss of the roof and first floor, and often the whole building, damage is comparitively slight. What makes the vital difference is the speed with which the modern fire service reaches the fire, and the ready availability of water, ladders and men. Devon fire controllers despatch at least five pumps to any report of a thatched roof on fire.

On 18th February 1991 an empty diesel train (a multiple unit) was travelling from Plymouth to Newton Abbot when the rear coach caught fire at Littlehempston near Totnes. The driver managed to uncouple the leading units before the fire engulfed the whole train. Firefighters from Totnes had to negotiate extremely difficult terrain to reach the incident. The rear coach of the train was completely destroyed and partially collapsed onto the track.

*30th September 1993 saw a serious fire on Topsham's ground, when the first floor of Swain's Court – a residential conversion of older outbuildings – became heavily involved. Here, flames roar out of a dormer window as a BA team enters an adjoining window with a hose line to try and prevent lateral spread.*

*BA wearing can be pretty exhausting – here are two Plymouth firefighters recovering after a 'hard wear' at the Lawson's fire illustrated on page 152. The firefighter on the right is Ray Hargreaves who became an assistant chief officer in Devon.*

*Not all fires in rural areas involve small or picturesque structures. This feed mill at Risdon, north of Okehampton, caught fire in the early hours of the morning, the fire involving the extensive system of feed pipework, trunking and conveyors. Here, a BA team from Chagford enter the top of the mill storage complex from the head of a 135 ladder to carry out ventilation and to tackle hotspots in the conveyor system above the bins. Crews from Okehampton, Hatherleigh, North Tawton and Chagford attended, together with a hydraulic platform from Plymouth and the hose-laying lorry and emergency tender from Barnstaple.*

Certainly the smallest house fire ever attended by the Devon Fire and Rescue Service was this unfortunate incident at the Babbacombe Model Village in Torquay. Ironically, the model that caught fire was atually the scene representing a house on fire! A short circuit in the wiring of the special effects lighting soon made the fire all to realistic. Here members of the Torquay crews inspect the damage the following morning.

Agricultural implements can often be prone to fire, and have a habit of doing so in the most inaccessible locations. To reach this burning Porta-Loda, crews from Okehampton and Chagford had to negotiate over a mile of rutted track and cross several steep and bumpy fields. Here the Okehampton crew are damping down the hot metal of the machine, which has also set part of the field on fire.

A Ford Transit motorhome burning fiercely on the forecourt of a petrol station at Newport, Barnstaple in 1999. A crew from Braunton fought the blaze, as Barnstaple appliances were already committed on another incident. Motor caravans and caravans present a particular hazard in a popular holiday area like Devon; they are somewhat fire-prone and usually involve LPG cylinders.

## SPECIAL SERVICES

Firemen from Exeter City Brigade make safe a lorry which overturned at Clyst Honiton on 9th October 1970. The appliance appears to be the Bedford TK PE running without the escape. Exeter already had yellow leggings and hi-visibility jackets at this stage; it would be some time before the rest of Devon caught up.

Firefighters from Topsham battle to release the driver of a car involved in a head-on collision with a lorry near Oaklands Garage on the Sidmouth to Exeter road. The twin hoses in the foreground are the hydraulic supply lines of the Hurst hydraulic rescue equipment, which is here being used to 'spread' the impacted front wheel and suspension away from the footwell area of the car.

Bottom Right: Like most major trunk roads, the M5 motorway sees its fair share of drama, but no incident had more potential for a major disaster than this December 1987 crash at Sowton, near Exeter, involving a fully-laden Calor Gas tanker carrying propane. The lorry overturned at speed on the southbound carriageway, bursting through the crash barriers to finish up some way down the northbound carriageway, straddling all three lanes and the A30 slip-road.

Miraculously, no other vehicle was involved, but the tanker developed a serious leak from the discharge valve. Propane is heavier than air and flows down into drains or other low-lying areas, where it forms a lethal fire and explosion risk. In this case, there was a campsite adjacent to the motorway embankment which was threatened, and the motorway was closed while firefighters from Exeter and Topsham stopped the leak by applying a water spray to the leaking valve. As gas leaked out from the pressurised tank, it expanded, giving a refrigerating effect which froze the water spray and stopped the leak until another tanker could be brought up and the cargo transferred. The accident caused widespead chaos on one of the busiest pre-Christmas shopping days.

One of the worst RTAs in Devon occurred on 22nd October 1989. The accident took place on the A30 Exeter–Honiton road beneath the railway bridge at the western end of the Honiton bypass, when a coach skidded on the sharp left-hand bend and crushed an oncoming car against the abutment of the bridge. All five occupants of the car died at the scene, and the retained crews from Honiton and Ottery St Mary, together with whole-time crews from Exeter, faced the harrowing task of freeing the remains of the victims.

Another tragic RTA occurred early in the morning of 21st April 1992 on Newton Abbott's station ground when a 32-ton articulated lorry ploughed into a concrete bridge pier on the A381, killing the driver on impact. The vehicle was delivering food to a supermarket in Torquay, and the unfortunate driver is believed to have fallen asleep at the wheel. Crews from Newton Abbot were quickly on the scene, but there was nothing they could do other than recover the body from the severely damaged remains of the tractor unit.

Probably the worst accident black spot in Devon has been the road junction at Woodleigh Cross on the A30 west of Exeter, where a minor road crosses this high-speed trunk road by a staggered crossroads. The junction has been the scene of numerous RTAs including several fatalities. Crews from Chagford and Exeter attended this 1994 incident, when a car collided at high speed with a lamp standard on the junction, severely trapping the driver. Here, firefighters stabilise the lamp standard using a short extension ladder and a hydrant key while their colleagues work with paramedics to free the driver. Regrettably, he did not survive. A flyover is now being constructed to alleviate the problems at this notorious location.

*This spectacular crash involving a milk tanker on the Winkleigh–Torrington road occurred in 1996. The vehicle left the road approaching a culvert over a deep gulley containing a stream, and plunged over the side of the embankment, landing upside-down in the stream. Miraculously, the driver was thrown clear and suffered only minor injuries, but a serious pollution incident was declared when milk started to leak into the watercourse. Milk is a very potent contaminant as it leaches oxygen from the water, killing fish and other aquatic life.*

*The incident was attended by Hatherleigh and Chulmleigh retained crews, who made the scene safe and assisted an Environment Agency team in containing the pollution and recovering the rest of the tanker's cargo. The appliance shown is 061 from Chulmleigh, one of the final batch of 'multis' bodied by Carmichael and delivered in 1980. It was replaced a short while later by a new MAN WrL.*

*This 1998 accident also occurred on the high-speed A30 at Merrymeet Junction, Whiddon Down, when a car struck the roundabout at high speed and rebounded into a road sign, killing the driver on impact. Crews from Chagford, Okehampton and Moretonhampstead rescued the remaining three passengers, one of whom was severly trapped in the rear of the vehicle. Three sets of hydraulic rescue equipment were used in this protracted extrication.*

*Firefighters from Exeter's Green Watch at the scene of a train crash in Riverside Yard, Exeter on 18th July 1991. The driver of a shunting locomotive was killed when his train struck another carrying stone from Meldon Quarry. Hydraulic spreading equipment is here being used to release the unfortunate man's body.*

*In 1988, the Cobbaton Combat Collection at Umberleigh bought several Russian-built T34 tanks that had been serving in the Czechoslovakian Army. En route to their final destinations, the haulier parked them up for a few days on the edge of the tiny village of Hele, near Cullompton. Over the next few days, the local children took great delight in climbing over, under and inside these 34 tonne monsters.*

*Each night, after school, the children became more and more adventurous: first getting into the turret, then engaging the ignition and starting it, and finally getting it into gear (all very hard to do – especially as all the instructions were written in Czechoslovakian). As the tank lurched forward across the parking area, the children 'baled out' in panic and left it to run on its own. The tank veered wildly from left to right as it went through a hedge into a field. At this point it had two options. If it went left, it would run onto the northbound carriageway of the M5 and join the traffic to Bristol, or, it could go right onto the main Westcountry rail link to London. This photograph shows the tank after having tried to scale the 12-foot retaining wall onto the railway link. Mike Nevitt, the Officer-in-Charge said 'I think it is amazing that you can go to the smallest, most remote Devon village and still find a 14 year old, Czechoslovakian-speaking tank driver!'*

## Appliances

Devon, with its wide mixture of risks and challenging road network, has always posed problems for those specifying fire appliances for the county. The result has been that Devon has had to 'go its own way' in a number of aspects of appliance design, and many innovations that have now become 'standard features' have Devon origins. The evolution of the various Devon 'specials' have been described and illustrated in the text, so this section concentrates on illustrating a few examples of the more interesting designs, and on portraying the current fleet.

*The location of this graveyard of old manual fire engines is not recorded, but the machine in the centre is an eighteenth century manual that served for many years at Colyton in east Devon.*

*Topsham Fire Brigade about 1900 with a late model large Merryweather manual pump drawn by a pair of horses. Relatively small and stocky animals with good agility were favoured for fire brigade work. This is very typical of many Devon town brigades at this time.*

When the more rural brigades converted to motor fire appliances they often purchased either second hand or rather outmoded machines that were available for a more economical price. This Dennis pump was acquired by the Okehampton parade in 1927, but is essentially to the 1914 design with solid tyres. Nevertheless, such machines were a huge advance on manual or steam-powered appliances.

Bideford's famous 'Grenville' – a solid-tyred Merryweather of 1927 vintage (late for a solid-tyred machine; pneumatics were usually deemed sufficiently reliable by then) with the usual 'Hatfield' 250-g.p.m. major pump and a further 'Hatfield' 150-g.p.m. trailer pump in addition. Seen outside the refurbished fire station opened in 1928.

Here is Torquay's 1920 version of the classic Merryweather motor pump – a later version with a horizontal air vessel above the pump, but without first-aid apparatus and hosereel. The machine has the pneumatic-tyre conversion common during the 1930s on older solid-tyred machines, and has a conventional firebell in place of Merryweather's pedal-operated gong. The escape is also by Merryweather, being an early sliding-carriage trussed design, and appears to be the one previously carried by the horsed escape van.

In 1935 the Newton Abbot Urban District Fire Brigade acquired a new appliance that was a rather obvious crib of the 1933 Exeter machine on the same type of chassis. Newton Abbot went for larger lockers and a three section ladder, but the machines were otherwise extremely similar. The same type of trailer pump was towed in both cases. At right is a rear view of the Exeter City 'New World' fire appliance showing the accommodation for the crew along the centre of the body work and the side mounting of the Bayley escape ladder.

Paignton were another brigade to acquire a modern motor fire appliance in the wake of the Riverdale Report, in the shape of this Leyland 'Cub' pump-escape CDV 592. This machine is unusual for such a late-model appliance in having traditional Braidwood bodywork with side seating rather than the (much safer) enclosed cross-bench design. This machine was named 'Bertha' and carried a Morris lightweight 50-foot trussed escape.

*Above: The unique TL/P stationed at Ilfracombe. This one-off appliance was placed in service by the Devon County Fire Service in 1965, using the 60-ft wartime Merryweather turntable ladders off the old Austin Utility TL GXN 203. The ladders were modified for power operation and mounted on the rear of a new Bedford TK chassis which was equipped with HCB bodywork incoporating a pump, 6-man crew cab and equipment lockers to create what the Americans would describe as a 'Combination Appliance'. It remained in service until replaced by a conventional TL in the early 1980s. The appliance is still in existence – the photograph was taken at a recent Blandford Fire Engine Rally.*

*Left centre and below: Another unique appliance with Devon origins – the experimental 'Brigadier' Wrl/Rescue built by Winkleigh-based Reynolds Boughton & Co, specialist vehicle builders in 1986. Reynolds-Boughton build many airport crash tenders, but this was their first essay into regular fire appliances. The machine had the engine mounted, bus-style, at the rear of the cab and also followed bus practice with large folding exit doors on the cab nearside. Otherwise, the machine followed the Devon 'multi-purpose' specification, and was trialled at Exeter in 1987, where these pictures were taken. However, the DFRS did not take to the design, and the sole example was finally sold to Buckinghamshire.*

## PEOPLE & EVENTS

Being a firefighter has always been about much more than merely responding to fires. Fire brigades are very much part of the fabric of society, a highly-visible expression of our humane attitudes. In the days of independent brigades, there was also a large element of civic pride in the local fire brigade, the size and quality of which was seen to reflect on the status and wealth of the town. These days, towns are still proud of their firefighters, but the support is mutual and manifests itself in many ways and through many different sorts of event – charitable, educational, civic and social. Here are just some of them.

*Above: Gals to the fore. Devon has welcomed an increasing number of female firefighters into the modern service but women in the fire service are nothing new, as this squad of NFS firewomen demonstrates. These girls have just finished their training at Torquay in 1943, but their role was no sinecure and many of them finished up very much 'in the line of fire'.*

*Right: Fair day in Bideford, and old and new fire engines parade around the sports ground. This manual pump is somewhat 'over-horsed and under-manned' – but it makes a fine sight nevertheless. Many people are fascinated by veteran fire appliances like this.*

*The children's Christmas party at Exeter Fire Station in 1934 with Chief Fire Officer Richards as Father Christmas. This popular event is still held at many fire stations throughout the County.*

*A temporary stucture was constructed to enable ladders to be pitched to carry out rescue drills at the 'Wings for Victory' display in Bideford during the last war. Note the brass helmets still being worn, and the faithful Bideford 1927 'Grenville' appliance – still on solid tyres, and still giving good service.*

These young 'recruits' in Totnes are getting their message across, transported through the streets in the annual carnival procession during the 1960s, starting outside the old Broomborough Hospital.

Devon County Fire Service Chief Fire Officer Willoughby Drake presents Long Service and Good Conduct Medals (awarded for twenty years' unblemished service) to members of 'A' Division at Ottery St Mary fire station in December 1958. The recipients were: Station Officer Ken Norman, Station Officer Fred Murrin, Leading Fireman Leslie Woodman, Fireman E. McCardle, Leading Fireman E. Foxwell and Leading Fireman W. Selley.

Children's Christmas party at Torquay Fire Station, Newton Road, in 1958, taken a year after the new station opened. The photo was taken in front of the 1939 Leyland/Metz Turntable ladder – a wonderful climbing frame by any standard – which had been moved from its original home in the cramped station behind Corporation Buildings in Market Street.

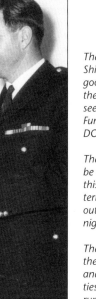

These two ladies are Mrs Olive Seaford – on the left – and Mrs Doris Shinner, who for many years ran a stall in Totnes Market selling goods in aid of the Fire Service National Benevolent Fund. Between them they raised thousands of pounds for the fund. Here, they are seen receiving a framed certificate for their good works from the Fund, presented to them by the then South Division Commander, DO Bob Chandler.

Their contributions throughout the years enabled South Division to be one of the highest fund-raisers in Devon for the 'Ben' Fund. To this day, Totnes Station is still one of the most successful stations in terms of contributions. Their annual Carol Service is always a sell-out, and they organise events ranging from whist drives and bingo nights to car boot sales.

The Fire Service National Benevolent Fund supports firefighters and their families through injury, disability or death in the line of duty, and runs recuperation centres with specialised physiotherapy facilities that have helped many an injured firefighter to get 'back on the run'. Their work is vital to the welfare of all firefighters and the profits from this book will benefit the fund.

On the run for charity. Exeter's White Watch (and Welephant) take to the streets on 25th June 1988 to raise money for the Great Ormond Street Children's Hospital. Here they are leaving Dane's Castle.

Members of Exeter's Blue Watch raised £1,653 for children with cystic fibrosis by pulling a fire engine through the streets of the city on 29th January 1992.

Fire service personnel have traditionally been involved in all manner of fundraising stunts. One of the most original was surely this re-enactment of the famous 'Lynmouth Lifeboat Pull', when a lifeboat was manhandled over the 15 miles of hilly road from Lynton to Porlock during a fierce storm in the early years of the twentieth century. The marathon effort was made to enable the boat to be launched in the quieter waters of Porlock Bay when conditions at Lynmouth were too rough to allow a rescue mission in response to an SOS from the steamship Forest Hall.

Here, a specially-constructed replica of a nine-teenth-century oared lifeboat retraces the route – in somewhat more clement weather, it must be said – pulled by firefighters from three North Devon stations with a direct connection to the sea: Coombe Martin, Ilfracombe and Woolacombe. The event raised several thou-sand pounds to enable the RNLI to equip the Ilfracombe lifeboat crew with up-to-date pagers. In coastal areas, the RNLI, coastguard and fire service work closely to provide rescue services.

KJY 999G, one of the Plymouth Leyland Beaver multi purpose appliances photographed immediately after repainting into Devon Fire Brigade colours in 1973. These machines always remained in Plymouth owing to their size, and were replaced by Dennis RS appliances in the early 1980s.

The Plymouth City emergency tender was a locally built machine with bodywork by Mumfords, fully equipped to the home office ET type 'A' specification. It was built in 1967 and remained in service until replaced by one of the new Dodge G12 ET/CU machines stationed at Greenbank and then subsequently at Crownhill.

The Plymouth City AEC/Merryweather 100 foot hydraulic turntable ladder of 1961, which replaced the wartime utility appliance at Greenbank. This appliance was re-chassised in 1981 with new Shelvoke and Drewry running gear; latterly it saw service as a reserve and training appliance. This photograph amply demonstrates why the Plymouth style of chrome hub cap was known to generations of firemen as a Sabrina.

*A 1953 Dennis F8/Dennis WrT tender based at Kingsbridge; it was withdrawn in 1977 and replaced by a 'Multi', by which time it was based at the volunteer station at Hartland.*

*Exeter's pride and joy in the last years of the independent city brigade was this Rolls Royce engined Dennis F49 pump, affectionately known as the Flying Pig; it was widely regarded as the fastest fire engine in the county.*

*Over the years the Dennis D series multi-purpose machines received a number of upgrades, such as strobe beacons to improve conspicuity. Here is a second series Dennis on the run as 421 at Seaton.*

The most modern turntable ladders in Devon is this Magirus thirty metre version with rescue cage mounted on an Iveco chassis and stationed at Crownhill fire station in Plymouth. It was purchased to replace the Metz ladder written off in a road accident in 1994. A similar but older ladder is now used for training and reserve purposes.

A Cummins-engined Dennis RS '237' appliance with JDC bodywork as a WrL/Rescue, seen at Paignton as 181.

The first series of Dennis DS 155/JDC-bodied compact WrL/Rescue appliances had more traditional fully-painted coachwork and black wheels. Here is 271 at Moretonhampstead – the first co-responding appliance in Devon.

*Devon's sole Camiva TL, built on a Dennis F127 'Low-level' chassis with bodywork by JDC. The french Camiva EMA30 ladders with rescue cage are of 30-metre (100-foot) reach and are fully computer-controlled to ensure ladder safety under all working conditions. The machine is now at Barnstaple as 014, but was placed in service as 174 at Torquay, as seen here.*

*Taken at Camel's Head fire station in Plymouth, 484 was the first of Devon's 28-metre Swedish-designed 'Bronto Skylift' Aerial Ladder Platforms. It is mounted on a Volvo FL10 chassis with bodywork by Angloco Fire Engineering of Batley, West Yorkshire.*

*The second of the Volvo FL10/Bronto 28.2 TI ALPs, built at a lower overall height that the original machine to clear the lower appliance bay roof at Station 32 Exeter, where it is stationed as 324.*

*A cuckoo in the nest. Appliance shortages in the early 1980s led to the purchase of a small batch of Volvo FL6.14 WrL/Rescue appliances with bodywork by Saxon – a large machine for Devon's narrower roads. Here is Teignmouth's 301; they also have a second WrL version as 302. Two more similar appliances are at Bideford, and two at Totnes, with one in the reserve/training fleet.*

*Tiverton has two more 'Cuckoos', a pair of Mercedes 1124F /Carmichaels, one with full WrL/Rescue capability, the other running as a WrT, 441 and 442 respectively. A third Mercedes/Carmichael is 012, the Barnstaple retained appliance.*

*Between the end of RS production and the introduction of the current Sabre, Dennis offered the Rapier, an advanced premium appliance with air suspension and a six speed automatic gearbox. There are three of these machines in the Devon fleet, used as the retained pumps at Exeter and Torquay and as the first-away appliance at station 28 Newton Abbot. This is the Exeter retained machine, 323.*

*Current front-line appliance for whole-time/urban stations is the Dennis SFD 133C Sabre/JDC, in either WrL/Rescue or WrT spec.*

The second batch of Dennis DS155 WrT/L have JDC body work with unpainted alloy sides. This is 121 from North Tawton.

First series Saxon bodied MAN country-area compact appliance. This is 371 based at Colyton in East Devon.

The latest batch of MAN country-area appliances has bodywork by JDC; it has the same MAN 10/224F chassis and is to full WrL/Rescue specification, but with far more effective visibility aids.

For difficult moorland areas there is a 4x4 version of the country appliance based on a Mercedes 917AF chassis with bodywork by Carmichael to WrT/Rescue specification. This is a co-responding appliance, 562 based at Princetown.

Devon has one example of a home designed light fire appliance with bodywork constructed by the Service workshops. The chassis is a Mercedes 814D 4x4 and the machine is based at Devon's last volunteer station at Kingston in the South Hams.

Demountable unit 010 with POD 10, the environmental unit for the northern area of the county based at Barnstaple.

This unique vehicle is the specialist rescue unit 488 based at Camel's Head in Plymouth. The appliance is based on a Mercedes Unimog 4x4 chassis with special low ground pressure tyres to enable it to cross boggy ground. The bodywork is by JDC and incorporates a powerful front-mounted winch.

*One of four 4x4 general purpose vehicles used to transport men and equipment to difficult locations. This Ford Ranger is based at Exmouth to cover risks on Woodbury Common.*

*One of the four new ICVs based in the County – 507 is the Plymouth area vehicle based at Greenbank Fire Station. The machines were built by the Service workshops using Mercedes Vito turbodiesel vans as a basis.*

*Fireboat Vigiles, the last piece of equipment acquired for the DFRS in the 20th century. Delivered in November 1999 and placed in service in March of 2000, it is one of the most advanced fire/rescue craft in the world.*

*Third World Aid. In April 1989 the Devon Fire and Rescue Service donated a Dennis 'D' fire appliance to the Gaborone City Fire Brigade in Botswana, central Africa. The ex-Plymouth vehicle was completely refurbished at the East Division workshops before being flown out. Pictured are the workshop mechanics who prepared the appliance: left to right – Peter Bird, Mike Bevan, the late Brian Phillips, Mike Hillier and Tony Chudley. Since then, Devon has continued to assist fire brigades in Africa, Albania and Colombia, South America with donations of equipment and training materials and by assisting in training of personnel. Another ex-Devon Dennis serves Tirana City Fire Brigade in Albania, and Devon personnel have made training and exchange visits to many countries.*

*Divisional Officer Paul Young (now Devon's CFO) presents the 1988 Divisional Winner's Shield for East Division to the winning team in the Annual Fire Service Quiz. The team from Exeter's Green Watch subsequently won the Brigade final and went on to the Regional level where they were beaten into second place. Left to right: Dene Schrimpf, Adrian Freeman, Paul Young, Mark Wilkins, Gary Clement and Graham Jackson. In the background are their Watch colleagues.*

*Fire station open days are another long-standing tradition and are events which serve many functions, from a good opportunity to offer fire safety advice to the forging of closer community links. Here, firefighters from Torquay stage a spectacular display, as well as offering people a chance to experience a 'flight' on a hydraulic platform.*

*Every year the firefighters of Torquay's Blue Watch embark on a charity fund raising event. This started many years ago as a bike ride around local stations – stopping over here and there for one or two nights to catch breath, have a few beers, and collect more money for the chosen charity. Each year, the week's events have become more adventurous, as shown in this picture of our intrepid colleagues in 1999 on top of Scafell Pike as part of their 'Three Peaks Challenge – an ascent of the highest mountains in England (Scafell Pike), Wales (Snowdon) and Scotland (Ben Nevis) – all, of course, undertaken on the watch's days off.*

*The charity chosen in 1999 was the local 'Friends of Special Needs Children' (FOSNEC) who specifically needed money for a water therapy unit in Torbay. This was by far the biggest challenge that Blue Watch had undertaken – and achieved. They climbed nearly 3,500m, travelled 1,400 miles and raised £3250. A great result by all concerned.*

## APPENDIX 1    DEVON FIRE BRIGADES BEFORE 1900

This is a list of those towns known to have had a fire brigade or fire engine at or before the turn of the century. It is by no means a complete list, as there may well be others listed in sources such as individual parish records that were not available at the time the original list of British fire brigades was compiled (1903). We have added such Devon brigades as were recorded to exist in other sources.

Ashburton (Widely held to third oldest British brigade, established in 1750)
Axminster
Bampton
Barnstaple
Bicton
Bideford
Bovey Tracey
Bradninch
Braunton
Brixham
Broadclyst
Buckfastleigh
Budleigh Salterton
Chagford
Chittlehampton
Chudleigh
Chulmleigh
Clovelly
Colyton
Combe Martin
Crediton
Cullompton

Dartmouth
Dawlish
Devonport
Exeter
Exmouth
Hartland
Hatherleigh
Holsworthy
Honiton
Ilfracombe
Ivybridge
Kenton
Kingsbridge
Kingsteignton
Modbury
Moretonhampstead
Newton Abbot
North Tawton
Okehampton
Ottery St Mary
Paignton
Plymouth
Plympton

Plymstock
Princetown
Salcombe
Sampford Peverell
St Marychurch
Seaton
Sidmouth
Silverton
South Brent
South Molton
Stonehouse
Tavistock
Teignmouth
Tiverton
Topsham
Torquay
Torrington
Totnes
Witheridge
Woodbury
Yealmpton

## APPENDIX 2    PLYMOUTH CITY FIRE BRIGADE IN 1950

Listing supplied by Sub/O 'Baz' Nolan of Plymouth and David Rumble

### Station A Greenbank

| Reg No | Year | Make/type | Pump Capacity |
|--------|------|-----------|---------------|
| JY 956 | 1932 | Dennis 45 H.P. Pump-escape | 700/900 |
| GLT 615 | 1943 | Austin K2 ATV/medium TP | 350/500 |
| CDR 287 | 1941 | Leyland/Merryweather 100-ft TL | |
| ADR 561 | 1938 | Bedford 27 H.P. Emergency tender (converted horsebox) | |
| GHX 681 | 1943 | Austin K4 ATV as Foam Tender | |
| unknown | 1943 | Ford 7V Radio van | |
| | 1944 | Beresford 8 H.P. light TP | 120/180 |

### Station B Penlee

| Reg No | Year | Make/type | Pump Capacity |
|--------|------|-----------|---------------|
| DR 7555 | 1930 | Dennis 30 H.P. Pump | 350/500 |
| GXA 740 | 1943 | Austin K4 Pump/Escape * | 250/350 |
| FDR 706 | 1942 | Leyland TD7/Merryweather 100-ft TL | |
| unknown | 1942 | Austin K4 ATV/TP as salvage tender | 350/500 |
| unknown | 1943 | Ford 7V Radio van | |
| XHO 272 | 1944 | GMC DUKW amphibious with MP & LPP | 350/500 120/180 |

**Station C Torr**

| Reg No | Year | Make/type | Pump Capacity |
|--------|------|-----------|---------------|
| AJY 747 | 1938 | Leyland 30 H.P. 'Cub' pump | 500/700 |
| GGN 749 | 1941 | Ford7V Pump/Escape* | 250/350 |
| GXM 93 | 1943 | Austin K4 ATV/WrT + light TP | 2 x 120/180 |
| GGU 815 | 1941 | Ford 7V Hose-laying van | |
| unknown | 1943 | Ford 7V Radio van | |
| unknown | 1943 | Austin K3 Canteen van | |
| | 1943 | Dennis 25 H.P. medium TP | 350/500 |
| | 1943 | Scammell wheelbarrow pump | 45/65 |

**Station 'D' – Boathouse**

| Reg No | Year | Make/type | Pump Capacity |
|--------|------|-----------|---------------|
| GGX 429 | 1941 | Austin K4 ATV/Medium TP | 350/500 |
| GHH 144 | 1941 | Austin K4 ATV/Medium TP | 350/500 |
| GLT 235 | 1939 | Ford7V/Sulzer Heavy SP Pump | 700/900 |
| | 1942 | Estuarial fireboat 'Iris' | 4 x 700/900 |

* Pump-escape conversions from wartime Utility escape carriers with medium pumps ex-TP nose-mounted on crankshaft ahead of radiator.

# APPENDIX 3    DEVON COUNTY FIRE SERVICE STATIONS IN COMMISSION, 1957

**'A' Division. South & East Devon. Headquarters station A1 Exmouth**

| | | | |
|--|--|--|--|
| Station A1 | Exmouth | W/T/Ret | PE, WrT |
| Station A2 | Topsham | Ret | WrT |
| Station A3 | Moretonhampstead | Ret | WrT |
| Station A4 | Chagford | Ret | WrT |
| Station A5 | Crediton | Ret | PE, WrT |
| Station A6 | Witheridge | Ret | WrT |
| Station A7 | Bampton | Ret | HrT + TP |
| Station A8 | Tiverton | Ret | PE |
| Station A9 | Cullompton | Ret | WrT |
| Station A10 | Ottery St Mary | Ret | WrT |
| Station A11 | Honiton | Ret | PE, WrT |
| Station A12 | Axminster | Ret | WrT |
| Station A13 | Colyton | Ret | HrT + TP |
| Station A14 | Seaton | Ret | PE, HrT + TP |
| Station A15 | Sidmouth | Ret | PE, HrT + TP |
| Station A16 | Budleigh Salterton | Ret | WrT |

**'B' Division. North Devon. Headquarters station  B1 Barnstaple**

| | | | |
|--|--|--|--|
| Station B1 | Barnstaple | W/T/Ret | PE, WrT, PST, BHAC |
| Station B2 | Ilfracombe | W/T/Ret | PE, WrT, TL (60-foot) |
| Station B3 | Combe Martin | Ret | WrT |
| Station B4 | Lynton | Ret | HrT + TP |
| Station B5 | South Molton | Ret | WrT + TP |
| Station B6 | Chulmleigh | Ret | WrT |
| Station B7 | Torrington | Ret | WrT |
| Station B8 | Holsworthy | Ret | WrT |
| Station B9 | Bideford | Ret | PE, WrT |
| Station B10 | Appledore | Ret | HrT + TP |

| Station B11 | Braunton | Ret | Wrt |
| Station B12 | Woolacombe | Ret | WrT |
| No number | Hartland | Vol | HrT + TP |
| No number | Clovelly | Vol | HrT + TP |

**'C' Division. South Devon. Headquarters station C1 Torquay**
**'D' Subdivision. West Devon. Sub-HQ station D1 Tavistock**

| Station C1 | Torquay | W/T/Ret | PE, PL, TL, FG, PST, CU, BAHC |
| Station C2 | Paignton | W/T/Ret | PE, WrT |
| Station C3 | Brixham | Ret | PE, WrT |
| Station C4 | Dartmouth | Ret | PE, WrT |
| Station C5 | Salcombe | Ret | HrT + TP |
| Station C6 | Kingsbridge | Ret | PE, WrT |
| Station C7 | Totnes | Ret | PE, WrT |
| Station C8 | Buckfastleigh | Ret | WrT |
| Station C9 | Ashburton | Ret | HrT + TP |
| Station C10 | Bovey Tracey | Ret | WrT + TP |
| Station C11 | Dawlish | Ret | WrT |
| Station C12 | Teignmouth | Ret | PE, WrT |
| Station C13 | Newton Abbot | Ret | PE, WrT |
| No number | Kingston | Vol | HrT + TP |
| Station D1 | Tavistock | Ret | PE, WrT |
| Station D2 | Hatherleigh | Ret | WrT |
| Station D3 | Okehampton | Ret | WrT + TP |
| Station D4 | North Tawton | Ret | HrT + TP |
| Station D5 | Princetown | Ret | HrT + TP |
| Station D6 | Yelverton | Ret | WrT |
| Station D7 | Ivybridge | Ret | WrT |
| Station D8 | Plympton | Ret | WrT |
| Station D9 | Plymstock | Ret | WrT |
| Station D10 | Bere Alston | Ret | WrT |

Key to appliance types listed:

PE = Pump Escape
PL = Pump/ladder
WrT = Water Tender
HrT = Hosereel Tender
TP = Trailer Pump. (These were all Home Office 'medium' 500 g.p.m.)
PST = Pump/salvage tender
BAHC = Breathing Apparatus tender
TL = Turntable ladder
CU = Control Unit

## APPENDIX 4    DEVON FIRE BRIGADE/DEVON FIRE AND RESCUE SERVICE STATION NUMBERS/CALLSIGNS FOLLOWING 1973 AMALGAMATION

**North Division**

| Station 01 | Barnstaple HQ | w/t ret | 2-pumps 1-ET 1HL |
| Station 02 | Ilfracombe | w/t ret | 2-pumps 1-TL |
| Station 03 | Appledore | Ret | 1-pump |
| Statoin 04 | Bideford | Ret | 2-pumps |
| Station 05 | Braunton | Ret | 1-pump |
| Station 06 | Chulmleigh | Ret | 1-pump |
| Station 07 | Combe Martin | Ret | 1-pump |
| Station 08 | Hartland | Vol/Ret* | 1-pump |
| Station 09 | Hatherleigh | Ret | 1-pump |

| | | | |
|---|---|---|---|
| Station 10 | Holsworthy | Ret | 1-pump |
| Station 11 | Lynton | Ret | 2-pumps |
| Station 12 | North Tawton | Ret | 1-pump |
| Station 13 | Okehampton | Ret | 1-pump |
| Station 14 | South Molton | Ret | 1-pump |
| Station 15 | Torrington | Ret | 1-pump |
| Station 16 | Woolacombe | Ret | 1-pump |
| | | | |
| Divisional reserves: | | | 4-pumps |

\* Became retained

## South Division

| | | | |
|---|---|---|---|
| Station 17 | Torquay HQ | W/T/Ret | 3-pumps 1 TL 1ET 1HL |
| Station 18 | Paignton | W/T/Ret | 2-pumps |
| Station 19 | Ashburton | Ret | 1-pump |
| Station 20 | Bovey Tracey | Ret | 1-pump |
| Station 21 | Brixham | Ret | 2-pumps |
| Station 22 | Buckfastleigh | Ret | 1-pump |
| Station 23 | Chagford | Ret | 1-pump |
| Station 24 | Dartmouth | Ret | 2-pumps |
| Station 25 | Dawlish | Ret | 1-pump |
| Station 26 | Kingsbridge | Ret | 1-pump |
| Station 27 | Moretonhampstead | Ret | 1-pump |
| Station 28 | Newton Abbot | Ret | 2-pumps |
| Station 29 | Salcombe | Ret | 1-pump |
| Station 30 | Teignmouth | Ret | 2-pumps |
| Station 31 | Totnes | Ret | 2-pumps |
| | | | |
| Divisional reserves: | | | 4-pumps |

## East Division

| | | | |
|---|---|---|---|
| Station 32 | Exeter | W/T/Ret | 3 pumps 1TL 1ET 1HL 1L4P |
| Station 33 | Exmouth | W/T/Ret | 2 pumps |
| Station 34 | Axminster | Ret | 1-pump |
| Station 35 | Bampton | Ret | 1-pump |
| Station 36 | Budleigh Salterton | Ret | 1-pump |
| Station 37 | Colyton | Ret | 1-pump |
| Station 38 | Crediton | Ret | 2-pumps |
| Station 39 | Cullompton | Ret | 1-pump |
| Station 40 | Honiton | Ret | 2-pumps |
| Station 41 | Ottery St Mary | Ret | 1-pump |
| Station 42 | Seaton | Ret | 1-pump |
| Station 43 | Sidmouth | Ret | 2-pumps |
| Station 44 | Tiverton | Ret | 2-pumps |
| Station 45 | Topsham | Ret | 2-pumps |
| Station 46 | Witheridge | Ret | 1-pump |
| | | | |
| Divisional reserves: | | | 4-pumps |

## West Division

| | | | |
|---|---|---|---|
| Station 47 | Plympton HQ | W/T | 1-pump |
| Station 48 | Camel's Head | W/T | 2-pumps 1HP |
| Station 49 | Crownhill | W/T | 2-pumps 1HFT 1ET |
| Station 50 | Greenbank | W/T | 2-pumps 1TL 1ET |
| Station 51 | Plymstock | W/T | 1-pump 1FB |
| Station 52 | Bere Alston | Ret | 1-pump |

| | | | |
|---|---|---|---|
| Station 53 | Ivybridge | Ret | 1-pump |
| Station 54 | Kingston | Vol | 1-L4P |
| Station 55 | Modbury | Vol/ret* | 1-pump |
| Station 56 | Princetown | Ret | 1-pump |
| Station 57 | Tavistock | Ret | 2-pumps |
| Station 58 | Yelverton | Ret | 1-pump |
| Station 59 | Training School | | 2-pumps 1 TL |

Divisional reserves: 4-pumps

Total brigade strength in appliances: 83 front-line pumping appliances, 4 TLs, 3 HLL 5ET 1HFT 2L4P, 16 reserve pumps, 2 fire training pumps, 1 training/spare TL

There were a number of other old appliances, unequipped, used for driver training purposes
* Became retained

# APPENDIX 5    THE DEVON FIRE AND RESCUE SERVICE, 1999

**North Division**

**Station 01 Barnstaple** – Divisional HQ
Core-manned/retained

011 Dennis Sabre/JDC Wrl/Rescue
012 Mercedes Carmichael Wrl
014 Dennis/Camiva 100-foot TL
015 Ford A 4 x 4/Fulton & Wylie hoselayer
010 MAN Prime Mover
01A Incident Support Pod Unit
01B Environmental Pod Unit

**Station 02 Ilfracombe**
Core manned/retained

021 Dennis Sabre/JDC Wrl/Rescue
022 Dennis RS Wrl/Rescue
027 Mercedes Vito/DFRS ICV

**Station 03 Appledore**
Retained

031 MAN/Saxon Wrl/Rescue

**Station 04/Bideford**
Retained

041 Volvo FL6/Saxon Wrl/Rescue
042 Volvo FL6/Saxons Wrl

**Station 05 Braunton**
Retained

051 MAN/JDC Wrl/Rescue

**Station 06 Chulmleigh**
Retained

061 MAN/Saxon Wrl/Rescue

**Station 07 Combe Martin**
Retained

071 MAN/Saxon Wrl/Rescue

**Station 08 Hartland**
Retained

081 MAN/Saxon Wrl/Rescue

**Station 09 Hatherleigh**
Retained

091 MAN/JDC Wrl/Rescue/Co-responder

**Station 10 Holsworthy**
Retained

101 MAN/JDC Wrl/Rescue/Co-responder

**Station 11 Lynton**
Retained

111 Dennis DS/JDC WrL
112 Mercedes 4 x 4/Carmichael WrT/Rescue

**Station 12 North Tawton**
Retained

121 Dennis DS/JDC Wrl/Rescue/
Co-responder

**Station 13 Okehampton**
Retained

131 Dennis RS/JDC Wrl/Rescue
132 Dennis RS WrT

**Station 14 South Molton**
Retained

141 MAN/Saxon Wrl/Rescue

**Station 15 Torrington**
Retained

151 MAN/Saxon Wrl/Rescue

**Station 16 Woolacombe**
Retained

161 MAN/Saxon WrL/Rescue/Co-responder

**South Division**

**Station 17 Torquay** – Divisional HQ
Wholetime/retained

171 Dennis Sabre/JDC WrL/Rescue
172 Dennis Sabre/JDC WrL
173 Dennis Rapier WrL/Rescue (retained)
174 Volvo/Bronto 282 Skylift ALP
175 Dodge 4 x 4/Angloco Hose-layer
177 Mecedes Vito/DFRS ICV
170 MAN Prime Mover
17A Incident Support Pod Unit
17B Environmental Pod Unit

**Station 18 Paignton**
Wholetime/retained

181 Dennis Sabre/JDC WrL/Rescue
182 Dennis RS/JDC WrT

**Station 19 Ashburton**
Retained

191 MAN/Saxon WrL/Rescue

**Station 20 Bovey Tracey**
Retained

201 Dennis DS/Dennis WrL/Rescue

**Station 21 Brixham**
Retained

211 Dennis DS/JDC WrL/Rescue
212 Dennis DS/JDC WrT

**Station 22 Buckfastleigh**
Retained

221 MAN/Saxon WrL/Rescue

**Station 23 Chagford**
Retained

231 MAN/Saxon WrL/Rescue/Co-responder

**Station 24 Dartmouth**
Retained

241 Dennis DS/JDC WrL/Rescue
242 Dennis RS/JDC

**Station 25 Dawlish**
Retained

251 MAN/JDC WrL/Rescue/Co-responder

**26 Kingsbridge**
Retained

261 MAN/Saxon WrL/Rescue

**Station 27 Moretonhampstead**
Retained

271 Dennis DS/Dennis WrL/Rescue/Co-responder

**Station 28 Newton Abbot**
Retained

281 Dennis Rapier WrL/Rescue
282 Dennis RS/JDC WrT

**Station 29 Salcombe**
Retained                                    291 MAN/Saxon WrL/Rescue

**Station 30 Teignmouth**
Retained                                    301 Volvo FL6/Saxon/WrL/Rescue
                                            302 Volvo FL6/Saxon WrT

**Station 31 Totnes**
Retained                                    311 Volvo FL6/Saxon WrL/Rescue
                                            312 Volvo FL6/Saxon WrT

**East Division**

**Station 32 Exeter**
Wholetime/retained                          321 Dennis Sabre/JDC WrL/Rescue
                                            322 Dennis Sabre/JDC WrL
                                            323 Dennis Rapier WrL
                                            324 Volvo/Bronto 28-metre ALP
                                            320 MAN Prime Mover
                                            32A Incident Support Pod Unit
                                            32B Environmental Pod Unit

**Station 33 Exmouth**
Wholetime/retained                          331 Dennis Sabre/JDC WrL/Rescue
                                            332 Dennis RS/JDC WrT
                                            335 Ford A 4 x 4/Fulton & Wylie Hoselayer
                                            337 Mercedes Vito/DFRS ICV

**Station 34 Axminster**
Retained                                    341 MAN/JDC WrL/Rescue/Co-responder

**Station 35 Bampton**
Retained                                    351 Dennis DS/JDC WrL/Rescue

**Station 36 Budleigh Salterton**
Retained                                    361 MAN/Saxon WrL/Rescue

**Station 37 Colyton**
Retained                                    371 MAN/Saxon WrL/Rescue

**Station 38 Crediton**
Retained                                    381 Dennis RS/JDC WrL/Rescue
                                            382 Dennis RS/JDC WrT

**Station 39 Cullompton**
Retained                                    391 MAN 14/Saxon WrL/Rescue

**Station 40 Honiton**
Retained                                    401 Mercedes/Carmichael WrL/Rescue
                                            402 Dennis RS/JDC WrT

**Station 41 Ottery St Mary**
Retained                                    411 Dennis DS/JDC WrL/Rescue

**Station 42 Seaton**
Retained                                    421 MAN/Saxon WrL/Rescue/Co-responder

**Station 43 Sidmouth**
Retained                                    431 Dennis RS/JDC WrL/Rescue
                                            432 Dennis RS/JDC WrT

**Station 44 Tiverton**
Retained                                    441 Mercedes/Carmichael WrL/Rescue
                                            442 Mercedes/Carmichael WrT

**Station 45 Topsham**
Retained

451 Dennis RS/JDC WrL/Rescue
452 Dennis Rs/JDC WrT

**Station 46 Witheridge**
Retained

461 MAN/JDC WrL/Rescue


**West Division**

**Station 47 Plympton**  West Divisional HQ/Service Training Centre
Wholetime

471 Dennis Sabre/JDC WrL/Rescue

**Station 48 Camel's Head**  Service Maritime Training Centre
Wholetime

481 Dennis Sabre/JDC WrL/Rescue
482 Dennis Sabre/JDC WrT
484 Volvo/Bronto 28-metre ALP
488 Land Rover/DFRS Specialist Rescue Unit

**Station 49 Crownhill**
Wholetime

491 Dennis Sabre/JDC WrL/Rescue
494 Iveco/Magirus 30-metre TL
495 Dodge/Saxon HFoT
490 MAN Prime Mover
49A Incident Support Pod Unit
49B Environmental Pod Unit

**Station 50 Greenbank**
Wholetime

501 Dennis Sabre/JDC WrL/Rescue
502 Dennis Sabre/JDC WrT
507 Mercedes Vito/DFRS ICV

**Station 51 Plymstock**
Wholetime

511 Dennis Sabre/JDC WrL/Rescue
516 Alnmarintec 11.4 metre fire/rescue boat

**Station 52 Bere Alston**
Retained

521 MAN/Saxon WrL/Rescue

**Station 53 Ivybridge**
Retained

531 MAN/Saxon WrL/Rescue/Co-responder

**Station 54 Kingston**
Volunteer

542 Mercedes 4 x 4/DFRS WrT

**Station 55 Modbury**
Retained

551 MAN/Saxon WrL/Rescue

**Station 56 Princetown**
Retained

562 Mercedes 4 x 4/Carmichael WrT/Rescue/
Co-responder

**Station 57 Tavistock**
Retained

571 Dennis RS/JDC WrL/Rescue
572 Dennis RS/JDC WrT

**Station 58 Yelverton**
Retained

581 Dennis DS/JDC WrL/Rescue

# A BRIEF GLOSSARY OF FIRE SERVICE TERMS & ABBREVIATIONS

**ADO:** Rank of Assistant Divisional Officer. Deputises for DO, has major areas of responsibility within Division (such as Group Commander in charge of several fire stations or Station Commander in charge of a major fire station), or equivalent areas of responsibility in management, training or fire safety.

**AFA:** Automatic fire alarm

**ALP:** Aerial ladder platform

**ARP:** Air raid precautions

**Assistance message:** A message sent by the OIC of an incident requesting additional appliances or other resources. The form of the message is proscribed; the total resources required are always given, without regard to what is already in attendance, thus: 'Make pumps six, TLs one', meaning: 'send additional appliances to give a total of six pumps plus a TL'

**ATV:** Auxiliary Towing Vehicle: wartime appliance used to tow a trailer pump.

**BA:** Breathing apparatus

**BACO:** Breathing apparatus control officer

**Bayley Ladder:** A design of lightweight wooden ladder with strings (sides) of two small sections of wood - one straight, one curved – braced together like a bowstring girder. Commonest in 35-foot form but also found in 25 and 45-foot versions. Introduced in the early 1920s and in widespread use until the early 1980s.

**Branch:** The fire service term for a nozzle used to control a jet, or firefighting water stream. The term is also used to describe the whole unit of branch, the firefighting hose feeding it and the men operating it.

**Branchman:** The firefighter controlling a branch

**CABA:** Compressed-air breathing apparatus.

**CFS:** Community fire safety. A wide-ranging programme of inspection, advice, education and practical help designed to reduce or eliminate fire risks and to equip people to deal with fire hazards.

**CU:** Control unit: a vehicle sent on to major incidents which incorporates a command centre for the incident with communications systems and relevant information. Control or command units are identified by red-and-white chequer banding and, at night, by a red/white flashing beacon. In Devon, these units were combined with the ETs; now superseded by ICVs.

**Fire appliance:** Fire fighting equipment of any type. Often used to describe actual fire engines, but can also refer to other fixed or portable firefighting apparatus such as extinguishers, fire blankets, sprinklers, etc.

**Delivery:** The output valve and connection of a fire pump

**DO:** Rank of Divisional Officer; a senior rank associated with command of a division or a large group of fire stations, or a major area of responsibility within the brigade management.

**Escape Ladder:** Generally, a ladder sufficiently wide, robust and stable enough to allow its use for rescue purposes, capable of taking
several persons at once. Traditionally, it was the sliding-carriage wheeled ladder of 3 sections extending to 50 feet by
means of winch and cable; nowadays it is the 13.5-metre 3-section lightweight alloy 135 ladder which is extended by
hand.

**ET:** Emergency Tender – a non-pumping appliance designed and stowed to meet special service calls and particular risks such as chemical spillage or incidents involving poisonous gases. Now replaced by a combination of rescue pumps and pod units.

**Eye (of pump):** The inlet of a firepump, to which suction hose is connected or into which a pressure-fed supply may be delivered.

**FcO:** Fire Control Officer (sometimes known as ConOp)

**Fireground:** The scene of firefighting operations. Also used to denote the area covered by a particular fire station, as in: 'The incident occurred on Station 30's fireground'. See also 'Station ground'.

**First-aid:** As well as the normal sense of rendering basic medical aid, 'first aid' in firefighting is the term used to describe equipment designed for instant use to make the initial attack on a fire. A first-aid appliance is a vehicle or fixed installation designed to reach an incident swiftly and to be able to deal with a small fire or to contain the situation until other appliances can be brought in to use. Modern fire appliances have first aid capability in the form of the onboard water tank feeding hosereels together with handheld extinguishers.

**Foam:** Firefighting medium consisting of a thick layer of closed-cell aqueous bubbles delivered onto the surface of a burning liquid or other material so as to extinguish by excluding air and cooling.

**Group Commander:** Title of an officer in charge of two or more fire stations. Can be held by any rank from StnO up to DO.

**GPV:** General-purpose vehicle – van or pick-up truck.

**HrT:** Hose-reel Tender – a vehicle carrying a limited water supply and a pre-coupled hosereel fed by a pump; a first aid fire fighting appliance.

**ICV:** Incident Command Vehicle – the replacement for the old control unit. A vehicle fitted out to perform all the functions of fire command, with communications and computer equipment, data retrieval systems, air-supported structure and power generation.

**Informative:** The message sent from the fireground to inform control of the nature and extent of an incident and the action being taken, including the tactical mode.

**HLL:** Hose-laying Lorry.

**Hosereel:** Three-quarter in bore high pressure rubber tubing in 60-foot lengths; three such lengths are normally wound on to a drum on each side of a pumping appliance and fitted with a hand-controlled branch. The hosereels are pre-coupled to the pump of the fire appliance and may be fed from the on-board tank supply. They are thus ready for instant use.

**HRJ:** Hose-reel jet – the use of first-aid water supply by means of a hosereel fed from the appliance pump and controlled by a small hand-held branch. Modern reels deliver water at both low (up to 10 bar) and high (10 -20 bar) pressures; the term HRJ implies high pressure is in use; otherwise refereed to as HR.

**Hurst:** The main type of full-capability hydraulic rescue equipment used in Devon.

**Instantaneous:** The type of hose coupling introduced during the last war and now in universal use. As the name suggests, it is a snap-together coupling rather than a screwed type.

**JCDD:** Joint Council for Design and Development – The Home Office committee which sets specifications for fire appliances and fire service equipment

**Jet:** Firefighting water stream from a branch or monitor

**JO:** Junior officer – usually leading firefighter.

**L4P:** Light 4 x 4 first-aid firefighting vehicle carrying a pump.

**L4V:** Light 4 x 4 not carrying a pump.

**LFf:** The rank of leading firefighter – typically, in charge of an appliance crew, deputising for SubO on both wholetime and retained stations. Equivalent areas of responsibility in training or fire safety departments.

**LPP:** Light Portable Pump: A self-contained petrol-driven pump of 150–250-g.p.m. capacity mounted in a carrying frame.

**Machine:** The (polite and repeatable) term by which firefighters usually refer to a fire engine.

**Major Pump:** A fire pump capable of delivering 500-g.p.m at up to 10 bars – the main pump on most fire appliances. The term is also used to describe any fire appliance carrying a pump of this type.

**Make-up:** This term is used in two contexts: Firstly, as a noun – a 'make-up' is an assistance message. Secondly, as a verb it has two distinct meanings depending on context. To 'make up' is to send an assistance message. The order 'Make up!', however, is the command to restow equipment after use.

**Mobile:** An appliance is mobile when travelling on the road and a message to this effect (mobile message) is always sent to control giving details of destination, purpose of journey, name of officer in charge and total number of crew.

**Monitor:** Fixed (non-hand-held) nozzle for passing large volumes of water; usually found as a Ground Monitor (free-standing, can be used on any level surface), a TL Monitor, on head of TL, and Fireboat Monitor, deck water gun on fireboat. Some industrial installations have permanent fixed monitors as part of inbuilt firefighting systems.

**On the Bell:** An appliance responding to a 'shout'

**OIC:** Officer in Charge

**PDA:** Pre-determined attendance. The number and type of appliances that will be sent to any particular address in the event of a fire call. Usually, the PDA is determined by the risk category or as a result of a risk inspection.

**PE:** Pump-escape, a dual-purpose fire appliance having a major pump and possibly a first-aid tank and hosereel, but also carrying an escape ladder. Succeeded in modern practice by the WrL.

**PCV:** Personnel Carrying Vehicle – ie., a crew-bus.

**Principal Officer:** An Officer of a rank sufficient to command a brigade: The Chief Fire Officer, Deputy Chief Fire Officer or Assistant Chief Fire Officer. One principal officer is always on call and is expected to take charge of any major incidents.

**Pump:** Strictly, a pump is the actual mechanism on a fire engine which pumps water, but it is also used by firefighters to describe any fire engine with pumping capability. A 'pump' is also a definition of a type of fire engine under the Home Office classification scheme, being a machine which has a pump but does not carry a full 400-gallon water supply or an escape ladder.

**RTA:** Road traffic accident

**Risk:** In fire service terms – anything which is likely to catch fire or generate a need for response. Thus, a building of any sort is a 'risk', but so is a highway or an area of moorland. Risks are assessed in categories on the basis of the nature of the area and the hazards and the danger to life involved; all addresses in Britain are placed in one of five 'Risk categories' or classified as a 'special risk'. The categorisation determines the PDA. In modern firefighting, risk is also the danger involved in any scenario, and is assessed by the OIC before he decides on tactical mode and commits crews to action.

**Shout:** A call-out: to go to an incident.

**Special Service:** An incident that does not involve firefighting.

**Standpipe, Key and Bar:** The standpipe is the fitting screwed onto a hydrant to enable hose to be coupled to the water supply. The hydrant is turned on by means of the key and bar.

**Station Commander:** A title rather than a rank, denoting the officer in charge of a fire station. The post can be held by any rank from SubO (on a 1-pump station) up to ADO or even DO for a principal station.

**Station Ground:** The area for which a particular fire station is responsible, not just in providing initial response to fire calls but also for inspecting and maintaining hydrants, carrying out risk visits and delivering CFS.

**StnO:** The rank of Station Officer. In charge of a watch on a wholetime station or, if retained, in charge of a 2-pump retained station. Equivalent areas of responsibility in management or training.

**Stop:** The message sent from the fireground to control to denote that no additional assistance beyond the resources already sent or requested will be required. A stop message gives: Name of officer sending, the address of incident, the nature and extent of the incident, the equipment in use, and the status of the attending appliances (available or committed), the tactical mode.

**SubO:** The rank of Sub-Officer. Second in command of a watch on a wholetime station or, retained, second-in-command on a 2-pump or in charge of a 1-pump retained station. Equivalent areas of responsibility in management or training.

**Tactical Mode:** The description for risk-assessment purposes of the type of operation on which crews are engaged. Thus, 'Offensive Mode' denotes active firefighting or rescue within a danger area; 'Defensive' denotes passive firefighting (from out side danger area) or crew standing by. 'Transitional' is where both Offensive and Defensive modes are in use.

**TL:** Turntable ladder – an aerial appliance having self-supporting ladders mounted in a turntable such that they may be pitched in any direction. Usually of 30-metre (100-foot) reach in three sections. May also have a rescue cage at the ladder head and usually fitted with a monitor (Large fixed swivelling nozzle) for use as a water tower.

**Trip Round the Bay:** Responding to a false alarm or other call where no action is taken.

**Turn-out:** The act of leaving the station in response to an incident. A 'turnout' is thus a call to an incident.

**Water Tower:** A TL or other aerial appliance used to direct a major firefighting jet onto a fire from high elevation.

**WrT:** Water Tender – a fire engine with major pumping capability which carries a tank water supply, usually of 400 gallons/1800 litres. Under the Home Office JCDD requirements, a water tender type A will have a demountable pump and a portable pump, while the more usual type B will have a built-in major pump plus an LPP

**WrL** Water tender/ladder – an appliance to full water tender specification which also carries an escape ladder.

**Zumro:** Makers of hydraulic rescue equipment, most particularly the compact equipment stowed on the MAN and Dennis DS appliance types.

# SUBSCRIBERS

Christopher D. Abbott, Newton Abbot

Nicholas J. Abbott, Torquay

Ian S. Alford

FF. G. Allcorn, 10 Holsworthy, Devon

Sub/O. T. Allcorn, 10 Holsworthy, Devon

Paul Allford, Totnes, Devon

Mr Dana Asdourian, Maine, USA

Glenn J. Askew

W.G. Back, Topsham

Tony R. Baglow, Ilfracombe

Mr Peter Bailes, Kansas, USA

Firefighter Christopher G. Bailey, Stn 28,
Newton Abbot

Ex Sub Officer William G. Bailey, Stn 28,
Newton Abbot

John F. Baker, Ashburton, Devon

Brian J. Baker, Sidmouth, Devon

Mr Terry Baker, Packall Lane, Brixham, Devon

Councillor Keith Baldry, Chairman Devon
Fire Authority

Mr Ray Banyard

Reg Barker, STN 38 Crediton, Devon

John Conrad Barnard

David R. Barrett

FF I. Bartlett, "Plod" White Watch STN 32 2000

Bert Bellworthy, Torquay Fire Brigade

F.F. Stefan Belsten, Torquay

Steve Billington, Exeter

L. M. Blackburn, Teignmouth

Eric C. Blogg, Ex Station Officer
City of Plymouth and Devon Fire Brigade

Robert F. J. Bradbury, Plymouth

John R. Bradbury, Plymouth

Michael A. Brice, Tiverton/Plymouth/Exeter

Mr David Brooks, Plymouth

Kenneth J. Brown, Dawlish, Devon

Steve Brown, Plymouth

John (Scouse) Bryan, Exeter

Daniel Buckley, Lebanon P.A. USA

Michael E. Bullen, Crete

Mike Bunn, Stratford Upon Avon

Martin Burdick, Shaldon, Devon

Harold Burnell, Brixham, Devon

Terry C. Burnell, Brixham, Devon

Sean Burnell, Brixham, Devon

Mike Burroughs, Plympton

K. J. Burrow, Bucks Cross, Devon

Paul Busscher, Plymouth. Collector of fire
memorabilia

A. S. Cann, Plymouth

Bob Caress, Phoenix Fire Protection Limited

Station Officer Derek Carley, Brixham, Devon

Colin Carter, Southampton

Mr David J. Case, Plymouth

Derrick W. Chalk, Torquay, Devon

Gary Chapman, Launceston, Cornwall

William S. Cherry, Crediton, Devon

Richard Cheu, Fair Haven, New Jersey  07704

Mr Ernest J. Clark, Saltdean

Leading Firefighter Geoff J. Cleverly-Hunt, Torrington

John Cockram, South Molton, Devon

Simon Cole, Barnstaple Fire Station

John Colley G.M., Blue Watch, Torquay (Retired)

Graham A. Collins, Brixham, Devon

Malcolm Cook, Cannington, Somerset

Geoffrey Coombe, Morchard Road

Firefighter M. J. Cowling, Dartmouth, Devon

Keith J. Cox, Totnes, Devon

George Crabb, Sidmouth, Devon

Dave Crawford, Red Watch, Torquay Fire Station

Station Officer P. J. Cregan, Somerset Fire Brigade

David G. Cross, Paignton, Devon

Arthur Cuff, A.F.S. 16 years, Station Exmouth

Wayne A. M. Davies, Ashford, Kent

Training Centre Devon Fire and Rescue Service, Plymouth

Stephen John Doidge, Yelverton, Devon

LFF Kevin Drew, Hatherleigh, Devon

Bryan Durrant, Whitestone

Ian Earle, Exeter, Devon

Michael J. Eascott, Plymouth

R. Edgecombe, Plymouth

Marilyn J. Elkins, Seaford, East Sussex

James S. Ellis, Paignton, Devon

B. J. Faithfull, Ex City of Plymouth and Devon Fire and Rescue 1963-90

Andy Fish, LFF Whitchurch, Cardiff - Former FF, Camels Head and Exeter

Elizabeth Fish, Exeter, Devon

Denise A. Ford, Surrey

Trevor S. Ford, Dartmouth

Beryl J. Forward, Greater Manchester Fire Service

D. O. Bud Francis, Defence Fire Service

R. P. Franks, Exmouth

Mervyn Freeman, Kingston, Devon

G. E. Freeman, Station Officer. City of Exeter 1950-79

Stn/O Barrie French, Dartmouth

LFF Paul Furler, Exmouth, Devon

David H. Galpin, Cheltenham, Glos

Mr Anthony C. Gatting, Exmouth, Devon

Terry Gaught, Stn 33 Exmouth

Hieth J. George, Exmouth

Miss A. D. Gillbard, Tiverton, Devon

P. A. Gillbard, Tiverton, Devon

Mr Brian Goddard, Ex. AFS Exmouth

Stephen J. Gooding, Cullompton

Norman F. Gooding, Cullompton

O418Ff Gough DJM, 41 Ottery St Mary

Clifford Gould, Cullompton

Peter Grant, Sidmouth, Exeter and Exmouth

Station Officer John H. Griffin

Alan Groom, Torquay, Devon
Sub.O. Paul Guy, South Molton, Devon

Kevin Hale, Saltash, Cornwall. Devon Fire Control

Mr Neil F. Handley, Plymouth

Svend Aage Hansen, Denmark

Firefighter Norman Harper Cullompton / Exeter /Exmouth, Devon

Ralph Havery OBE, F.I.Fire E, Chief Officer, Plymouth/Devon F.Bs 1962-

Terry Hawkins, Torquay

Terence B. Hawton, Hampshire

Councillor Geoffrey Heathcock JP, Cambridgeshire

Mr T. Henderson, Thornbury, Bristol

Tony Heywood

Dennis Hill, Keynsham

John Hills, STN 33 Exmouth, Devon

John F. Hiscocks, Ottery St Mary

John Howes, Devon Fire and Rescue Service

Peter Howison, STN 38 Crediton

M. S. J. Hughes, Plymouth

Cllr. Bernard Hughes, Exmouth, Devon

Mr Charles P. W. Huitson, Plymouth

Graham Isaac, Paignton, Devon

Raymond Isaac, Barnstaple, Devon

Sub. Officer Alan Isaac, Barnstaple, Devon

Kevin Ivey, Plymouth

Andrew R. Janes, Taunton, Somerset

L/ff Matt Johnson, East Division Training

Mr Roger Johnston, Plymouth

Robert Dearden Jones, Gravesend, Kent

Sub Officer A. Jones, Torquay, 2000.

Charles A. J. Keevil, West Hagbourne, Oxon

John J. Killoran, Exmouth, Devon

Philip A. Kilshaw OBE, Poole, Dorset

Roy King, Newton Abbot, Devon

S. R. King, Street, Somerset

Mr Mark A. R. Kitchen, Torquay

Frank A. Knott, Torquay, Devon

John Laird, Barnstaple, Devon

Denis F. Lander, Exmouth, Devon

Pat Langdon, Blue Watch Exeter

Kevin Langworthy, Dartmouth

Brian Langworthy, Dartmouth

Mr A. Le Count, Ex Plymouth Fire Brigade

LFF Paul Lee, Brixham

Gerald William Leworthy, Barnstaple, Devon

Ex FM Dave Lock, Mark, Somerset

Michael Loosemore, Waiuku, New Zealand

Derek L. Loveridge, Exmouth

Roy Luck, Plympton

Dave Maddern, Exeter, Devon

Raymond Marley, Bampton  Sub Officer Retired

Derek Marriott, AFS Exmouth and Headquarters
(17 years)

Anthony (Harry) McGeehan, Station Officer Retired,
Tiverton, Devon

Mr Jim McLaughlin, Massachusetts, USA

Jan Mead, Torquay

Harold Meadowcroft, Devon Fireman
from 1940 to 1970

Michael Mitcham, Barnstaple, Devon

Doris E. Mitchelmore, Paignton

Mrs Jean E. Mogridge

Simon L. Mogridge, Birmingham

Paul Morrey, Kingsteignton, Devon

Mr M. Mullenger, Saltash

Terry Nettleship, Plymouth

Nick Noden, Brixham

Finbar E. Nolan, Plymouth

The North Devon Athenaeum

Richard M. Osborne, Ilfracombe

Rod (Moses) Ousley, Exeter

Councillor Ian Oxley, Torbay Council - Member
Devon Fire Authority

P.C.C. Motor Bodies, Newton Abbot, Devon

Tony "Baby Scouse" Perischine, Exeter White Watch

Chief Bill Peterson, Plano, Texas

L/FF J. D. Pledger, 1154 Torrington

J. F. Pratt, Dunstable

Chris Pratt, Cullompton

D.O. Bob Prince, Barnstaple, Devon,
Divisional Commander (North)

Christopher J. Pritchard, Kentisbeare

Paul Pym, Ex Station 45, Topsham

Mark Quick, North Tawton

Bob Radford, Exeter

Thomas W. Radford, Teignmouth, Devon

Jan Ragless, Topsham

Donald K. Ramsey, Torquay, Devon

Brian Read

Ed Reburn, Plymouth

Graham and Sue Reed, Exeter, Devon

Peter D. Regan, Exmouth, Devon

Paul Rendell, Okehampton, Devon

LFF Terry Reynolds, Hatherleigh Station 091

Carole M. Rice, Exmouth, Devon

Assistant Chief Fire Officer Len Richards, East Sussex

Ian Richards, Budleigh Salterton

Michael J. Ricketts, Plymouth.  Firebrigade Society.

Phil Rikken, Plymouth

Dave Roberts, Tiverton, Devon

Keith Robson, Anderby Creek

Mr Colin C. Rockey, Kingston

R. G. P. Rose, Barnstaple, Devon

Mr Kirk Rosenhan, Mississippi, USA

Malcolm D. Ross, Dawlish, Devon

Ian E. Rothwell, Retired Stn O., Windermere

Philip J. Rowe, Kingsbridge, Devon

David J. Rumble, Plymouth

Alex Ryles, Gateshead

Maurice William Salter, Exeter, Devon

Raymond Sandercock, Paignton, Devon

Sub. O. W. Sanders, Barnstaple

James A. Sanderson, Plymouth, Devon

LFF Andrew Sauerzapf, South Molton, Devon

Mr Robert E. Savage, Retired Devon Fire Rescue Service

Kevin Sedgeman, Kingsbridge, Devon

Frank Sedgemore (Dec'd), Fireman, Budleigh Salterton, Exeter City Brigade

Divisional Officer T. Shaddick, Barnstaple

Sub/O Colin Shaw, Bere Alston, Devon

Patrick A. D. Sheen

T. Shute, Exeter, Devon

Mr Karl Sillitoe, Market Drayton

L/FF Joseph Small, Bovey Tracey (Retired)

Phil Smith, Firefighter - 38 Crediton

Robert Smith, Coleford, Gloucestershire

Ron Smith, Plymouth

Mrs Maureen E. Smith, Exmouth

Lester Solway, Weston-Super-Mare, Somerset

Ian Somerville, Winsham, Devon

Mr Percy Sowden

Nicholas P. A. Spreckley, Exeter, Devon

Mr Bernard J. Stevens, (Ex Fireman) Totnes

Mr Brian Stevens, Totnes, Station 31

C. R. Stidworthy, Teignmouth

Mr Mark A. Stone, Paignton

Mr Brian J. Sullivan, Plymouth

Clive Sutton, Plymstock

Sub/O Chris Swindle, Station 41

Colin Swinfen-Styles, Torquay

G. J. Sydenham, Teignmouth

Tom Taylor, Plymouth

Gary Thompson, Retained Torquay from 1990

Dave Thorn, Ivybridge, Devon

Sub Station Officer N.N.P. Toms, Camels Head Fire Station

Alan J. Tonkin, Crediton, Devon

Peter M. Trott, Station 48. Camels Head

DO. Paul Trueman, Plymouth

Owen J. Turl, Topsham, Devon

John Twigg, Rockbeare, Exeter, Devon

Richard Underhill, Ex Station 45, Topsham

Norman Vaine, Tiverton, Devon

Ian Vosper, Exeter, Devon

John F. W. Walling, Newton Abbot, Devon

Matthew Warren, Torquay

Arthur H. Way, Seaton, Devon

David E. W. Webb Firefighter, 1966-1998 Warwickshrie and Devon F.B.

Ron Weeks, Exeter

John P. Weller, Topsham

Stephen E. West, Exmouth, Devon

Ray Whalley, FBS Plymouth

Michael White

Mike White (the younger)

P. J. Whitehouse, Deputy Chief Officer, Devon Fire and Rescue Service (retired)

Neil J. Whitemore, Dartmouth Station 24

Cllr Graham Wickham, Newton Abbot

Roger Wilcox, Ilminster, Somerset

Gerta Wilkins, Paignton, Devon

ACFO Geoff Wilkins, Devon

Dave Williams, Dawlish, Devon

Chris and Mary Williamson, Retained, Modbury

Retired Sub Officer Geoff Wills, Bovey Tracey

Sub Officer Roy Wills, Bovey Tracey

Ex LFF Leslie A. Woodman, 351 Bampton

Chris Woodwark, Farnham Common, Bucks

Mr D. Woolwright, Saltford, Bristol

E. E. Woon, Plymouth

A.D.O. Trevor Wright, Torquay

A. R. Wyle, Devon

CFO Paul Young, Devon

Scott M. Young, Barnstaple, Devon

David and Marilyn Youngs, Exeter, Devon

John and Pat Youngs, Welwyn, Herts.